The Moderator's Survival Guide

The Moderator's Survival Guide

Handling Common, Tricky, and Sticky Situations in User Research

Donna Tedesco
Senior User Experience Researcher

Fiona Tranquada
Senior Usability Consultant

AMSTERDAM • BOSTON • HEIDELBERG • LONDON
NEW YORK • OXFORD • PARIS • SAN DIEGO
SAN FRANCISCO • SYDNEY • TOKYO
Morgan Kaufmann is an imprint of Elsevier

Acquiring Editor: Meg Dunkerley
Editorial Project Manager: Heather Scherer
Project Manager: Priya Kumaraguruparan
Designer: Greg Harris
Morgan Kaufmann is an imprint of Elsevier
225 Wyman Street, Waltham, MA, 02451, USA

Library of Congress Cataloging-in-Publication Data
Tedesco, Donna.
  The moderator's survival guide : handling common, tricky, and sticky situations in user research / Donna Tedesco, senior user experience researcher, Fiona Tranquada, senior usability consultant. pages cm
  Includes bibliographical references and index.
  1. Commercial products--Testing. 2. Computer software--Testing. 3. User centered system design.
4. Focus groups. 5. Interviewing. 6. Forums (Discussion and debate) I. Tranquada, Fiona. II. Title.
  TS175.5.T43 2013
  004.2′1–dc23
                              2013019705

British Library Cataloguing-in-Publication Data
A catalogue record for this book is available from the British Library.

ISBN: 978-0-12-404700-6

Cover design by CoDesign, Boston

For information on all MK publications visit our website at www.mkp.com

DEDICATION

Donna:

For Mom and Dad, with love

Fiona:

For Justin and Alison, who haven't stopped believing

CONTENTS

Introduction 1

Part 1   Your Moderation Toolkit   8

ACKNOWLEDGMENTS

This book has been a true labor of love, and we are grateful for the support from everyone who helped us pull it all together.

First, we'd like to thank Meg Dunkerley and Heather Scherer from Morgan Kaufmann for your hard work, direction, and patience. We are especially grateful for the amazing feedback provided by our reviewers, Mary Beth Rettger, Whitney Quesenbery, and Chauncey Wilson. Thank you for combing the manuscript thoroughly with your expert lens and delivering helpful feedback with such sharp wit.

Thank you to our Survival Story contributors for giving us and the readers some entertaining and interesting outside perspectives to sprinkle throughout the book.

Our book cover and spine art looks as good as it does thanks to the mad talent of Karen LeDuc and Matt Kanaracus at Codesign, Boston. Thanks also to Mark Ainscow for your brilliant photography skills and responsiveness to our frenzied requests. Thanks also to our photography models, Reeve Goodenough and Deirdre McGruder.

We have infinite gratitude for our very talented filmmaker, Chris Portal. We can't thank you enough for volunteering dozens of hours of your time and immense talent to prepare, film, edit, and produce the companion videos to this book. (If anyone wants to admire Chris' other work, go to *http://www.chrisportal.com/*.) We have equally large amounts of thanks for our talented "sound guy," Dennis Ganz. We will miss working with both of you—and always remember our 12-hour filming days filled with boom mics and pocket dollies, inordinate amounts of coffee, and the "Harlem Shake."

Thanks also to our numerous actors: Mark Ainscow, Gary Aussant, Margy Bergel, Laura Bowden, Reeve Goodenough, Jeff Goodwin, Cory Madaris, Ellen Mangan, Deirdre McGruder, Lauren Mckenzie, Susan Mercer, Debra Reich, Dorienne Rosenberg, Scott Williams, and David Wong. We appreciate you volunteering so much of your time to help us refine the scripts, rehearse, and finally film (for hours on end). You did a great job and kept us laughing (with you, not at you). And, of course, big thanks to the User Experience Center at Bentley University for generously allowing us to film in and around their space.

Thank you to everyone in the user research community who provided inspiration and feedback as we pulled this together, especially those in the Boston area who joined us for our workshops and guest teaching gigs. Your enthusiasm helped us refine our message and kept us going through the hardest times.

Finally, we want to thank others who we pulled in for advice and reviews of various materials: Gina Ackeifi, Steve Borowick, Lena Dmitrieva, Elizabeth Goldman, Penny Gronbeck, David Kaplan, Samantha Louras, Stephen Reinach, Elizabeth Rosenzweig, and Tomer Sharon. You all are the best.

Donna

First, thank you to my coauthor Fiona who is super smart, talented, and fun to work with. This has been an incredible experience and I'm thankful that we worked so well together. A shout out to my peeps at Fidelity and MathWorks for being so supportive and listening to gripes about my long nights and weekends of working on this book. Thank you to my family and friends for being so great through this entire process. Thanks to Rebecca for keeping me sane and motivated when I most needed it. My appreciation goes to Tom and Bill for making my first book-writing experience so awesome that I wanted to do it again.

Fiona

Thanks to all my coworkers and students at the User Experience Center for their support and encouragement throughout this process. And thanks to Donna for persuading me to write this in the first place and being such a great coauthor. My family and friends have been incredibly patient and supportive through this whole experience, which I deeply appreciate. Special thanks to my mom, dad, and Aunt June for everything over the years, and to Justin and Hazel for picking up the slack as I spent countless hours in a haze of writing and editing.

SURVIVAL STORIES

LIST OF VIDEOS

All these videos are available on our website at *http://www.modsurvivalguide.org/videos*. You can also use your QR reader to scan the code for each video.

Video	QR Code	Description
1		Watch Video 1 to see an example of a moderator interacting with a self-blaming participant during a usability study. The participant is very nervous about the session and is looking for affirmation.
2		Watch Video 2 to see an example of a moderator working with a participant who is distracted by external circumstances during a usability study. The participant is reluctant to leave the session early even though he is distracted and has trouble focusing.
3		Watch Video 3 to see an example of a moderator interacting with a distracted participant during a remote usability study. The participant ends up sharing more than she intends.
4		Watch Video 4 to see an example of a moderator dealing with a flirtatious participant during a usability study. The participant starts off being friendly but becomes more forward as the session progresses.
5		Watch Video 5 to see an example of a moderator dealing with an interrupting observer during a contextual inquiry. The moderator pulls the observer out of the room to reiterate the session ground rules.
6		Watch Video 6 to see an example of a participant who is expecting an interview instead of a contextual inquiry. The moderator clarifies her expectations, but has to repeat them a couple of times as the session progresses.
7		Watch Video 7 to see an example of a moderator realizing that the participant scheduled for an interview lacks the necessary experience. The moderator discusses what to do with a stakeholder and finds a way to adapt the session.

LIST OF SITUATIONS

These are all of the situations discussed in this book, sorted by frequency (frequent, occasional, or rare).

Frequent

4.1	Participant does not seem to meet a key recruit criteria
5.1	Participant thinks that she is participating in a focus group
6.1	Participant is reluctant to say anything negative
6.2	Participant does something you don't understand
6.3	Participant is not thinking aloud
6.4	Participant is not able to complete a necessary task
7.1	Technical issues arise with your setup and/or equipment
7.2	Remote participant experiences difficulty joining
8.1	Participant looks for affirmation
8.2	Participant asks for your opinion
8.3	Participant looks or sounds uncomfortable and/or nervous
8.4	Participant is self-blaming
8.5	Participant asks, "Did other people have trouble with this?"
9.1	Participant is running late
9.2	Observers are loud and distracting
9.3	Participant receives a call during the session
10.1	Participant starts going on a tangent
11.1	Remote participant is obviously distracted
12.1	Participant is extremely entertaining and friendly
12.2	Something personal, inappropriate, or confidential is visible

Occasional

4.2	Participant either refuses to or can't do a key task
4.3	Participant has an unexpected physical feature
5.2	Participant doesn't want to be recorded or has other concerns
5.3	Participant has different expectations for the compensation

5.4	Participant brings you to a conference room or other space
5.5	Participant treats a contextual inquiry like an interview
6.5	Participant ignores or pretends to understand your question
6.6	Participant not approaching workflow naturally
6.7	Participant does not have any negative feedback
6.8	Participant believes he has successfully completed a task
6.9	Observers are not engaged in the session
7.3	Facility loses its internet connection
7.4	Remote participant drops off the call
7.5	Prototype or product changes unexpectedly
8.6	Participant is unwilling or unsure
9.4	Participant cancels or is a no-show
9.5	Observer unexpectedly interacts with the participant
9.6	Session interrupted accidentally by an observer or someone else
9.7	Session interrupted by someone the participant knows
10.2	Participant consistently focuses on irrelevant details
10.3	Participant does something very unexpected
10.4	Participant is slow or thorough
10.5	Participant gives vague responses to questions
10.6	Participant is difficult to hear or understand
10.7	You don't have time to complete everything
10.8	Participant struggles excessively with a task
11.2	Participant is distressed by a personal line of questioning
11.3	Participant insists that she would never do something
11.4	Participant is frustrated by the prototype's limited functionality
11.5	Participant seems annoyed at your neutrality
12.3	Participant is obviously distracted by external circumstances
12.4	Participant tells you something personal
12.5	Participant has a disconcerting or distracting physical attribute
13.1	Participant curses or makes inappropriate comments
13.2	You know the participant, or the participant knows you

Rare

11.6	Participant does not seem to respect you or take you seriously
11.7	Participant becomes insulting or has an agenda
11.8	Participant becomes agitated by a product's usability issues
12.6	You have to point out something potentially embarrassing
12.7	Participant seems upset
12.8	Participant has an unexpected disability or service animal
13.3	Participant knows an unexpected amount about you
13.4	Participant flirts with you
13.5	Participant does something awkward or uncomfortable
13.6	Participant makes a strangely specific request
13.7	Participant makes request during a site visit
14.1	Fire alarm goes off or the facility needs to be evacuated
14.2	A natural disaster (e.g., earthquake, tornado) occurs
14.3	Participant starts to looks ill or otherwise unwell
14.4	You begin to feel unwell while moderating a session
14.5	You notice a bad smell or have an allergic reaction
14.6	Participant seems to be drunk or stoned
14.7	Participant touches you
14.8	Participant's environment contains dangerous items
14.9	Participant is doing something illegal or threatening

AUTHOR BIOS

Donna Tedesco is a senior user experience researcher with over 10 years of user research experience. She has published and presented at local, national, and international conferences, and is coauthor with Bill Albert and Tom Tullis of the book *Beyond the Usability Lab: Conducting Large-Scale Online User Experience Studies*. Donna received a B.S. in engineering psychology/human factors from Tufts University School of Engineering, and an M.S. in human factors in information design from Bentley University.

Fiona Tranquada is a senior usability consultant with over 10 years of user research experience. She has published and presented at local and national conferences and is an active board member for the Boston chapter of the User Experience Professionals Association (UXPA). Fiona received a B.A. in professional writing and creative writing from Carnegie Mellon, and an M.S. in human factors in information design from Bentley University.

INTRODUCTION

Why we wrote this book

Throughout the years that we've known each other, we've spent a lot of time thinking and talking about the unique challenges of moderating user research. In the usability lab between sessions, driving to and from field visits, at professional meetings, and in the local coffee shop, we picked each other's brains. We shared stories about our experiences with participants, the approaches that our colleagues used, and any recent research on moderating techniques (although the latter always felt lacking). A book on this topic has been percolating for quite a while because, as you can probably guess, we're big moderating geeks.

When we started to mentor new user researchers, we found ourselves sharing tips on more than just how to moderate, like how to handle anything that comes up during a session including what specifically to say in those situations. Even the most experienced researchers struggle to balance the competing and ever-changing needs of a session, which means less experienced researchers are often thrown off-balance by the unexpected as well as the expected.

While there are a lot of great resources on how to plan user research and how to be a good moderator, there is little written about how to handle unexpected, tricky, or sticky situations that occur during a user research session. Although we've seen hints of these guidelines in the literature and heard them in conversations with colleagues, we found almost nothing that codified this topic. Loring and Patel (2001) wrote a great paper about handling awkward usability testing situations, but we wanted something that went into more detail and incorporated other types of one-on-one user research. The closest full-length work we've found is *Moderating Usability Tests* by Dumas and Loring (2008), which is an important, helpful, and well-written book about moderating fundamentals. If you haven't read it already, we recommend that you do so in conjunction with this book!

We wrote this book as a survival guide for anything that comes your way during a user research session. Our focus is on actionable and specific steps that you can take—including many examples of what to say—and how to decide what's best for your situation. We also want to start a conversation about these topics and help encourage more mindful moderation.

Who this book is for

This book will be most useful for anyone who performs one-on-one user research. These roles typically include user researchers or other related professionals or students involved in the design and evaluation of systems or experiences.

We're assuming that you already know the basics about moderating and running a user research session. You should also be familiar with logistical responsibilities such as recruiting participants, creating clear and concise informed consent forms, and welcoming the participant when he arrives for his session. If you need a refresher on the fundamentals, Appendix B lists some helpful resources for getting up to speed.

Beyond that, it doesn't matter whether you're a new moderator or a seasoned veteran; we believe there are nuggets of wisdom and food for thought in this book for everyone.

What you'll learn

Our goal is that after reading this book, you'll be inspired and empowered to make the best decisions for you, the participant, and your research. In many cases, your decisions will come down to "it depends" (as do so many things in user research), but we'll help you think through and accommodate the things those decisions should depend *on* in various types of situations. This book should be a quick, handy resource for you—think of it as your moderating Swiss Army knife that you can employ as needed.

You'll learn the steps involved in making these decisions and taking the appropriate action, including:

➤ What to consider any time you encounter a common, unexpected, tricky, or sticky situation.
➤ How to approach the situation and adapt your response as necessary depending on the study type, study goals, and the participant's comfort level.
➤ What kind of things you can say to help address the situation.

You can see specific examples of these principles in action in Part 2. In those chapters, we describe the spectrum of situations that you may encounter, ranging from the very common to the very rare. Note that we focus only on situations that occur during a research session and exclude any interactions that may occur in study preplanning, in-between sessions, or in postsession or poststudy debriefing. (That's enough material for another book!) Obviously, we can't provide a comprehensive list of every possible situation that you might encounter. At the same time, some of the situations listed here may never happen in your career. Essentially, these situations were selected to highlight how your responses need to adapt depending on what's happening around you.

Through these examples you can envision what you might do in similar situations. Even if you never encounter, say, an earthquake during a session (and we hope you don't), reading up on what to do in that situation will hopefully bring awareness and consideration for how to handle other types of emergencies.

One-on-one user research methods

This book focuses on user research methods where a moderator is interacting with a single participant, typically as an evaluation of or conversation about a product. We cover situations that occur during both in-person sessions (with the participant and moderator in the same location) and remote sessions (with the participant and moderator in different locations).

The three methods that we refer to are:

➤ *Usability studies.* During a usability study, you watch a participant as he attempts to complete tasks using a product (or a prototype of a product). The goal of a usability study is to evaluate how easy or difficult that product is to use.

➤ *Contextual inquiry.* During a contextual inquiry, you observe the participant in his native environment and ask the participant to show you how he does something. The participant guides the session, but you ask questions along the way to clarify and validate his observations. The goal of a contextual inquiry is usually to gain a deeper understanding of the user's process, including what the user finds important and necessary.

➤ *Interview.* During an interview, you ask a participant a series of questions. The goal of an interview is to gather detailed information from participants about a specific topic or set of topics. User research interviews, as opposed to market research interviews, usually focus on the participant's experience using products with the goal of collecting requirements and feedback to improve the product or experience.

Language used in this book

For the sake of simplicity, we've made the following terminology choices that you'll see throughout the book:

➤ *Product.* The product, prototype, or service being evaluated as part of the user research. It can be a computer system, mobile device interface, physical product, or a process. In a usability study, the product can be in the form of a low- or high- fidelity prototype or live environment. Basically anything and everything is fair game—as long as it's the focus of the user research.

➤ *User researcher.* Synonymous with user experience researcher. This refers to you, the moderator, even if your title is something else.

➤ *Your organization.* If you're an employee of the organization (e.g., company or business) that you're doing research for, your organization refers to your employer. If you are a consultant working on behalf of a client, your organization refers to your client.

➤ *Study* and *session.* A *study* is made up of a number of *sessions* with participants. For example, a usability study of a product might include six individual sessions with participants. We most commonly refer to sessions in the context of being back-to-back in a full day, but sessions could also intermittently span the course of many days or weeks.

➤ *Study plan.* The moderator's guide, study protocol, or test script that a user researcher puts together for a study and follows for each session. This can be as formal as a 10-page typed document or as informal as a few handwritten notes on a piece of notebook paper.

➤ *Stakeholders.* Your stakeholders are your key decision makers. If you're a consultant, your stakeholders are your clients. If you are an in-house user researcher, your stakeholders could be business partners, developers, project managers, and/or anyone else you need to work with closely as you design your study. We refer to *stakeholders* when we're talking about making decisions for your study.

➤ *Observers.* Observers include your stakeholders and anyone else observing the session, whether they're in the room with you, in another room (e.g., in a usability lab), or remote. We refer to *observers* when we mean anyone watching the study.

➤ *He/she.* For ease of reading and equality for all, we alternate pronouns throughout this book between "he" (this introduction and even-numbered chapters) and "she" (odd-numbered chapters). Please keep this arbitrary rule in mind when reading, as the situations listed don't have implicit gender-based assumptions. Every situation could happen with any combination of male and female moderators and participants.

How this book is organized

This book is structured in three parts.

Part 1 discusses your responsibilities as a moderator, provides high-level guidelines for handling situations during a session, and introduces moderation patterns. This part is broken into traditional chapters that you may want to read in their entirety.

Part 2 takes the principles from Part 1 and applies them to over 90 situations, grouped by topic. Each situation stands on its own, so Chapters 4–14 don't necessarily need to be read end-to-end. You can look up particular situations, browse through types of situations, or read a bunch at a time. Each situation is organized the same way:

➤ *Description*—what the situation is

➤ *Method(s)*—the type of method that this situation occurs in (usability study, contextual inquiry, interview)

➤ *Frequency*—how often a moderator might encounter this situation (frequent/occasional/rare)

➤ *Pattern(s) to apply*—which moderation patterns may be appropriate and helpful

➤ *What to do*—instructions for how to react and resolve the situation

➤ *What to say*—specific wording guidelines for talking with the participant

➤ *What not to say or do*—pitfalls to avoid

➤ *How to avoid*—tips to minimize the chance of this situation happening or, if that's not applicable, tips to help prepare you for the situation

➤ *See also*—cross-references to other situations that are similar to this one

Part 3 offers tips on how to minimize the chances of certain types of situations occurring and how to sharpen your moderating skills, no matter your experience level!

The appendices include a handy aggregated checklist of the most useful phrases that a moderator can use during a session and a list of things that you can do before a session to minimize the chances of something unexpected or sticky happening. These checklists are also available on our website (*http://www.modsurvivalguide.org*).

Here is a detailed breakdown of what each part of our book covers:

Part 1: Your Moderation Toolkit

Chapter 1: Moderation Matters: Power, Responsibility, and Style. This chapter discusses the qualities that are most helpful for a moderator during a research session and the different moderating styles that you can choose depending on the needs of the session.

Chapter 2: In the Trenches: Six Steps for Handling Situations. This chapter provides a high-level view of the steps you should take to understand what type of situation the participant is dealing with and respond appropriately.

Chapter 3: Mix and Match: Your Moderation Patterns Toolbox. This chapter defines specific steps that you can take to change the course of a session and when each pattern works best.

Part 2: Your Survival Guide

Chapter 4: Recruiting Mishaps: Participants You Weren't Expecting. This chapter covers situations where the participant does not fit your recruiting criteria or has some other feature that makes proceeding with the session a challenge.

Chapter 5: Participant Misconceptions: Not What the Participant Was Expecting. This chapter covers situations where there is a mismatch between the participant's expectations for the sessions and what you've planned.

Chapter 6: Some Guidance Required: Participants in Need of Shepherding. This chapter covers situations where the participant or your observers are not fully engaged with the session or require some other type of guidance to ensure that you get the feedback you need.

Chapter 7: Make It Work: Handling Technical Obstacles. This chapter covers situations where you encounter challenges with the technical setup, including prototype and remote session difficulties.

Chapter 8: Is This Right? Responding to Uncertain Participants. This chapter covers situations where the participants seem hesitant or unsure about their feedback.

Chapter 9: What's Going On? Recovering from External Interruptions. This chapter covers situations where your session is interrupted by an observer or someone else.

Chapter 10: Get on Track: Overcoming Momentum Blockers. This chapter covers situations that can slow down your session or throw it off track.

Chapter 11: Take the Wheel: Guiding Wayward Participants. This chapter covers situations where the participant becomes annoyed or defensive at you or the product.

Chapter 12: A Delicate Touch: Addressing Sensitive Situations. This chapter covers situations where something about the participant or his behavior has to be approached delicately.

Chapter 13: Uncomfortable Interactions: Responding to Awkward Situations. This chapter covers situations where the participant says or does something that makes you feel uncomfortable.

Chapter 14: Safety First: Minimizing Emotional and Physical Distress. This chapter covers situations that pose a risk to your and the participant's emotional or physical well-being.

Part 3: Improving Your Skills

Chapter 15: An Ounce of Prevention: Avoiding and Mitigating Situations. This chapter highlights steps you can take before the session to increase the odds of everything running smoothly.

Chapter 16: Sharpening Steel: How to Improve Your Skills and Help Others Improve Theirs. This chapter provides actionable tips on how to improve your moderating skills.

Sidebars and survival stories

Scattered throughout the book you'll find sidebars and survival stories:

➤ Sidebars go into more detail about specific topics related to moderating and challenges you may encounter throughout a session.

➤ Survival stories are written by other user researchers who are generously sharing experiences that they've had while moderating. We're thrilled by the variety of stories and the interesting situations they've encountered and hope you'll find them as entertaining and thought-provoking as we have.

Companion website and videos

Additional material, videos, and other bells and whistles are available on our website, *http://www.modsurvivalguide.org*.

We've put together seven videos, each of which shows a different situation or combination of situations. The videos do not show full sessions; instead, each video shows snippets of a session where a situation occurs and the moderator reacts. For dramatic effect, we show a few different snippets of the session to show the potential progression of a situation and how the moderator's response changes.

These videos are all listed on this page of our website: *http://www.modsurvivalguide.org/videos*. You'll also see these videos referenced throughout the book within certain situations. Each video reference will include a short description, the URL, and a QR code. If you're so inclined, you can scan the code with a QR reader using your mobile device. This will bring you directly to the page that hosts and discusses that video in more detail.

If you're an educator who is using this book for a class, please check out our page for educators on our website: *http://www.modsurvivalguide.org/educators*.

And, of course, we always welcome your feedback and questions, which you can submit by going to our contact page: *http://www.modsurvivalguide.org/contact*. You can also follow and talk with us on Twitter: *@ModSurvivalUX*.

Part 1
Your Moderation Toolkit

CHAPTER 1

Moderation Matters:
Power, Responsibility, and Style

1.1 "Are they laughing at me?"

I used to work at an institution of higher learning. We did a lot of usability testing, up to 120 studies a year. One particular day we had a client who wanted to test a website, but wanted their entire department staff to observe the testing. Our observation room sat 12 and it was mostly filled. Being late in the day, the observers were getting slap-happy after watching users identify the same usability problems over and over again. It was our last session of the day when we encountered a slightly more eccentric partici-pant than normal.

As she was tackling the tasks, she was quite entertaining in some of her feedback, and you could hear, through the adjoining wall to the observation room, muffled commentary becoming louder. I proceeded to instant message my colleague in the room to have the observers keep it down, but by the time she read my note, it was too late. My participant's eccentric nature had come out via an absolutely hysterical comment that I, as the moder-ator, had to literally bite my tongue to not laugh at. While I controlled my own reaction, a volcanic eruption of laughter could be heard through the wall. As my participant heard them, her face changed immediately, followed with "Are they laughing at me?"

I no longer wanted to laugh. I was paralyzed with "What do I do?" I lied. I told her no, they're not laughing at her, but rather that everyone who has come in here today has had a similar experience with this task, so we'll have to redesign the website. It was the best I could do at the time, but I'm not sure she believed me. During the next several tasks, there were no sounds from the observation room; they were as silent as she had become. At the end, I walked her out and apologized on behalf of the observers.

—Michael Dutton

To read about some factors to consider in a situation like Michael's, see sections 9.7 and 15.8.

1.2 Power and responsibility

Michael's story emphasizes how important a role you have as the moderator of a user research session. Your position on the session's frontlines means that when tricky, sticky, and unexpected situations arise, you're the one who has to decide what to do and then take action.

When you encounter an awkward or uncomfortable situation with a friend or someone else you know, you can inform your response with your knowledge about that person. You rarely have any additional knowledge to help you when the same situation happens during a user research session. And, of course, you have additional complications to consider.

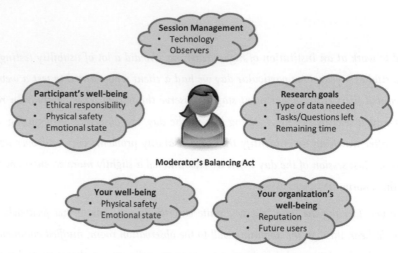

Figure 1.1 As the moderator, you're balancing a lot of competing needs during the session.

During a session, your reactions as a moderator must balance the following competing needs (Figure 1.1):

➤ The participant's emotional and physical states. Is she nervous or uncomfortable? Is she looking like she is unwell or experiencing physical discomfort?

➤ Your emotional and physical states. Are you uncomfortable with anything happening in the session? Are you reacting to an allergen in the environment? Is there an external circumstance occurring that might threaten your physical safety or that of the participant's?

➤ The study's research goals. Are you measuring an experience, looking for issues that need to be fixed, or trying to understand the participant's process?

➤ General session management needs. Are your remote session technology and recording equipment working correctly? Are your observers behaving well, especially if they're in the same room as you?

➤ Protection of your organization. Are you ensuring that the participant leaves with a positive experience so she doesn't say nasty things about your organization on social media? Are you doing your best to get feedback from participants that will help improve the experience for future users of your organization's products or services?

Throughout a session, this balance may shift and you, as the moderator, have to adjust accordingly. The way you handle a situation at the beginning of a session may be very different than how you'd handle the same situation later on, even with the same participant.

Take the example of the usability study session from Michael's story. At the beginning of the session, his duty as the moderator was mainly to elicit feedback that satisfied the study's goals. Some minimal encouragement may have been needed along the way to keep the participant content, but his larger concerns were to stay neutral and keep the observers engaged in the session. But as soon as the participant heard laughter from the adjacent room, she became uncomfortable, embarrassed, and all too aware that her performance was being watched.

At this point, the balance of competing needs shifted away from the session goals and more toward the participant's emotional comfort. Because the participant's comfort was at risk, Michael's attention as a moderator had to focus less on collecting feedback and more on making sure that she was okay and would leave the session feeling comfortable (rather than upset at him or his organization). Under normal conditions, telling the participant that everyone else had the same experience with the task might have been considered biasing. But Michael sacrificed that data integrity to help the participant relax and to avoid tarnishing the reputation of his organization. Also, he needed to ease tension between himself and the participant for his own emotional comfort.

Finding the right balance of these needs can be difficult and stressful, especially if you're new to moderating. There are times when you'll feel pressure to help the participant—it can be painful to watch her struggle—but you may have to resist that urge and maintain neutrality so that the data you're collecting are unaffected. On the flip side, sometimes you'll feel pressure from the stakeholders to stick to your study plan but you'll have to deviate from that plan to comfort an upset participant.

This responsibility is why you, as the moderator, are important. You have the power to impact both the study results and the participant's emotional state. More than anyone else involved in the research, your interpersonal and troubleshooting skills can mean the difference between a successful session and an awful one. But, as we've learned from countless movies, this power comes with great responsibility. You'll have to take that power and use it wisely in all kinds of common, tricky, and sticky situations. We hope this book will be your moderating Swiss Army knife: the right set of tools to help you deal with anything that comes your way during user research sessions.

1.3 The session ringmaster

Empathy. Flexibility. Creativity. Sense of humor. Aura of authority. To successfully handle tricky and sticky situations while moderating, you must embody and balance all these qualities. You may recognize these skills as being similar to those of a circus ringmaster. The ringmaster actively listens to and monitors everything that is going on around her, directs the audience's attention, and controls the overall pacing and flow of the show.

This response may have biased the participant by reinforcing her feelings about the product, possibly changing her feedback and behavior for the remainder of the session.

Let's talk about these qualities in more detail:

➤ *Empathy* helps you recognize what the participant is feeling. Remember that no matter what else you're dealing with outside of a session—argumentative stakeholders, temperamental technology, travel problems, etc.—the participant is a person and not just a way for you to get feedback. Put yourself in her shoes and think of how you'd want to be treated if the positions were reversed. Be genuinely interested in her well-being and in what she has to say. Use your empathy to identify when she is upset or frustrated and respond in a sincere, compassionate way to help her feel comfortable again.

➤ *Flexibility* is necessary because as these situations occur—a participant becomes sick or angry, an observer barges in, or technology fails you—you can't just railroad your way through the study plan. Sticking stubbornly to your original plan may just exacerbate the situation, leading to uncomfortable participants and biased results.

> Newer moderators tend to have the most difficulty with the principle of flexibility. See the sidebar "Tips for New Moderators."

➤ *Creativity* or improvisation is called for when unexpected situations arise. In fact, we know a few improv actors who are great moderators. A very simple formula called "Yes, and …" underlies improv. The principle behind "Yes, and …" is to acknowledge and accept what you have to work with and build upon it rather than fight it. This concept is especially well-suited for user research activities. If a tricky or sticky situation arises, embrace it (flexibility, or the "yes") and think quickly about how to handle it (creativity, or the "and …"). Creativity is not an easily learned thing, and for some it's more natural than for others. But you can set up a framework conducive to creativity by embracing the improvisation mindset.

➤ A *sense of humor* is important in unpredictable situations. When everything feels like it's falling apart during a session, it's better for you to laugh than cry! We don't mean that you have license to be obnoxious or make inappropriate jokes to the participant—of course you need to stay professional. Rather, we mean that you should appreciate the humor of the situation but only on the inside. Try not to get upset or nervous if something doesn't go as planned. Take a breath and remind yourself that you have the tools necessary to handle this. In the worst case, you'll have a great story to share with your colleagues later (after removing any confidential information, of course).

> When used carefully, subdued humor can take the edge off an awkward situation. *Carefully* is the key word. Only use humor when appropriate and there is no way for the participant to feel that you're laughing at *her*.

➤ An *aura of authority* means that, as the moderator, you must establish yourself to both the participant and the observers as the one in control of the session. Remember that you're ultimately responsible for what happens here! Your body language and tone of voice are vital in establishing this authority. You must also be comfortable keeping the session on track. For example, if the participant is taking longer than you expected to show you her process during a contextual inquiry and you need additional feedback before the session ends, you must politely but firmly move on. Remember to balance your authority with your empathy so that the participant feels comfortable and confident while sharing her feedback.

> While you have control over the session, the participant should feel that she is leading the conversation (i.e., she has "speakership"). See Dumas and Loring (2008) for more on this.

While you put the participant in the spotlight during user research, don't forget that you're ultimately in control. Harness your inner ringmaster, plus or minus the top hat and coattails.

> ## "YES, AND ..."
>
> The "Yes, and ..." principle is central to improvisation. Let's imagine that you start a scene with, "Happy birthday. I made you a cake," and my response is, "That is not a cake. That is a dinosaur and my birthday was last month." This response makes it harder for you to respond with something that builds the scene along smoothly. I've probably set you up for an awkward situation.
>
> Let's start again. You say, "Happy birthday. I made you a cake." Now my response is, "Thank you so much! Mmm, the bacon frosting is my favorite part." Once again, the goal is to build upon the scene, however weird, instead of controlling it. Rather than saying, "No, it's not bacon frosting! It's butterscotch," you might say, "Yeah. It goes great with the wasabi filling." This is saying "Yes, and ..."! You took weird and made it weirder—which makes for an exciting and (um, potentially) hilarious improv scene.
>
> We're not saying that if the participant strikes up a bizarre conversation, you should follow it to see where it goes (unless the topic relates to your goals). But if something unexpected happens, roll with it. If a prototype breaks, troubleshoot on-the-fly or find a way to get the participant's feedback without it. If an observer barges in, address it and resume the session. If the participant talks about bacon frosting, keep a poker face and bring the session back on track (again, unless bacon frosting is in scope!). Use flexibility and creativity to smoothly move the "scene" along.

1.4 The science and art spectrum

You're conducting a usability study. The participant is attempting a task that asks her to book a flight on a travel website. She gets to a page where she is considering the fares and says, "I don't usually just book a flight. I typically explore the flight-plus-hotel combination deals and purchase one of *them*."

Do you ask the participant to continue the original task of picking a flight? If you did, you'd be able to compare all participants' data fairly. Or do you go off-script and follow the participant into whatever she would typically explore? You'd then get some valuable information about other areas of the website that you might not get from other participants.

You've just stumbled into one of user research's great debates: Is moderating a science or an art? This debate usually arises in the context of usability studies when the participant is asked to attempt tasks with a product. Those who contend that moderating is a science believe that every moderator–participant interaction is an opportunity for bias and skewed data. Such moderators propose only interrupting participants during tasks if absolutely necessary, and keeping those interruptions confined to minimal phrases, or what Dumas and Loring (2008) refer to as "acknowledgement tokens" like "so" and "mmhmm." Even if the participant is upset or distracted, your interaction with her would not change.

We don't see the art and science approaches as a binary choice, but rather as the endpoints of a spectrum. Depending on the study goals and method, your approach may fall anywhere along that spectrum.

Because the majority of studies we've conducted have been formative (where the goal is to improve and learn rather than measure), our approach leans toward the art of moderating. This approach allows for more natural interactions with participants and, in our experience, lets you be more responsive when the unexpected occurs and acknowledgment tokens alone won't cut it. In types of user research other than usability studies, there is an even stronger need for there to be some art to moderating. A certain flexibility level is fundamental for moderating those methods. For example, an interviewee may raise a topic relevant to your study goals that you had not originally planned on discussing, and you'd like to follow up. Or during a contextual inquiry, you may not anticipate how the participant will do some of her work, so you may need to muster up some on-the-spot questions about what she is doing.

We've found that the science approach works best for summative research (where the goal is to measure or validate a product) and when biometric or eye-tracking devices are used. However, even for summative research, you need to prioritize the participant's well-being, even if it means sacrificing your data's integrity. For example, if the participant starts crying during your summative usability study, you should respond compassionately instead of maintaining your neutral acknowledgments. While this may mean your task time measurements or other metrics may be affected, your ethical priority is toward the participant.

Where your approach should fall on the science/art spectrum depends on varying contexts, such as:

➤ The type and nature of the research—is it a usability study, contextual inquiry, or an interview? While bias is a concern for all methods, influencing participant behavior during usability studies or contextual inquiries might be a bigger concern than influencing attitudes stated in an unstructured interview.

➤ If it's a usability study, is it summative or formative? A summative study requires strict assessment, usually measuring the user experience with metrics like task time and task success. Interruptions and exploratory questions may come at a cost in data quality. A formative test is meant to be more exploratory and anecdotal, so there is usually room for more conversation and creative follow-up tasks/questions.

Some user researchers in the science camp have criticized the think-aloud protocol as a biasing factor in usability studies, citing research like Boren and Ramey (2000). Instead, they watch as the participant works silently and ask detailed follow-up questions later.

As we cover specific situations and recommendations later in this book, we'll be explicit about any assumptions we're making about the type of research and its goals. We'll also explain the trade-offs you must consider and the potential outcomes of your choices. Feel free to adapt our advice to align with your own philosophy and circumstances, and use it to guide you in making more informed decisions.

1.5 Your moderating style

Moderating isn't just about controlling the session and responding to any situations that occur. It's also about the approach you take and the interpersonal skills you use when interacting with the participant. We define this approach as your moderating style. Just like how people come in all shapes, sizes, and combinations of qualities, so do our moderating personas.

Your style of interacting with participants is a combination of your core personality traits and the disposition you take while moderating. Your style may involve a combination of two or more characteristics, such as sociable, friendly, relaxed, lively, jovial, detached, business-like, quiet, inquisitive, alert, eager, dutiful, respectful, controlled, or subdued. Perhaps your natural style of moderating is friendly, but quiet and business-like. Or relaxed, yet respectful and inquisitive.

Think about what your natural moderating style is like. In your ideal session, with your ideal participant, how would you interact with her? What "vibe" would you be sending? Once you've identified your style, you'll be able to recognize how your behavior might come across to different types of participants.

Table 1.1 lists some of the different moderating styles we've seen and used in the past, defines their characteristics, and warns about potential biases and pitfalls that come with them. Of course there are variations and gradations of each style, but these hit the key differences.

As you can see from Table 1.1, there are advantages and disadvantages to every moderating style. There is no single ideal moderating style—the style that you use can and should change from study to study, session to session, or even during the course of a session. Also, these styles are not mutually exclusive. Figure out what kind of style (or styles) will work best with your research goals in a particular study, and be flexible if the participant or situation calls for it.

1.6 Effective adaptation

To move beyond your natural style and become a truly excellent moderator, you must learn to adapt your style when necessary. Much like Sun Tzu's *The Art of War* (n.d.), the art of moderating requires recognizing and responding to changing conditions. The "Yes, and …"

> Think of your style as a sort of moderating fingerprint.

> One way to help identify your style is to watch videos of yourself moderating or ask your colleagues for their objective assessment. See Chapter 16 for more ideas.

Moderating Style	Description	Good When	Possible Pitfalls	Tips
Friendly Face	▶ Centers on being comforting and encouraging to participants. ▶ Comes across as relatively casual and responsive to participants, often using nonverbal feedback such as smiling and nodding, and can help participants feel comfortable and happy to be part of the research activity.	▶ Participants are timid and self-blaming. ▶ Participants are participating out of obligation. ▶ Participants seem disengaged.	▶ Talking too much or letting the casual, conversational style become influential. ▶ Slipping into the role of a buddy, saying biasing things like, "I know, that does seem weird," or "Don't worry, everyone's had trouble with that." ▶ Steering participants off topic so they become more interested in laughing or chatting with you than giving the feedback you need.	▶ Be genuine. If participants feel that you're being disingenuous, they may close up and give curt feedback, or make snarky remarks or facial expressions.
Down to Business	▶ Treats the session with a serious, professional tone. Often limits interaction with the participant and minimizes probing or follow-up questions. ▶ Shows the participant that you're in control of the session and have an important agenda to cover.	▶ Participants act too casually, are chatty, or otherwise seem to need structure. ▶ Participants continue asking for assistance. ▶ Participants need constant reinforcement that they're the "driver" and you're mostly a silent observer. ▶ Your study is using a quantitative method where you're measuring aspects of the experience.	▶ Becoming too formal or quiet, which can make participants feel nervous or like they're being tested. This nervousness may prevent them from interacting naturally with a product or opening up as much as they would have otherwise.	▶ Monitor your tone. If it becomes overly serious or academic, participants may become more nervous. ▶ Avoid condescension. Participants may view a serious tone as condescending, especially if they're colleagues at the same organization or participants who are high profile (e.g., VIP customers).

Inquisitive Mind	▶ Focuses on the feedback you're given and follows up with questions and activities to learn as much as possible about everything. ▶ Runs session with a mindset like that of a student, eager to learn. ▶ Tends to "go rogue," and loosely follow study plans.	▶ Participants are knowledgeable but need prompting to go into detail. ▶ Your study is using more qualitative methods (e.g., interviewing). ▶ Your study is during the discovery phase of a design process where you "don't know what you don't know," so any information is useful.	▶ Taking participants off-track from their thoughts or natural interactions by your continuous questioning. ▶ Encouraging participants to go on tangents that may not be useful, or open the floodgates for complaining or nonconstructive venting.	▶ Monitor your study plan. With this style it's easy to mismanage your time. ▶ Consider whether your intended questions stem from wanting useful information for the research, or just being curious.
By the Book	▶ Takes great lengths to create a study plan that follows a prescribed order and purpose, and tries not to deviate from the plan. If you didn't create the plan but are using it to run a session, you'll probably follow it very closely. ▶ Tends to be the opposite of an inquisitive mind style, and is usually a style inherent to newer moderators.	▶ Participants are experts in a highly technical domain and you're not. ▶ Your study is using a quantitative method where order and timing are important. ▶ Your study plan is complex and carefully thought out, with limited flexibility and lots of dependencies between tasks or questions.	▶ Following a "script" can sometimes mean missed opportunities for useful feedback. ▶ Causing participants to tense up and act or respond unnaturally because they feel like they're being tested. ▶ Biasing participants and making them feel stupid if you have to show them how to do something before moving to the next task (due to dependencies in the tasks).	▶ Make participants feel heard. Since you may not have follow-up questions that reassure participants that you heard their feedback, use eye contact and a friendly tone to make them feel heard and valued. ▶ Avoid redundancy. Make sure you're not eliciting feedback on topics that participants already addressed earlier in the session, just because it's in the script. If you do want to cover those topics again, preface your questions with phrases such as "You may have already answered this, but ..."

Table 1.1: Examples of moderating styles, their strengths, and weaknesses.

19

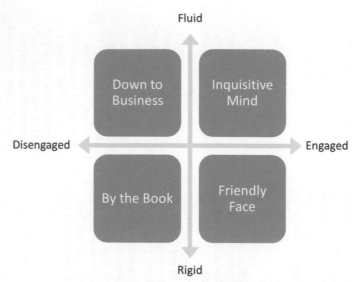

Figure 1.2 Different moderating styles are appropriate depending on your research goals, how prescribed your study plan is (fluid to rigid), and how you want to approach the participant (engaged vs. disengaged).

approach calls for rolling with the punches. Likewise, your preferred moderating style may not be suitable for a particular kind of study, participant, or situation, and you may have to transition to another on-the-fly. This is when your flexibility is really put to the test!

The best style to use depends both on how you need to interact with the participant (as discussed in Table 1.1) and where your study goals fall on the quadrant shown in Figure 1.2. Each style falls somewhere within the range of rigid versus fluid (based on your research goals and how much you need to follow a prescribed structure of your study plan) and engaged versus disengaged (how you need to interact with the participant at any given time).

You've read about the differences between moderating styles in Table 1.1, but let's hash out a more detailed example here. Consider a contextual inquiry where you have a chatty participant who you're trying to keep focused on demonstrating her workflow. Contextual inquiries are typically fairly fluid, and you're a fairly friendly and casual moderator, so you've started with a style similar to Inquisitive Mind. However, given the participant's talkativeness, continuing to be so informal and familiar could create issues. The participant may become even more chatty and off-topic, pulling her away from the natural workflow you're trying to observe. The session may quickly snowball into an interview or conversation. The best way to adapt here is to transition to a Down to Business style with the goal of slightly disengaging from the participant. You don't want to disengage so much that the participant becomes uncomfortable, just enough so that she knows you're there for the serious business of watching her work.

We talk more about the moderation pattern of disengaging from the participant in section 3.6.

Conversely, other situations may require you to draw a participant out and build engagement. Consider a fairly scripted interview where the participant is quiet and reserved. She seems like she is either shy or nervous about the session. Even if you're more of a By the Book moderator, you may need to turn on the Friendly Face to help her feel more comfortable. A genuine smile and sincere tone of voice can help pull the participant out of her shell without biasing her feedback.

There is no precise way to pinpoint a participant's or moderator's personality, making it difficult to give one-size-fits-all advice for moderating. But our hope is that we've made you more aware of different moderating styles and how these styles can impact a session. To be truly effective you need to adapt and switch to other styles as needed. Being aware of moderating styles and their comparative strengths and weaknesses will help you shape and polish your own approach.

TIPS FOR NEW MODERATORS

When you're just starting to moderate, you may feel overwhelmed by everything that you need to track throughout a session. New moderators tend to be very By the Book because of these concerns. You may cling tightly to a scripted study plan, worried that you'll miss a question or ask something the wrong way. While these are reasonable concerns, this devotion to a script may mean that you'll miss a change in the participant's body language or tone, potentially missing an issue until it's too late to successfully resolve it.

These are some recommendations we give to new moderators to help them balance their attention so that the participant doesn't go unnoticed:

➤ If you have a scripted study plan, review it carefully before moderating your session. If possible, watch a team member moderate from the same script before your first session so you can get a real feel for the overall flow. This familiarity will make it easier for you to pay more attention to the participant instead of being so focused on the script.

➤ Add a note at the bottom of each page of your study plan to remind yourself to look up at the participant.

➤ Limit your note taking so you can pay more attention to the participant. Use your pen to check off questions/tasks as you go through them so you have a quick visual indicator of what you've covered already and what's remaining.

For additional tips on improving your moderating skills, see Chapter 16.

SURVIVAL STORY: "THE CHAIR'S ARMS WERE TOO FIXED AND NARROW"
NICOLLE DIVER

A couple of years ago, I was conducting a usability study on a financial services website in a traditional lab setting. The lab was set up with two rolling office chairs next to each other and facing a computer with a prototype of the website we were testing. The participant, Greg, was a very large person. Greg entered the room and attempted to make himself comfortable in one of the rolling chairs. Unfortunately, the chair's arms were fixed and too narrow for Greg to sit back fully in the seat. Greg awkwardly sat on the front edge of the chair and waved hello to the team of observers behind the one-way mirror.

Greg provided helpful feedback, but appeared nervous throughout the interview. He questioned if the feedback he was offering was helpful and second-guessed some of his answers. As we approached the final third of his session, Greg used his arms as leverage against the table to adjust his position. The rolling office chair shot out from underneath him, leaving Greg flat on his back on the floor! Instantly embarrassed, I asked a mortified Greg if he was hurt and jumped out of my chair in an attempt to help as he stood up. By the time a male colleague rushed into the lab from the observation room, Greg and I were settling ourselves back in our chairs at the desk. At this point, I was keen to end the session, but it was clear (despite a beet red face) that Greg preferred to finish the session and not dwell on the fall. I continued the discussion regarding the task we were testing and discreetly cut out any remaining tasks. Instead of heading to the observation room to see if there were any additional questions, I completed the wrap-up questions as if nothing had happened. I walked Greg out of the office with the usual small talk about the weather and a friendly thank-you.

We were lucky that Greg did not injure himself or cause any damage to anything aside from his bruised ego. Greg was not the first participant to find our standard-issue office chairs too small.

Key takeaways are to have the most accessible seating option possible and, in the event of an embarrassing situation, do your best to help the person regain their dignity. Try to find a chair that is as adjustable as possible—not just up and down, but also with either no arms or adjustable-width arms. And remember, the participant won't know if you cut the last task or skip a few questions. By acknowledging the embarrassing event in a polite and professional way and then moving on, Greg left the session reassured that we got the information we needed despite his bruised ego.

CHAPTER 2

In the Trenches:
Six Steps for Handling Situations

Once you've understood your role as the moderator and the different styles of moderating, you can start thinking about how to handle the different kinds of situations that may arise during the session. Some of these situations will challenge your interpersonal skills; others will push the limits of your troubleshooting and crisis-handling capabilities. Although there are common circumstances you're almost guaranteed to encounter, we can't predict what else might happen. Even after our years in user research, we're still surprised (and sometimes delighted, shocked, or horrified) by what happens when we're one-on-one with a participant. This chapter provides a set of guidelines (as shown in Table 2.1) to help you decide exactly what to do when something unexpected, sticky, or tricky happens during your session.

1. Take a moment to evaluate the situation before jumping to action.
2. Resolve any threats to physical safety.
3. Verify that you're not causing or magnifying the situation.
4. Check the participant's comfort level.
5. Use careful language and tone to probe on the situation and begin to resolve it.
6. Regain control to bring the session back on track.

Table 2.1: Step-by-Step Guide for Handling Any Situation.

2.1 Take a moment to evaluate the situation before jumping to action

You're running an interview with a remote participant over the phone. The session seems to be going well until the participant doesn't respond as quickly to your questions. You hear him whisper to someone in the background but can't understand what he says. What, if anything, should you do?

When you encounter anything outside of expected session circumstances, take a moment to step back and evaluate the situation. As the moderator, you keep track of so many things that it can be difficult to take that time. But doing so is vitally important. Why?

➤ You need to make sure that you understand the cause of the situation so you can address it appropriately. Rushing to do or say something may lead you to inadvertently make the situation worse or further compromise the results of the session.

➤ The situation may resolve itself. In this remote session example, a few moments may be enough for the participant's whispering to stop and for you to be able to move on with your questions. Also, consider the example of a usability study participant who becomes confused or frustrated. A delay of a few extra seconds is often enough time for a participant to find his bearings and continue without any intervention from you. This delay may also be all a distracted participant needs to reengage with a task or question on his own.

➤ If the situation persists, those additional seconds will keep the participant from seeing you sweat (or, in a remote session, hearing you fumble your words as you try to figure out what to do). Remember that, as the moderator, you establish the pace for the session. Take this moment to think through your options and prepare what you're going to do and say if the situation continues.

This moment may feel like a lifetime to you, but it doesn't necessarily feel that way to the participant! Even in a potentially life-threatening situation (e.g., a fire alarm goes off), take a moment to gather as much information as possible before proceeding. Your need to respond appropriately should outweigh your instinct to react immediately. Remember that you're responsible for the participant's well-being as well as your own.

Think of this moment as securing your own oxygen mask before assisting other passengers.

If the situation is especially tense or you're not quite sure what's going on, you may want to take your moment in another room, away from the participant. Taking a break is an incredibly powerful tool that we'll discuss more in section 3.7. A break gives you a chance to think about what's happening in the session without the pressure of monitoring everything else. If you have observers, you can use this break to check with them and get a "gut-check" on what you think is happening and why. The participant may also benefit from a few minutes to cool off, or deal with his distractions.

Table 2.2 shows examples of what you can say if you need to take a break. Note that you can use these phrases even if they aren't entirely true—consider them mild deceptions for the greater good. Pretexts are discussed further in the sidebar "Using a Pretext."

For a usability study with a multiroom setup:

➤ "We're at a good stopping point right now. Let's take a short break and resume the session in five minutes." (If appropriate given your setup, you can add: "Feel free to leave the room to get a drink or go to the restroom while I'm gone.")

For an onsite and remote sessions:

➤ "I'm so sorry, but would you mind if I took a quick five-minute break to get a drink?" or "This seems like a good stopping point. Why don't we take a quick five-minute break?"

Table 2.2: What to Say: Taking a Break.

USING A PRETEXT

While you should avoid misleading the participant, there are times when the truth is going to be harmful. For example, if you notice that the participant does not have the characteristics you need and you want to consult with your stakeholders (who are in another room) about what to do, you should not express your concern about his qualifications directly to the participant. Being honest may hurt his feelings or make him nervous about participating. Instead, make an excuse to leave the room.

Technology can be blamed for many things and provides a convenient excuse if you need to leave the room or end the session early. Just make sure that you have something realistic to blame so that your reason for leaving isn't obvious. For example, if you say, "The computer isn't working correctly," the participant may realize that you're lying because he can see that it actually is working. But if you say, "Our prototype isn't working the way it's supposed to," he doesn't have any reason to know that it is just an excuse.

Examples of what you might say include:

➤ "It seems like we may be having technical issues with our recording equipment. Let's take a short five-minute break while I run next door to look into it."

➤ "I apologize, but I just noticed that there is something wrong with our prototype. Please excuse me for a few minutes while I go to the other room and see if anyone from our team knows what's going on."

➤ "I'm sorry, but it looks like the product I wanted to get your feedback on isn't working. I have a few more questions for you, but after that, we'll end the session early. You'll still get your full compensation though!"

If you don't feel comfortable blaming the technology or it isn't applicable (e.g., in an interview where you aren't using any equipment), you can use the study itself as a pretext:

➤ "I meant to give you your compensation at the start of the session. Let me actually go grab that now. Let's take a break for a few minutes."

➤ "I just noticed that I'm missing a page of my questions. Let's take a quick break so I can run next door and print that out."

➤ "The rest of these tasks/questions aren't applicable to you/your role, so we're going to skip them. This means we may be done a little bit earlier than expected, but don't worry, you'll still receive your full compensation!"

2.2 Resolve any threats to physical safety

In the middle of a contextual inquiry, you hear a low rumbling sound. You take a moment to evaluate the situation, and quickly realize that you're experiencing an earthquake. What do you do next?

For more about how to handle earthquakes and other natural disasters, see section 14.2.

When a situation involves a physical threat, you need to respond to and address the threat as soon as you've taken a couple of seconds to understand what's going on. Respond quickly and appropriately, even if that means that you're unable to continue the session. The safety of you and the participant takes priority over your data collection needs!

Keep in mind that the participant may not know what to do, especially if he is in your facility. You must take responsibility for his safety as well as your own. For example, if a fire alarm goes off or your building is evacuated, bring the participant with you as you follow standard evacuation procedures. While the participant may end up seeing your observers, your top priority is to keep him from physical harm instead of maintaining the integrity of the session.

In the example of an earthquake, you should instruct the participant about where to go (e.g., under a desk or in a doorway). If you're moderating a usability study from an adjacent control room, and you think it's safe to spend another couple of seconds using the microphone, tell the participant that you're experiencing an earthquake and instruct him to go under the desk or in the doorway immediately.

The participant's perception of his safety is just as important, even if you think he is safe. For example, we've heard of moderators continuing a session through a small earthquake or a fire drill without saying anything to the participant. Be sensitive to the participant's comfort and keep him informed.

If you're in the participant's space, follow his lead to exit the building safely or follow the appropriate safety protocol for the event that you're experiencing.

Depending on the severity of the situation and safety of the environment, you may want to cancel or end the session rather than asking the participant to wait around until the situation is resolved. If you do this, be sure to give him his full compensation and thank him for the feedback provided. If the environment is safe, and the participant is not visibly shaken and willing to continue, offer to take a short break before resuming so you and the participant can both regain focus.

2.3 Verify that you're not causing or magnifying the situation

During an interview, the participant starts making snide remarks after each question you ask. You're not quite sure why he is responding that way. The issue doesn't resolve itself, and taking a break doesn't help. There is no physical danger to resolve but you're worried about the participant's attitude and its effect on the feedback he is providing. What, if anything, should you do?

Let's step into some awkward territory for a minute, but we promise, it's for your own good! Sometimes a situation is magnified, if not created, by something that you're doing. Part of being a good moderator is being humble enough to constantly evaluate and reflect on how you're interacting with participants. Before you jump to a conclusion about why the participant is behaving in a certain way, try to detect anything you may have done that led to this behavior.

Table 2.3 shows some examples of problematic moderator behavior that we've observed, the moderating styles (as identified by Table 1.1) that may encourage this behavior, and the effect it can have on the participant's comfort level.

As discussed in Chapter 1, there is a delicate balance between the goals and method of your study, the type of participant you have, his current emotional state, and the appropriate moderating style to use. These last two elements in particular can change multiple times

Moderator Behavior (Moderating Style)		How the Participant May React
Over-the-top fake (Friendly Face)	You're trying to be very kind and respectful toward the participant while maintaining a friendly tone. However, you don't realize that you come across as patronizing or disingenuous.	The participant becomes irritated and curt with his feedback. He may feel like you're not taking his responses seriously.
Buddy-buddy (Friendly Face)	You want the participant to be comfortable, so you start acting like the two of you are old pals. You laugh together and find yourself making jokes. He tries to make you laugh and looks to you for affirmation, as with any natural friendly exchange. For an example of what this may look like, see Figure 2.1.	The participant begins to try to please you, unknowingly reflecting your attitudes and biases. His efforts to please you throw him off his natural course of interaction and keep him from answering questions fully and honestly.
Obliviously abrasive (Down to Business)	You maintain a serious, expectant tone as you ask questions. However, your tone comes across as overly stern. You also stare intently at the participant without looking away or blinking while he talks. For an example of what this may look like, see Figure 2.1.	If the participant is naturally talkative and high profile, he may feel insulted or put off by your serious tone. If he started out nervous, your tone may only increase his discomfort. The intent staring may unnerve him to the point of asking to leave.
Death by silence (Down to Business; By the Book)	You're trying to be as neutral as possible so you take a very minimalistic approach to moderating. You're completely silent most of the time, using only brusque probes (e.g., "And …?"), even though the participant is obviously nervous and uncomfortable with the silence.	The participant starts to blame himself and apologizes for "doing a bad job." Because you don't respond, he becomes more uncomfortable.
Clock watcher (By the Book)	You're trying to stay on schedule, and look at the clock or your watch at the most inopportune times. You ask a question from your study plan and, while the participant answers, look at the clock, look ahead in the study plan, or obviously pay no attention to the participant's answer.	The participant gets frustrated and makes sarcastic or snide remarks because he doesn't feel like you're listening to him.

Table 2.3: Examples of Problematic Moderator Behavior and Its Effects.

Figure 2.1 Examples of moderating behaviors. The Obliviously abrasive (left) and the Buddy-buddy (right). © 2013 Mark Ainscow, used with permission.

throughout the session. You should always carefully monitor how the participant responds to avoid making him uncomfortable. Again, part of the art of moderating is in evaluating your technique throughout the session and adapting it as necessary.

LEARNING TO ENJOY THE SILENCE

Most moderators are uncomfortable with silence during a study, especially new moderators! You may feel especially uncomfortable if you're using a think-aloud protocol, since it may seem like the participant forgot your instruction to share what he is looking for or expects to see.

However, silence can be a valuable tool. Sometimes allowing a participant to quietly process and then answer the question or resume thinking aloud is more valuable than probing immediately for his thoughts whenever he becomes silent. For example, most people have difficulty thinking aloud while reading thick blocks of web content, so hold off on your questions while the participant is obviously reading. Similarly, not answering the participant's question right away can lead the participant to answer it on his own. However, if he shifts toward you, or repeats the question while raising his voice, it's time to say something.

It takes practice to become comfortable with this approach, but it pays off when the participant doesn't feel rushed or harassed by your frequent reminders to talk about what he is thinking.

To find out if you're creating or contributing to a problem:

1. Check your body language:

   ➤ Are you too close to or too far from the participant?

   ➤ Are you maintaining eye contact, or are you making too much eye contact?

➤ Have you been yawning or glancing at your watch?

➤ Are you sitting upright, or are you slouched down in your chair?

➤ Have you been frowning or grimacing instead of maintaining a friendly, neutral expression?

2. Replay what you've said during the session:

➤ Have you neglected to reassure the participant that you're listening to him? Have you been chiming in with the occasional "mm-hm" to encourage him to continue talking?

➤ Have you been talking too much, and not letting the participant talk?

➤ If running a usability study with a think-aloud protocol, did you give the participant enough time to respond before reminding him to think aloud? (See the sidebar "Learning to Enjoy the Silence" for more on this.)

➤ Did you stop using the participant's language and start using language from the product's user interface, domain, or any other jargon he may not understand?

➤ Are you using close-ended or leading questions that "give away" the answer you want or expect to hear?

➤ Have you been laughing with or making jokes with the participant?

If the participant is remote, you might need to provide acknowledgments more frequently to reassure him that you're still there and paying attention.

3. Replay your paralanguage—*how* you said what you said:

➤ Did you sound judgmental about an opinion or detail that the participant shared?

➤ Did you insinuate that the participant did something incorrectly?

➤ Could your tone be heard as patronizing or disingenuous?

4. Evaluate your note-taking behavior:

➤ Are you shuffling papers while the participant attempts tasks or answers your questions?

➤ Have you been taking notes only when the participant says or does something "wrong" or unexpected?

5. Check the physical setup of the room:

➤ Is the temperature too hot or too cold?

➤ Is there anything in your equipment setup that the participant seems to be struggling with (e.g., a monitor that is pushed too far back on the table, or a chair that is set too high or too low for the participant)?

Participants are quick to notice anything different, so if you suddenly started writing when you hadn't done so previously, he may feel that he is doing something wrong.

We'll talk more about how to build awareness of your own behaviors while moderating in Chapter 16.

2.4 Check the participant's comfort level

Once you've verified that the situation you're seeing hasn't been caused or exacerbated by your own behavior, check to see if the participant's degree of comfort has declined to an unacceptable level.

Most user research starts out being somewhat uncomfortable for the participant. He may arrive without knowing exactly what he'll be asked to do, or he may worry that he is being tested in some way. If you are coming in to his space, he'll be unable to get away from the typical hassles of his environment, which may become magnified by the uncertainty of what he'll be asked to do during the session.

Unless you're doing very specific research that deliberately puts users in uncomfortable situations, you want to minimize, if not altogether eliminate, anything that compromises the comfort or safety of the participant. Part of your job as a moderator is helping the participant feel comfortable participating and providing his feedback, and ensuring that he remains comfortable—physically and psychologically—during the session.

PROTECTING PARTICIPANT RIGHTS

Most professional organizations whose members interact with nonmembers in a professional capacity, including the User Experience Professionals Association (UXPA), have a code of conduct or set of ethical guidelines to govern their members' behavior. These guidelines are in place to ensure the ethical behavior of the professional (i.e., you as the moderator), and protect the rights of the nonmember (participant).

As a user researcher, you need to keep your ethical obligations to the participant front and center throughout the session. Remember, when the participant comes to your session, he may have little to no information about what he'll be doing and why he'll be doing it. It's your job to provide him with this information before he begins, and obtain his consent to participate.

This informed consent lets the participant know what he'll be doing as part of the study, what he'll receive for participating (compensation), and his rights (e.g., to take a break or leave at any time). Even though you should have him sign a consent form before the session begins, review the key points verbally as part of your briefing at the beginning of a session.

We recommend reviewing the UXPA's code of conduct at http://www.usabilitypro fessionals.org/about_upa/leadership/code_of_conduct.html, which outlines how to behave ethically as a user researcher. As a quick cheat sheet, here are the key things to remember when interacting with your participants:

➤ Do no harm, and if possible, provide benefits. As discussed in Chapter 1, there is always some level of stress associated with participating in user research. However, your responsibility as a moderator is to keep that stress—whether physical, mental, or emotional—from reaching an unreasonable level.

➤ Act with integrity. Be respectful toward the participant, no matter who he is or what he does.

➤ Respect the participant's privacy, confidentiality, and anonymity. Make sure he provides his informed consent, and that he knows the steps you'll take to avoid disclosing his personal information.

Ensuring the participant's physical comfort is usually fairly easy to accomplish. Let him know that he is welcome to take a break at any time and, if possible, offer him a beverage. If he seems uncomfortable in the research space (e.g., because the chairs are at an awkward height or size for him or the air conditioning is running high), make whatever adjustments you can to keep the environment as welcoming and stress-free as possible.

The participant's psychological comfort can be more challenging to maintain, especially when he is asked to interact with a product that has major usability issues or he is being interviewed about a sensitive or private situation. However, keep in mind that if a participant is struggling or growing frustrated with a usability study task, his comfort is not necessarily being threatened. In fact, that struggle often fulfills a common goal of user research, which is to identify problem areas. The participant's struggle serves the purpose of making the product better for future users.

If, however, the participant berates himself for being stupid or unable to figure something out, or exhibits more than one of the signs of an uncomfortable participant (Table 2.4), you need to alleviate his discomfort. Remember that a participant who leaves a session feeling disgruntled or unhappy is an unhappy customer (or potential customer). Given how easy it is to share negative reviews and experiences via social media, you want to avoid any potential damage to the credibility of your research or your organization.

If the participant seems uncomfortable, be careful not to assign any blame to him. Remember that he is likely in an unfamiliar environment (to him), or may be stressed to show a stranger (you) around his comfortable environment. He may be under a lot of stress unrelated to the session, such as childcare issues or tight work deadlines. Even if there is nothing external

Pay attention to context when evaluating the participant's comfort level. He may be sweating because he is nervous, or because the thermostat is set too high. But if he is sweating and calling himself stupid, he is probably uncomfortable.

> ➤ He increases his physical distance from what's being evaluated (e.g., chair pushed away from the table or keeping a physical product at arm's length).
> ➤ He crosses his arms.
> ➤ He blames himself or apologizes for being "stupid" or inexperienced.
> ➤ He has difficulty speaking clearly.
> ➤ He exhibits signs of emotional distress, such as tremors, crying, or excessive sweating.
> ➤ He constantly glances around the room or at the cameras.
> ➤ He asks to end the session early.
> ➤ He pays excessive attention to distractions (e.g., his email is open in the background and he keeps checking it).

Table 2.4: Signs a Participant May Be Uncomfortable.

 Watch Video 1 to see an example of a moderator interacting with a self-blaming participant during a usability study. The participant is very nervous about the session and is looking for affirmation.

Visit our website (http://www.modsurvivalguide.org/videos) or use your QR reader to scan this code.

causing his discomfort, the research session itself can create some stress no matter what you do to avoid it.

To help the participant feel more comfortable,

➤ Reassure him that he is not being tested, and that anything that frustrates him is valuable information for the product team. Remind him that his feedback will make the product easier to use for future users. For a contextual inquiry or interview, you can reassure him that his feedback is confidential and will ultimately be used to make his own life/work better.

➤ If you're running a usability study, avoid using the term *test* when referring to your research. A test is something that can be failed, and may place additional pressure on the participant. He may not understand that you're testing the product and not him. Instead, use *study*, *session*, or *evaluation of* <product>. Likewise, you may consider calling each usability task a *scenario* instead of *task*.

➤ If the participant crosses his arms or moves away from you (or the product being evaluated), ask him to tell you what he is thinking. This question gives him permission to express the reasons for his discomfort, and may reveal if he is uncomfortable because of something you asked him to do.

➤ Ask the participant if he would like to take a short break, or go ahead and suggest a break.

Even if you tell the participant upfront that the test refers to testing the product, he may not internalize this. He may stay on edge if you continue to refer to the study as a test.

If the participant reaches a point where he asks to leave or end the session early, you're obligated to wrap things up. Be sure to give him his agreed-upon compensation and thank him for his time and help. You can check on him afterwards (using whatever means you originally scheduled him for the session; if he was scheduled by a recruiter, ask the recruiter to follow up). If appropriate (e.g., if he was distraught due to external circumstances), you can even offer to reschedule for a more convenient time.

SETTING CONTEXT FOR YOUR BEHAVIOR

The first few times a usability study participant hears you respond to his questions with questions ("What were you expecting?"), or when you do not respond at all, he may become unnerved ("I don't know, that is why I'm asking you!"), or even sarcastic ("You're not going to tell me, are you?"). Your lack of response may lead him to feel that he is being tested, as much as you say otherwise.

You can set the context for your behavior at the beginning of the session, and reinforce it along the way. In your presession instructions, tell the participant something like, "If you ask me questions, I may not really answer you or I may be vague. If I'm doing that, I'm not being unfriendly; I'm just trying to stay neutral...." Another helpful thing to say the first time he asks you a question is, "So I'll actually turn that question around on you; what would you expect to happen there?" By doing this, the participant can start anticipating your moderating approach and will feel less like he is being evaded or tricked. Also remember that your paralanguage—how you say what you say, like your intonation, loudness, or tempo—can have an effect on the message communicated. There is a big difference between responding to a question with, "*What* do you think?," "What do *you* think?," and "What do you *think*?" The first may come across as inquisitive, whereas the second and third might come off as rude or patronizing.

If a participant keeps asking questions over the course of a session, we sometimes resort to subdued humor to make light of the situation. For example, we may kindly say, "I'm going to plead the fifth here—like I said, I'm just here to observe. Tell me what you'd *expect* it to do?" (works if you're in the United States), or "I'm going to turn that around on you again! What do you think?" Again, if your delivery and paralanguage is kind and not patronizing, usually the participant will laugh along, stop expecting answers from you, and resume voicing expectations on his own.

2.5 Use careful language and tone to probe on the situation and begin to resolve it

Once you've established that you're not causing or magnifying an issue, you'll probably need to talk with the participant to try to understand more about, and hopefully resolve, the situation. One of the most important principles in moderating is to let the participant do most of the talking, but when you do speak—whether it's to provide direction, probe for more detail, or give neutral reassurance—you need to choose your words, and your tone, carefully.

To choose the appropriate language, we suggest reviewing and memorizing some prefabricated responses that represent moderating best practices. Prefabricated responses are valuable for interacting with participants while maintaining neutrality and consistency. By memorizing at least some of these phrases and reviewing a list before your study, you save the cognitive effort of improvising appropriate responses on the spot. As we start reviewing specific situations in Part 2, you'll be amazed at how flexible these short phrases can be.

The phrases we use most often include:

➤ "What would you expect?"
➤ "What are you trying to do right now?"
➤ "What are you thinking right now?"
➤ "How did this compare to your expectations?"
➤ "What are your thoughts on how that worked?"
➤ "That link isn't working for today's session. What would you expect to happen if you clicked it and it was working?"
➤ "Thank you for that feedback, but for the sake of time, please move on to …"

For more examples of these phrases, see Appendix A.

Since you need to be careful about providing positive feedback to participants, we've found the following phrases to be relatively neutral. When used judiciously, the phrases are capable of acknowledging to the participant that you've heard his feedback and are giving him a small amount of reassurance that the feedback was helpful:

Saying something is "helpful to know" is usually received as more of a token of gratitude for feedback, whereas "good" or "great" can be perceived as *qualifying* the participant's feedback.

➤ "Okay."
➤ "Okay, thank you," or "Okay, thanks for that."
➤ "That is good to know," or "That is helpful for us to know."

Careful use of these phrases will address the majority of typical issues you see during your research. Just as important as what to say is what *not* to say, which we give examples of in the sidebar "What *Not* to Say." Of course, you'll encounter situations where these neutral phrases may not cut it, or if a participant doesn't act as expected when given one of those phrases. In these cases, keep in mind these three guidelines:

1. *Be as unbiased and nonjudgmental in your response as possible.* No matter how inflammatory or provoking the situation is, or how much you agree (or disagree) with what the participant is saying, it is your responsibility to remain neutral. Remember that it's not just what you say, but also how you say it, both in intonation and body language. For example, if the participant is describing a personal or cultural belief that you find repugnant or inappropriate in response to your interview question, try to keep your face still and your voice at an even neutral tone as you ask your next question.

2. *Build on what the participant says rather than negating it.* As mentioned in Chapter 1, one of the fundamental principles of improv is to never disagree with something that has been said, but instead to say "Yes, and…." This principle means that you're always building on what someone else is doing rather than negating it. In a research session, your "Yes, and …" is less about agreeing with what the participant has said and more about acknowledging that he is been heard. For example, if the participant asks if he has performed a task correctly, respond with a prefabricated phrase instead of ignoring the questions. For example, "So I'll actually turn that question around on you: Do you feel that you've found the information that you're looking for?"

3. *Be as graceful as possible when redirecting or reacting.* When the participant wanders off track or no longer provides useful feedback, your paralanguage will set the stage for his reaction. You don't want to imply that he has done something wrong. Here's one of our favorite examples of a moderator–participant exchange that we've seen, showing how your word choices and intonation can have a negative effect:

Moderator: How would you do <*task*>?

Participant: Oh, I would do <*this*>.

Moderator: (pause, intonation rising) Oh. You *would*?

The rising intonation implies a questioning of the participant, and may cause him to feel judged or that he should rethink his answer. Instead, a graceful reaction would be to say "okay" with a neutral tone and move on, or ask him if there are other things he would try if the first attempt didn't work. If he is interacting with a prototype, you could also let him attempt the task, ask how it compares to what he expected, and then ask if there are any other ways he might try to do the same thing.

We discuss this kind of situation where a participant makes inappropriate comments in section 13.1.

WHAT *NOT* TO SAY

There are some phrases that you need to be careful with, as their connotations may have unexpected consequences on the participant. Table 2.5 lists these phrases, and why they usually don't fare well.

Continued

What Not to Say	Why
"Let me give you a hint."	Reinforces that the participant needs help.
"Why would you want to go there?" or "What made you do it *that* way?"	Implies that the place the participant wants to go, or did go, is not correct.
"Talk to me about …"	Depending on how it's said, or how much it's overused, can sound commanding or condescending.
"No, don't <do/click> that."	Reinforces that the participant is doing something he shouldn't.
"We/they did that because <*special case could happen or special constraint limited us*>."	Implies that you were part of the design team, and/or are defending the design choices.
"That is great feedback." or "That is good feedback."	Implies that other feedback is not great.

Table 2.5: Examples of What You Should Not Say While Moderating

2.6 Regain control to bring the session back on track

Hopefully, what you've done so far has jumpstarted the session. However, if the participant feels out of control or continues in a direction that is not useful to your research goal, it's your job to steer him back. As the moderator, you're always responsible for maintaining control of the session. This means accepting responsibility for changing the tone or providing whatever support is necessary to bring the session back on track.

Remember that you're not the participant's buddy. You didn't set up this time with him for a gripe or therapy session. It's your job to keep him from treating it that way. At the same time, some of the art of moderating includes redirecting a session and treating the participant's feedback with grace and respect.

So how do you reestablish control of the session? For most one-on-one methods, a specific restatement or refocusing of a task or question is enough to get the participant back on track:

➤ "Thank you for going into that level of detail. For the sake of time though, I'd like you to return to <*attempting/answering task/question*>…."

➤ "Thank you for explaining that, it's helpful for us to hear. We're a bit pressed for time so I'd like to direct your attention to…."

The pattern for redirecting the participant is more fully explained in section 3.3.

You can also bring the participant to a different task or question if you think he may be getting stuck or hung up on something in particular.

If your first attempts to regain control don't work, you may need to use stronger language to rein the participant back in:

➤ "I apologize for interrupting, but it's really important that I get your feedback on this *<task/topic>*. If you don't mind, let's return to that, and if there is time at the end of the session, we can return to this discussion in more detail."

Also, check that your body language projects an appropriate authority level. Maintain eye contact with the participant and angle your body toward him—this will help draw his attention and increase the odds that he'll pay attention to you. However, never touch the participant, even as a way to get his attention or give him comfort. Remember that many people do not like being touched by strangers and the inherent power imbalance within a moderating session can make any touch completely inappropriate.

> We talk more about how to use your body language in section 3.5.

If the session is veering out of control through no fault of the participant (e.g., technical problems), avoid sharing your frustration with him and do your best to keep that emotion out of your voice. The participant may feel like you're directing that irritation at him.

Another reason you may need to regain control is when the participant does not meet the desired criteria and you must adapt accordingly. One approach to this situation is to transition the session into a different type of research. This works especially well if the participant is an important customer, or part of a user group, who you want to feel validated and listened to. For example, a usability study with a customer who doesn't match your target user profile may be transitioned into an interview that will provide more information about his profile. Be sure to discuss these options with your stakeholders so they know what's happening and can provide input on other types of feedback they might be interested in receiving. If, however, the participant will be unable to provide any kind of useful input (e.g., if his role is entirely unrelated to your target), you may need to politely end the session.

> This technique is also referred to as *shifting the focus*, which we discuss more in section 3.8.

No matter what situations you encounter, the steps discussed in this section should help you figure out the best approach to address and resolve them. When in doubt, think back to what you would want done if your positions were reversed—how would you want *your* moderator to handle the situation? Chapter 3 details some of the specific interaction patterns that you can apply to help with this resolution.

SURVIVAL STORY: "I KNOW WHAT SHE NEEDS!"
CAROLYN SNYDER

I was running a paper prototype usability study at the client site. It was codiscovery. User #1 had already shown up. User #2 arrived with her angelic, sleeping two-month-old baby in tow. She was surprised when I reminded her that the session would take two hours. She was under the (sleep-deprived) impression it would just take a few minutes.

What I should have done was explained that we couldn't accommodate infants, apologized for the misunderstanding, paid her, and sent her home. Instead, I asked the client if they were okay with a baby in the room. They were surprised, but didn't object. (For the record, most of them were mothers themselves, and User #1 was female.)

Halfway through the session, the baby began crying. "I know what she needs!" the new mom proclaimed. Trying to be delicate, I asked, "Would you like privacy?" (For those keeping score at home, this was my second mistake: I should have taken her to another room.) "Nope, I'm good," replied the mom, and put her baby to her breast right there in front of me, the other participant, and a handful of in-room observers. For the record, I am a proponent of public breastfeeding, but along with many other behaviors, it falls under the category of "Things I Would Never Do at the Office."

I spent the rest of the session agonizing over how the client would respond. They chose not to make an issue of it (I have wonderful clients), but even now, nearly 20 years later, I still think about all the ways it could have ended badly.

It did cross my mind to send her home. But in the moment, it was surprisingly hard to choose that fork in the road. Being an eager young user experience consultant, I put a higher priority on getting feedback for the client than on the comfort of the participant, client, and even myself. I lacked the confidence to make a unilateral decision and take responsibility for it. I do still make mistakes, but I've learned to own them.

CHAPTER 3

Mix and Match:
Your Moderation Patterns Toolbox

As we start describing situations that you may encounter (in Part 2), you'll notice that we repeat some recommended actions over and over again. You can think of these actions as *moderation patterns* that can be applied to almost any situation, and modified, as needed. Table 3.1 lists all the patterns that we'll discuss in this chapter. Some of these may seem obvious to you, especially if you already have some moderating experience under your belt. Even so, our goal is to help you think about when each pattern is appropriate to use based on the circumstances of the session and your desired outcome.

Most of these patterns aren't mutually exclusive—you can use one or multiple at a time or within the same session. Given that you may encounter situations that build on each other (e.g., experiencing technical problems while the participant is already distracted by external circumstances), you may need to apply multiple patterns within a short time period.

> At the beginning of each situation in Part 2, you'll see a heading for "Pattern(s) to apply" followed by any relevant patterns.

➤ Take responsibility
➤ Clarify the task/question
➤ Redirect the participant
➤ Reassure the participant
➤ Build engagement
➤ Disengage from the participant
➤ Take a break
➤ Shift the focus
➤ End the session early

Table 3.1: Moderation Patterns. Each pattern defines a type of interaction that you can use during a user research session to affect its outcome and direction.

3.1 Take responsibility

Taking responsibility means recognizing that, as the moderator, you're in charge of the session, and then using that power wisely.

When to use

When something happens during a session that a participant may not know how to react to, or when a misunderstanding is encountered, you should step up and take responsibility. This pattern may be appropriate:

➤ To keep the participant from feeling badly about something she did.

➤ If the participant seems to have misunderstood something you asked her about, or to do.

> ➤ If the participant is approaching emotional or physical discomfort or physical danger.

> ➤ If there is an emergency where you have to assist the participant to ensure her safety.

What to do

This pattern means that you take responsibility for anything that, from the participant's perspective, is unexpected during the session. For example, if you need to skip tasks or end a session due to something about the participant's behavior (e.g., she brings a baby with her to the session or misunderstands a question), you can blame yourself for not having the setup to support her situation or for not choosing the best words. Putting the responsibility on you keeps the participant from feeling badly about herself.

This pattern also means that if something in the session seems to be going wrong, you should take, or absorb, responsibility for it. If the participant is complaining, don't agree or disagree with her—just absorb and accept her feedback. If something else goes wrong, don't blame your designers, developers, recruiters, or the participant—even if something is objectively their fault. As far as the participant is concerned, the buck stops with you.

You also need to take responsibility for the participant when it comes to her physical comfort and safety, especially in life-threatening situations such as fires or earthquakes. Especially if she is at your facility, it's your job to watch over, keep track of, and direct her until she is safely on her way home.

Keep in mind that you may also need to use this pattern with your observers, especially if your observers are in the same room as you and the participant. If the observers are distracting or causing problems, you must take responsibility and resolve the situation to ensure the comfort of the participant.

Take responsibility is a pattern that can be used in almost any kind of session. It's a good principle to keep in mind as unexpected situations arise.

See pattern in use

You can see this pattern being used in situations such as:

> ➤ 5.8 Participant brings a child or a pet to her session

> ➤ 14.1 Fire alarm goes off or the facility needs to be evacuated

3.2 Clarify the task/question

By clarifying what you mean by a task/question, or asking the participant to reiterate her understanding of what you asked her to do, you'll reduce misunderstandings and improve the odds of getting the kind of feedback you need.

When to use

Use this pattern when you want to make sure that the participant is clear about what you asked her. This pattern may be appropriate:

➤ If the participant obviously did not understand the task/question.

➤ If you think the participant may not have understood the task/question.

➤ If the participant seems to be avoiding a task/question.

What to do

First, verify that the participant misunderstood the task/question by asking her to tell you, in her own words, what she is doing or describing. For example, if you asked a participant during an interview to tell you about the last time she purchased a computer and she starts talking about a recent restaurant she visited, you can say, "So tell me why you're describing your restaurant experience." You might find out that she didn't hear your question correctly, or that she visited this restaurant before she went to a store to purchase her last computer.

If the participant misunderstood what you were asking her, reword or rephrase the task/question as needed to ensure that she understands what she is being asked to do. In a usability study, you can ask her to re-read the task out loud, and ask if she has any questions about the task. You may also need to provide some guidance on the type of feedback you're looking for (e.g., functionality rather than visual design, thinking aloud, etc.) or point the participant toward an area of the product that she hasn't found on her own.

While this pattern is fairly straightforward, it can be used in a wide range of situations to help keep the participant on the desired track. But be careful of its misuse or overuse; for example, if you're prompting the participant to re-read a task every time she goes off the optimal or successful path for a task, she may catch on and it could start to influence her behavior.

This pattern is especially useful in situations where the participant is behaving or answering questions in an unexpected way. Several of these situations are described in Chapters 6 and 10.

See pattern in use

You can see this pattern being used in situations such as:

➤ 6.5 Participant ignores or pretends to understand your question

➤ 10.2 Participant consistently focuses on irrelevant details

3.3 Redirect the participant

Sometimes the participant pursues a path that will be less useful to you, or the energy that she sends out doesn't mesh with what you need from her. Use redirection to help align the participant with your goals.

When to use

Use this pattern when you need to take the participant's focus and emotions and redirect them in a direction more appropriate for your study. This pattern may be appropriate:

➤ If the participant seems fixated on something other than what you need to receive feedback on.

➤ If the participant seems to be going down a path that will not be useful based on your study goals, and you want to bring her attention back to your original intent.

➤ If you need to give the participant an assist so she is able to continue a task during a usability study.

➤ If the participant is obviously disgruntled or unhappy with the organization/product, and you can tell that her complaints will get in the way of your feedback.

➤ If the participant seems overly enthusiastic with the organization/product and loses focus.

What to do

You'll see redirection referenced in many situations throughout the book, but it is especially key in situations where participants are uncertain. These situations are listed in Chapter 8.

This pattern redirects the participant toward an outcome more appropriate to the research you're performing. The most common application of this pattern is the moderator staple of turning a question back around to the participant. For example, if she asks, "Where would I go to do that?" you may respond, "Where would you expect to go?" If the participant asks a question that is more difficult to turn around—for example, "Am I doing this right?— this pattern lets you provide a vague neutral answer that then redirects her to a topic more relevant to the study. For example, "Like I said, we're definitely not testing you here. Let me ask you about…."

You may also need to provide a usability study participant with an assist if she struggles with a task that you need to get feedback on, or if she is unable to complete a task that future tasks depend on. In these situations, you're redirecting the participant from the path she is currently taking to the one that you need her to use so you can accomplish your study goals.

An *assist* can mean anything from a gentle prompt to pointing out what the participant hasn't seen on her own. For more on the different types of assists, see section 6.2 and the sidebar "The Diversionary Assist."

This pattern also lets you provide some space for the energy exuding from a disgruntled or overly enthusiastic participant. One way to do this is to, at the beginning of the session, let a disgruntled participant spend a limited amount of time venting to get the negativity out of her system. For example, if you're interviewing her about how she decides to purchase a product and she immediately starts ranting about her experience on a specific e-commerce website, interrupt gently: "My goal for this session is to talk at a higher level about your decision making process. But since it seems like you've had a recent experience with this website, let's take five minutes now for you to tell me about it, and then we'll get back to my list of questions. Does that sound okay?" Once the participant has vented, tie her emotional state into what you're asking her to do. For example, "I know you've had problems with this website in the past, and that is exactly why we're doing this research—to understand how and why you use websites like this so we can find ways to make your experience better."

See pattern in use

You can see this pattern being used in situations such as:

➤ 11.7 Participant becomes insulting or has an agenda

➤ 8.1 Participant looks for affirmation

THE DIVERSIONARY ASSIST

Giving usability study participants an assist requires a delicate balance. You need to find a way to provide the assist that doesn't make the participant feel stupid for missing the correct answer, and that avoids implying that there *is* a correct answer. A technique that we've found to work well—something we think of as an advanced moderating maneuver—is to redirect the participant temporarily with an unrelated question or task and come back to the main topic later. This diversion often makes the participant forget what she was just doing and allows you to ease into the necessary topic without making her feel stupid or unsuccessful.

For example, let's say the participant is looking for a way to chat with a representative on an e-commerce website but has not yet found it in the About Us section. Instead, she has been exploring all of the other areas. You need her to eventually get to the chat section because you want to get feedback on the chat functionality. You might first say something like, "Let's move on for now. I want to go back to what you did earlier…" and then spend a few minutes on another topic. The other topic could be something the participant did earlier, another task that can be done independently of the previous one, or a broader question about the website in general. After this redirection, you're ready to drive her to the chat feature. You can then guide her to the About Us link and ask, "What would you expect to see in this area?" If you don't have time, just direct her: "Why don't we click into this area." The participant may catch on or not (you'd be surprised at how often participants don't), but she'll usually make light of it if she does—"Oh, *that* is what I was looking for earlier!"

3.4 Reassure the participant

Sometimes the participant gets upset or needs to be comforted, either because of something happening inside the session or from something else going on in her life. Reassuring her can bring her emotional state to a more comfortable level so you can continue with the session.

When to use

Participants may become stressed or nervous about their performance during the session and need some gentle reassurance. This pattern may be appropriate:

➤ If the participant blames herself or is self-deprecating.

➤ If the participant seems nervous, uncomfortable, or hesitant.

➤ If the participant asks if she is doing a task correctly.

What to do

Remind the participant that you're not testing her in any way, and that you're a neutral observer who wants her honest feedback, both positive and negative. If you didn't design the product, you can let her know that as well. You can provide similar assurances during an interview or contextual inquiry to assure the participant that you're a neutral party who is interested in her experience. If the participant needs additional reassurance, let her know that the feedback that she is providing is helpful and will help the team make the product better.

For more on what kind of feedback is appropriate to provide, see the sidebar "Should You Tell a Participant That Her Feedback Is Helpful?"

This pattern also includes reassuring the participant that she has control within the session to take a break if necessary and leave whenever she wants. Your reassurance should make her feel that you'll do your best to make—and keep—her comfortable, even if you don't explicitly say so. Remember your ethical obligations to the participant and do your best to ensure that she'll leave the session feeling no worse—and ideally better—than she did when she arrived.

See pattern in use

You can see this pattern being used in situations such:

➤ 8.4 Participant is self-blaming

➤ 10.8 Participant struggles excessively with a task

SHOULD YOU TELL A PARTICIPANT THAT HER FEEDBACK IS HELPFUL?

You may tell a participant that her feedback is the kind of feedback you're looking for or that it is helpful. We feel it's useful to provide this reassurance because it allows you to be more proactive than reactive about reassuring her.

Unfortunately, there are a few common misuses of this approach:

➤ *Feigned interest:* If your tone sounds rote or machine-like, telling a participant that her feedback is good or helpful can come across as disingenuous.

> ➤ *Frequency:* If you tell the participant that her feedback is good or helpful every time she says or does something, you start to sound like a broken record and she may lose trust in you. Similarly, providing this feedback at the wrong times could annoy her and possibly bias the study. For example, the participant may catch on if you only tell her that her feedback is useful when she says or does something in particular.
>
> ➤ *Wording:* Saying "that is great feedback" or "that is good feedback" qualifies the participant's feedback, which again may attune her to when you *are* or *are not* "praising" her feedback.
>
> Be careful and methodical about how you provide any kind of affirmation. Instead of responding to everything that the participant says or does, pause periodically after a number of tasks or questions and tell her, "This is helpful for us to hear, and is the type of feedback we're looking to get. Thank you. Let's move on to...." You only need to do this once or twice during a session, ideally toward the beginning of the session when participants are most guarded and can benefit from this feedback.
>
> When providing any other feedback to the participant, stay neutral with responses such as "Okay," or "Okay, thank you for that" instead of adding qualifiers. Additional guidelines for carefully using language and tone are discussed in section 2.5.

3.5 Build engagement

Sometimes a participant just doesn't seem connected to what you're asking her to do or talk about. By building engagement, you can help her feel more invested in the session. This emotional investment may make her more willing to provide the feedback you need.

When to use

Use this pattern to help draw an unengaged participant into the session. This may be appropriate if:

➤ The participant seems nervous or reluctant about providing feedback.

➤ The participant is not engaging with the product being studied.

➤ The participant seems distracted or uninterested.

What to do

One way to build engagement is to adjust your body language, making sure that you're taking the position of an active and interested listener (Figure 3.1). Sit up straight, angling your body slightly toward the participant. If you're in the room with her, adjust your seat so you can maintain comfortable eye contact and she doesn't have to look up or down at you.

Figure 3.1 Build engagement. A neutral moderating position (left), and an attempt to engage (right). © 2013 Mark Ainscow, used with permission.

Keep your facial expression friendly and neutral. An occasional smile is okay, and you may notice the participant smiling back in return! Check your tone as well, remembering to sound genuinely interested in what she has to say.

If the participant seems disengaged with the product she is using, try to establish a personal connection between the participant and what she is doing. Encourage her to talk about herself or her experiences, and then tie her response into a rephrasing or refocusing of the task. For example, if you're running a usability study on a mobile game that the participant seems to find uninteresting, ask her to tell you about mobile games that she does enjoy. After hearing her response, ask her to compare the experience of her favorite game to the one she is using as part of the study.

A bonus about making the personal connection is that the participant may forget about her initial emotional response (nervousness, etc.). But be careful to keep your efforts on building engagement linked to the session. This pattern is not about making friends with the participant; it's about turning a topic or task that she finds boring, uninspiring, or irrelevant into something that she can provide feedback on.

The survival story "His frustration was clearly growing" shows an example of a moderator discovering that his participant has trouble reading.

In having this conversation with the participant, you may discover other reasons for the lack of engagement, such as low literacy or computer skills or a mismatch with your screening criteria. If this is the case, you may decide to shift the focus of the session to accommodate her unexpected skill level or criteria mismatch, or you may need to end the session early.

The Friendly Face and Inquisitive Mind moderating styles discussed in Chapter 2 are most appropriate to use during this pattern.

See pattern in use

You can see this pattern being used in situations such as:

➤ 8.3 Participant looks or sounds uncomfortable and/or nervous

➤ 11.1 Remote participant is obviously distracted

3.6 Disengage from the participant

Sometimes a participant can get a little too personal or too enthusiastic in her interactions with you. Disengaging lets you politely pull away from that attention and establish a more neutral tone for the session.

When to use

This pattern may be appropriate:

➤ If the participant is being overly chatty or is oversharing personal information.

➤ If the participant is making you uncomfortable in any way, either through her attitude, something she is saying, or something she is doing.

Do not use this pattern if you feel that there is any danger presented by the participant's behavior. Instead, take a break if you feel able to leave the room, and end the session early.

What to do

This pattern lets you gain some emotional distance from the participant (Figure 3.2). Move to a more formal tone of speaking, and reposition your body slightly away from her. Also try not to make too much eye contact with her, and focus more directly on the product or your notes. If you're doing a contextual inquiry or usability study, you can also move yourself slightly behind the participant. This position makes it more difficult for her to directly interact with you and forces her to focus on the product. If you're in a multiroom usability lab, you can also moderate from a different room. If you decide to switch to the other room in the middle of the session, simply say, "For the next few tasks, I'm going to be in the other room."

You'll find this pattern especially useful in many of the awkward situations described in Chapter 13.

A variant of this pattern is to make a task or question less personal. This is useful if it seems that the personal nature of your question is causing the participant's discomfort. For example, if you're interviewing a participant about how she found a nursing home for her father but she is having a hard time talking about the process she went through, ask

Figure 3.2 Disengaging from the participant. A neutral moderating position (left), and an attempt to disengage (right). © 2013 Mark Ainscow, used with permission.

her instead to describe the last time she had to find a new doctor for herself. After she has talked for a bit about something more neutral and seems more comfortable, you can tie her response into your original personal question. For example, "You said that personal recommendations were extremely important in how you found your dermatologist. Tell me about if, and how, personal recommendations played a role in how you decided on a nursing home for your father?"

The Down to Business and By the Book moderating styles are most appropriate for use while applying this pattern.

See pattern in use

You can see this pattern being used in situations such as:

➤ 12.1 Participant is extremely entertaining and friendly
➤ 13.4 Participant flirts with you

3.7 Take a break

Taking a break lets you hit the session's "pause" button. This pause can reset the flow of the session and give you and the participant some time and space.

When to use

Use this pattern when you need to take some time, either for yourself or the participant. This pattern is appropriate:

➤ If the participant is stressed or upset and seems to need some space.
➤ If you're feeling stressed or upset by anything happening in the session.
➤ If you need to get a second opinion about the participant from your observers so you can determine how to proceed with the rest of the session.
➤ If you need to let the observers know that they're being loud or disruptive.
➤ If something in your technical setup needs to be change or fixed.

Remember that your emotional well-being is just as important as the participant's!

What to do

Let the participant know that you're taking a short break. If the reason you need to take a break won't upset or offend the participant, you can provide that as a reason. For example, "The batteries on my audio recorder seem to have died. Let's take a break for a few minutes while I replace them." Alternatively, you can leave the reason vague, or stretch the truth if necessary. For example, "I need to check into something about the prototype."

The idea of using convenient excuses to take a break or end a session early is discussed in the Chapter 2 sidebar "Using a Pretext."

If you're taking the break to give the participant space, offer to show her where the restroom is or get her something to drink. If you're leaving her in the room and the recording equipment is still running, remind her of this so she doesn't think she has some privacy and start making personal phone calls. Similarly, if the participant is remote and her screen is being shared, have her turn off the screen sharing first or remind her that her screen is still visible.

If possible, have a backup survey or questionnaire related to the study that you can give to the participant if you need to take a break and want to provide her with something useful to do. Section 15.2 describes this idea in more detail. Having this kind of backup also has the advantage of making the participant feel productive and useful—an advantage over leaving her staring nervously at herself in a one-way mirror!

See pattern in use

You can see this pattern being used in situations such as:

➤ 7.1 Technical issues arise with your setup and/or equipment

➤ 14.4 You begin to feel unwell while moderating a session

3.8 Shift the focus

Shifting the focus lets you adjust your study plan and research method to something that is a better fit for the participant's qualifications or emotional state.

When to use

Use this pattern if you realize that your study plan is not going to work with the participant you have. This may happen if:

➤ The participant is reacting poorly to the current form of research (e.g., because she says she would never perform the tasks you're asking her to do and she can't be persuaded to try anyway).

➤ The participant doesn't match your recruiting criteria, but is either high profile (e.g., a customer VIP) or if, based on your study goals or timing, it's better to get some data than getting nothing.

Keep in mind that this pattern may not be appropriate if:

➤ Your research goals are very narrowly defined and there is no value in adjusting the session (in which case, you should end the session early).

➤ The participant doesn't match your recruiting criteria and you have a backup/floater participant available who you could run instead (in which case, you should end the session early with your current participant).

What to do

Once you realize that your study plan isn't working, decide if you can adjust the method to a form of research that better matches the participant's qualifications or mental state. For example, if you're running a usability study of a bank's online account opening process and the participant says she'd only open an account at a branch, you might adjust your questions and tasks to more of an interview format to learn if she has opened an account at a branch before, what the experience was like, and how it could be improved. Or, if you're interviewing a nurse about her interactions with patients but learn that she primarily deals with administrative tasks instead, you can change the focus from asking her questions to watching the workflow she has to follow to accomplish her tasks.

It sometimes helps to use this pattern in conjunction with taking a break so that you have time to talk to your stakeholders about your revised plan.

To be successful at this pattern, you must have a solid understanding of the research goals and how your findings are going to be used. This understanding is key in determining if this pattern is appropriate and, if so, how to best shift a session's focus to yield useful feedback.

See pattern in use

You can see this pattern being used in situations such as:

➤ 4.2 Participant either refuses to or can't do a key task

➤ 7.3 Facility loses its Internet connection

3.9 End the session early

Ending a session early is your last resort when other strategies have not—or could not have–been successful.

When to use

If the participant is not responding to your efforts to make her more comfortable, or if external circumstances make it difficult or impossible to continue, you may need to end the session and cut your losses. This pattern may be appropriate:

➤ If the participant is a misrecruit and there is no way to adjust the session to get feedback from her.

➤ If the participant seems excessively upset or unable or unwilling to continue.

➤ If you're worried for your safety or that of the participant's.

➤ If technical or environmental issues make it difficult or impossible to continue.

What to do

In the case of technical or environmental issues, you have a built-in reason for ending the session. For example, if you have to evacuate your facility because of a fire, the intensity of the situation and unstable environmental conditions means you should let the participant leave.

Ending a session early for any other reason requires careful communication skills, as you don't want the participant to think that you're ending it because she did something wrong. If you did not provide her with a list of tasks or questions ahead of time, you can just skip any unfinished items and go straight to ending the session without any additional explanation. If she can tell that you're skipping something, you can use a pretext such as, "The rest of these tasks/questions aren't applicable to you/your role, so we're going to skip them." Other pretexts that may come in handy to explain a shortened session include:

➤ "You went through everything faster than expected!"
➤ "We're having some technical difficulties, so rather than having you wait around, we're going to end early so you can have time back in your day."

The point at which you decide that a session is not worth saving—your breaking point—will be different for each study and the factors that are key to the study's success. Think about it ahead of time and discuss it with your stakeholders: What are the deal-breakers that would make you end a session rather than continuing it?

This discussion will also help you figure out if you can shift a session's focus instead of ending a session. See section 15.2 for more about this.

See pattern in use

You can see this pattern being used in situations such as:

➤ 4.1 Participant does not seem to meet a key recruit criteria
➤ 14.6 Participant seems to be drunk or stoned

3.10 Choosing the best pattern for your situation

Now that you have all these patterns at your disposal, how do you decide which to use, and when? As you can see in Table 3.2, the patterns fit into the steps described in Chapter 2 for how to handle situations. Different patterns are more useful than others depending on what step you're on.

As discussed in Chapter 2, you should always keep in mind your ethical obligations to ensure the comfort and safety of the participants, your organization, your team, and yourself. In addition to these obligations, consider the following when you decide what to do during a

	1. Take a moment to evaluate the situation before jumping to action	2. Resolve any threats to physical safety	3. Verify that you're not causing or magnifying the situation	4. Check the participant's comfort level	5. Use careful language and tone to probe on the situation and begin to resolve it	6. Regain control to bring the session back on track
Take a break	X	X	X	X		
Shift the focus				X		X
Build engagement			X	X	X	X
Clarify the task/question					X	X
Redirect the participant					X	X
Reassure the participant		X		X	X	
Disengage from the participant			X		X	X
End the session early		X		X		
Take responsibility	X	X	X	X	X	X

Table 3.2: Patterns That Can Be Used At Each Step for Handling Situations.

session, specifically, how hard you work to bring a session back on track instead of ending the session early:

1. *Your research project's goals.* Think about what your stakeholders are trying to learn from this research, who they need to learn it from, and what will help them get the answers they need. For example, is the goal to discover issues, or to validate a product? How important are specific participant criteria? Being clear on these goals, and knowing that you and your stakeholders are on the same page about those goals, will let you make more efficient decisions.

2. *Maintaining data quality.* Based on your research goals, what sample size do you need? How many participants have you run already? How much consistency (of recruit criteria and of tasks/questions) do you need between participants? For example, if you're running a qualitative usability study and have recruited twelve participants (assuming you'll have two no-shows), you may be more willing to let the twelfth participant explore other areas of the product outside what's in the study plan than when you're running the second participant.

Because of all these factors, it's impossible to spell out exactly which pattern is best to use in every situation. Instead, use these questions to identify what's best for *your* situation.

We hope this chapter has given you an understanding of the tools available in your moderating Swiss Army knife and the key considerations that might affect how, when, and why, you'd use each of them. In Part 2, you'll see these tools applied across a wide variety of situations.

SURVIVAL STORY: "THE GROUND STARTED TO MOVE" COLIN BAY

Back when I worked at a Fortune 500 company, I was running a usability study in one of our labs when I had a real surprise. The participant was in the test room and I was on the observation side of the mirror (which was probably a 20-yard walk from the participant), speaking through our intercom system while I took notes. In the middle of a task, the ground started to move and quickly reached peak magnitude. It was a 3.9 earthquake, centered about 10 miles away.

I should probably explain that I've been in many small to medium earthquakes before and was well aware that the company I worked for, cautious in the extreme, built their factories and office buildings to the most exacting standards of safety. In fact, we had recently had an earthquake inspection in which some very minor items, such as a bookcase in a usually inhabited hallway that wasn't bolted to the wall in quite the right way, were flagged as needing urgent attention.

So when I could tell that the tremors weren't that big, I wasn't especially worried, and have to say, to my embarrassment today, that I kept on taking notes. After typing the next sentence or two, I glanced up and was nonplussed to find that the participant had disappeared. She was just gone! I finally figured out that she had done the smart thing that I hadn't: ducked under the desk for safety. When the shaking was over, I ran down the hallway and into the participant's room to see how she was doing. She came out from under the desk and was clearly ready to go home.

It's obvious to me now that I failed in my primary responsibility of looking out for the participant's well-being. Had that been my first thought, I would have grabbed the microphone, ducked under the desk myself, and talked to the participant during the earthquake to make sure she was okay and to keep her reassured. But at least I was right about ending the session, as the participant was too shaken to continue comfortably.

SURVIVAL STORY: "HIS FRUSTRATION WAS CLEARLY GROWING" DAN SEWARD

I was conducting a task-based usability study for a tourism website with a "general public" audience, which left the door wide open for our recruiter. We'd had some wacky participants, but the website was testing fairly well and meeting design goals. One of our last participants was a soft-spoken auto mechanic who became embarrassed when he was handed a card with a written task description. After looking at the card, he mumbled that he didn't understand the (fairly straightforward) task. Thinking that something was just unclear, I read the task out loud to him and he immediately took the mouse and went to work.

The way he used the website was odd. I didn't understand some of the navigational choices he made. He also began a pattern of verbally giving up on tasks, but at first he responded well to gentle encouragement and was able to complete most of the items in a roundabout way. About two-thirds of the way through an hour-long session, his frustration was clearly growing—he was giving up on tasks more quickly and changing the subject (repeatedly describing how he used Facebook). As a moderator I was getting frustrated with his attitude, but did my best not to show it, and gently pushed him back on task. Finally, he looked at me sideways and explained that he "didn't read very well," and actually apologized for coming to a research activity that required reading. We certainly hadn't specified a literacy level in the recruiting brief—only whether someone had a particular amount of experience using the Internet.

Suddenly, our session made a lot more sense. First, I immediately and sincerely thanked him for coming in and giving it a try. I expressed that the website was designed for anybody with Internet access to use, and that his feedback was really valuable. I offered him one of the remaining tasks, but it was clear from his body language (slumped shoulders, darting eyes) that he had thrown in the towel. So I let him off the hook a few minutes early; he visibly relaxed, and I could see that it was definitely a relief.

The session truly was valuable. Prior to this session, shamefully, we hadn't considered low-literacy users. Our participant reinforced the value of visual navigation cues, imagery, and video throughout the website, and showed that low-literacy users would be unlikely to benefit from some of the text descriptions of hotels and attractions. In the end, the session was a tricky but useful surprise.

Anecdotally, I learned that low-literacy participants are unlikely to disclose their abilities without prompting, and that they might need a particular type of encouragement to work through testing tasks. And, paradoxically, I learned that it might be worth screening *for* this sort of participant, if your testing material truly is intended for general audiences.

Part 2
Your Survival Guide

CHAPTER

Recruiting Mishaps:
Participants You Weren't Expecting

Recruiting mishaps can happen despite your best efforts. A participant who doesn't meet your criteria or who has some other unexpected quality means that your session may immediately start with a go or no-go decision. These situations require you to make quick decisions about whether and how to proceed with the session, and to make any necessary accommodations for any unexpected participant characteristics.

4.1 Participant does not seem to meet a key recruit criteria

> Your recruit criteria were very specific about certain qualifications that participants should have. However, when the participant arrives, he seems to not actually meet those qualifications.

Method(s): Any
Frequency: Frequent
Pattern(s) to apply: Take responsibility; Reassure the participant; Shift the focus

What to do

➤ First, verify that the participant does not actually meet the desired criteria. One way to do this is to let the participant know that the information you have about him indicates that he has a specific qualification, and ask him directly if that is correct. If you're looking for participants who perform a certain type of task, ask the participant to describe his role and, in particular, what he does regarding the task that you're interested in. Another way is to be subtle with your line of questioning, so that it comes off as normal background questions. That way if you immediately take a break and/or end the session, the participant won't feel like it's his qualifications that caused the problem.

➤ Keep in mind that once the participant arrives, you're obligated to provide him with compensation (unless there was another agreement in place; see section 15.2 for more about your compensation decisions), so you might see if there is a way to adapt the session to include the participant's feedback, or shift the focus of the session entirely to another method. To decide this, see if the participant's actual qualifications would still be useful for your research. For example, based on your research goals, you may know that talking to a novice manager will provide useful feedback even though your primary target for recruiting was experienced managers. If your stakeholders are observing in person, you should take a moment to discuss this with them privately. Especially if your project has time or budget restrictions, you may not have a chance to replace the participant with someone who's a better fit. Be prepared to argue the case for your observers as to why the participant still may yield useful and valid data.

➤ If you need to let the participant go and not proceed with the session, consider being candid about why you're unable to proceed. This approach may be appropriate if the criteria was role-based—for example, "I apologize for the misunderstanding. For the purpose of this study, we need to talk with managers who have direct reports."—or any other reason where the participant won't feel like he "failed." However, if the reason is potentially sensitive, use a pretext such as having "technical difficulties." Be appropriately apologetic to the participant, especially if he was excited about giving his feedback, and provide him with his full compensation.

➤ If the participant is a very important person (VIP) or customer, or a colleague hooked in with your project team, you probably can't get away with the technical failure pretext. Check with your observers/stakeholders on the best way to handle this particular participant. They may encourage you to proceed anyway so the participant feels like he has had a chance to provide feedback that will be taken seriously, even if it isn't in line with your original research goals. One way to get this feedback is to adjust your study plan to learn more about what the participant does or is interested in doing.

What to say

➤ "Before we continue, I just want to verify a few things about your *<experience/expertise/role>*. According to the information provided by our recruiter...."

➤ "I'm sorry, *<participant name>*, but for the purpose of this research, we need to talk with people who *<criteria>*. Thank you so much for your willingness to come in today, and here is your agreed-on compensation."

Ending early:

➤ "I'm sorry, but it looks like the prototype I wanted to get your feedback on isn't working. I have a few more questions for you, but after that, we'll end the session early. You'll still get your full compensation though!"

What not to do or say

➤ Don't be accusatory about the participant's qualifications (or lack thereof). He may take it personally. When verifying the participation criteria, do so in a subtle and nonjudgmental way.

➤ Don't assume that the participant lied about his qualifications. The screener questions could have been poorly worded, or your recruiter may have been more lenient than he should have been. After the session, go back and review the requirements with the recruiter.

➤ Likewise, don't assume that it was the recruiter who messed up. Until you're able to look into what happened, you won't know the truth of the situation. When interacting with the participant, always take the responsibility for the misunderstanding yourself, even if you're pretty sure the fault lies with your recruiter.

How to avoid

➤ Ensure that the recruiter has detailed information about each of your desired criteria and how to evaluate whether or not the participant matches the criteria. Avoid using "give-away" questions

CHAPTER 4

4.1 Participant does not seem to meet a key recruit criteria (cont.)

in a recruiting screener where a respondent can guess what the correct answer is. For example, instead of asking a yes/no questions such as, "Do you use an iPad?" ask the more open-ended, "Do you use any mobile devices or tablets? If so, which ones?"

➤ Verify the participant's qualifications at the beginning of the session, especially if any of your criteria are deal-breakers that would require you to end the session.

➤ Consider having backup or floater participants available. This way, if a participant doesn't meet your requirements, you can still get feedback from someone during the session time. For more on backups and floaters, see section 15.1.

➤ Talk to your team ahead of time to understand their tolerance for misrecruits, and create an action plan for how to address them. It will be helpful to set expectations upfront, so that you can have a quick and efficient discussion during an actual session.

 Watch Video 7 to see an example of a moderator realizing that the participant scheduled for an interview lacks the necessary experience. The moderator discusses what to do with a stakeholder and finds a way to adapt the session.

Visit our website (http://www.modsurvivalguide.org/videos) or use your QR reader to scan this code.

See also

➤ 4.2 Participant refuses to or can't do a key task

➤ 4.4 Participant is unfamiliar with the equipment

➤ 11.3 Participant insists that she would never do something

➤ Survival Story: "An unexpected picture started to emerge"

➤ Survival Story: "I would have trusted my gut" in Chapter 11

RECRUITING MISHAPS: PARTICIPANTS YOU WEREN'T EXPECTING

4.2 Participant either refuses to or can't do a key task

As part of the recruiting process, participants were told that they would be asked to do a specific task during the session. For example, you need the participant to log in to his bank account and perform nontransactional tasks, so the recruiter told him that he must be able to log in to his account for the session. When you ask the participant to do this, he either can't (e.g., because he has forgotten his login information) or won't (e.g., because he changed his mind).

Method(s): Usability study; Contextual inquiry
Frequency: Occasional
Pattern(s) to apply: Take responsibility; End the session early

What to do

➤ If you were explicit about participants needing to do something specific during the session as a condition of the recruit, and the participant is unable or unwilling to do this, end the session. The exceptions are if there is a way for you to reschedule the participant, shift the focus of the session, or you have some other backup plan in place. You'll need to provide the participant with his compensation unless you were crystal clear throughout the process that the compensation was contingent on performing this task. However, even in this circumstance, err on the side of the participant, especially if you have any sense that he misunderstood what he signed up for.

➤ If the participant is willing to do the key task but is unable to (e.g., because he forgot his password), see if there is a way for you to help him get whatever information he needs to proceed. For example, if he forgot his password, ask him to go through the Forgot Password or Password Reset process. If this process involves him using the phone or answering sensitive questions on the screen to reset account information, leave the room to avoid overhearing personal identifying information and/or be sure that nothing is being screen-shared or recorded during that time. If the participant seems reluctant to make this attempt, do not force him, and instead end the session.

➤ Offer to reschedule if the participant is genuinely disappointed about not being able to participate. Be sure to confirm and reconfirm your expectations for what he'll need to do during the rescheduled time!

What to say

➤ "I'm sorry, but we need participants to do <*task*>. Unfortunately, this means that we're not going to be able to have you participate today. If you're able and willing to get the information and come back, we'd be happy to reschedule you."

What not to do or say

➤ Don't assume that the participant lied about his willingness to do this task when being recruited. The screener questions could have been poorly worded, or your recruiter may have been more lenient than he should have been. Take responsibility for any miscommunication.

How to avoid

➤ If you're making the participant's compensation contingent on his ability to attempt the key task, confirm this task with him several times before the session. Be as explicit as possible about what he may need to have prepared for the session, especially if it will involve accessing potentially sensitive information. As soon as the session begins, verify that the participant will be able to attempt the key task before he signs the consent form (and thus before being recorded or observed by others).

➤ Alternatively, you can avoid conflict altogether and compensate any participant who shows up for testing, regardless of whether he is willing or able to move forward.

➤ Despite your best efforts, accept that you may have a participant arrive who still falls into this category. Have a backup plan in place for these participants in case any misunderstandings occur. Your backup plan may include having backup or floater participants available, shifting the focus to a different type of study, or setting up a test account that a participant can use to attempt tasks on his own. For more discussion on backup participants, floater participants, and backup plans, see sections 15.1 and 15.2.

See also

➤ 4.1 Participant does not seem to meet a key recruit criteria

➤ 4.4 Participant is unfamiliar with the equipment

➤ 6.4 Participant is not able to complete a necessary task

➤ 11.3 Participant insists that she would never do something

4.3 Participant has an unexpected physical feature

Your room's physical and technical setup works well until you get a participant who has a physical feature that requires an adjustment. For example, the participant may be left-handed, have an injured arm in a sling, or be a very large or small person.

Method(s): Any in-person method
Frequency: Occasional
Pattern(s) to apply: Take responsibility; Reassure the participant

What to do

➤ If the feature is something you notice on your own (e.g., very tall, left-handed), make any adjustments to your facility as soon as possible. For example, show the participant how to lower the chair, or move the mouse from the right to left side). When you make the adjustments, place any blame on you or your facility for not being set up correctly.

➤ If a participant is very large and has trouble fitting into his chair, offer to get him a different one without making a big deal about it. A chair without any arms can work very well. While most participants won't take you up on your offer, those who do will be very grateful.

➤ If the participant apologizes for inconveniencing you, reassure him that it's no inconvenience and that you're looking forward to his feedback.

What to say

➤ "I apologize that we're not set up as well as we could be. Let me show you how we can adjust the chair to a more comfortable height."

➤ "Is there anything I can do to make you more comfortable?"

➤ "Sorry, but before we continue, I'm going to help you lower/raise the chair so our recording equipment can capture you."

What not to do or say

➤ Don't call unnecessary attention to the participant's physical attributes.

➤ Occasionally, a participant will call attention to his own attribute to acknowledge it. If he does so, try not to follow up with personal questions. Focus any questions on understanding how you can better accommodate him. If the participant makes fun of himself for some sensitive attribute, do not laugh along. Smile politely, and then move on to your study plan.

➤ Don't complain about any extra work created by making the accommodations for the participant.

4.3 Participant has an unexpected physical feature (cont.)

How to avoid

➤ Familiarize yourself with the adjustments that your facility and equipment can support. For example, most chairs and desks can be lowered or raised, other types of chairs are usually available from somewhere, and a mouse (and its control panel settings) can be moved from the right side to the left side.

See also

➤ 10.6 Participant is difficult to hear or understand

➤ 12.5 Participant has a disconcerting or distracting physical attribute

➤ 12.8 Participant has an unexpected disability or service animal

➤ Survival Story: "The chair's arms were too fixed and narrow" in Chapter 1

4.4 Participant is unfamiliar with the equipment

Your session requires the participant to interact with a computer, mobile device, or similar type of equipment. When asked to use this equipment, the participant indicates or demonstrates that he lacks basic familiarity with it. You can tell that proceeding with him will be impossible unless you spend some time acquainting him with the basics of the equipment.

Method(s): Usability study
Frequency: Rare
Pattern(s) to apply: Reassure the participant; Shift the focus; End the session early

What to do

➤ First, figure out if the participant is just unfamiliar with the platform that is being used. For example, participants who are used to older Apple computers and mice may not understand how to use a Windows two-button mouse, but have an understanding of how a mouse is supposed to work. If this is the case, provide a short explanation of how the device works on this platform or, if possible, switch to what he is used to (e.g., if you're testing an application on an Android operating system and he only knows how to use an iPhone with iOS, you may want to switch devices if you're able to do so).

➤ If the participant is truly unfamiliar with the equipment, experiment with a short five-minute explanation and demonstration of what to do. Depending on what your research is focused on, that short time period may be enough to get him to a level where he can proceed. Make it clear to the participant that you're training him just for this first five minutes, after which you'll no longer be training but rather observing.

➤ Let the participant attempt the first task, with you providing minimal technical support as necessary. Ask him to think aloud so you can track whether any problems he runs into are based on the interface he is interacting with or his unfamiliarity with the equipment.

➤ If the participant continues to struggle, shift the focus of the session to limit the use of this equipment and end early. Handle this as gracefully as possible. See section 10.8 for additional tips for dealing with struggling participants.

➤ If at any point the participant seems like he is feeling bad or inadequate, reassure him that he is not being tested and that the feedback he is providing is helpful.

What to say

➤ "You seem a bit uncomfortable with the *<equipment>*. Have you used anything like this before?"

➤ "I'm going to take a few minutes to help get you set up on this *<equipment>*, since we'll be using it later in the session."

What not to do or say

➤ Don't show any surprise or shock regarding a participant's experience level. Remember that you don't know anything about the participant's background, and it can be dangerous to make assumptions.

How to avoid

➤ Consider adding some basic equipment experience into your recruit criteria. We've found that recruiting participants who spend at least five hours a week using the Internet doing varied activities (e.g., not just checking email but reading online, purchasing from e-commerce websites, etc.) typically ensures that they can use a computer and a mouse.

➤ Depending on your study goals, this situation may not be something that you want to avoid. The perspective that a very new or inexperienced user provides can be extremely valuable. However, for a typical usability study, the extra time spent helping an inexperienced participant results in less time getting the feedback that you need, so you'll have to weigh this trade-off on a study-by-study basis.

See also

➤ 4.1 Participant does not seem to meet a key recruit criteria

➤ 4.2 Participant either refuses to or can't do a key task

➤ 4.5 Participant has difficulty reading

➤ Survival Story: "She looked agitated" in Chapter 8

4.5 Participant has difficulty reading

> The participant meets the recruiting criteria for the study, however, when you give him a task to read, he is hesitant and slow and struggles with the words. He has similar difficulties when trying to interact with the product, especially if there is a lot of text. You might notice that he talks about expectations instead of using the product, even when you explicitly ask him to do so. It seems that he may have low-literacy abilities, be a non-native English speaker, or have some kind of reading disability. As the participant struggles, he may grow increasingly nervous and uncomfortable, or seem embarrassed.

Method(s): Usability study
Frequency: Rare
Pattern(s) to apply: Reassure the participant; Shift the focus; End the session early

What to do

➤ If the participant is having difficulty or seems nervous reading tasks aloud, read the task to him or ask him to read it quietly to himself and then verbally reiterate the task. You may find that despite having issues reading the tasks, he may approach the tasks with the product without issue.

➤ If the participant continues to struggle with the tasks and is getting increasingly nervous or frustrated, shift the focus of the session to reduce the amount of reading required. For example, if he communicates well verbally, turn the session into an interview. If necessary, use a pretext to explain the shift (e.g., tell the participant that the prototype isn't working as intended so you need to change the format).

➤ Whether or not you shift the focus of the session to another method, end early. If possible, try to do it in such a way that the participant doesn't realize that you're ending things early (e.g., by saying that you got through everything faster than anticipated).

What to say

Switch over to reading tasks to participants:

➤ "Let's say that your next task is to...."

➤ "I apologize—I didn't word this task very well. Let me try to rephrase it...."

Change the focus to an interview:

➤ "It looks like our prototype is not working as we planned it to, so if you don't mind I'm going to just ask you some questions."

End the session early:

➤ *At beginning of the session:* "I'm sorry, but we're going to have to cancel the session due to some technical difficulties. Thank you so much for coming in, and here's your compensation."

➤ *If a little later in session:* "That is actually all I had for you today, so you'll get some time back in your day! Thank you so much for your feedback, and here's your compensation."

What not to do or say

➤ Don't show any surprise or shock regarding a participant's literacy level.

➤ Avoid anything that might make the participant more nervous or embarrassed about his performance, such as pointing out that he seems to be having trouble reading.

How to avoid

➤ During recruiting, let participants know that they will be interacting with a product rather than just answering questions.

➤ If low-literacy participants are part of your target recruit, be sure to set up your study plan appropriately to accommodate their abilities. For example, you should not require them to read tasks.

See also

➤ 4.4 Participant is unfamiliar with the equipment

➤ 10.8 Participant struggles excessively with a task

➤ Survival Story: "His frustration was clearly growing" in Chapter 3

4.6 Participant or others ask you to help

You're onsite to conduct a contextual inquiry. Because they see you as an extra set of hands, the participant or your other contacts onsite ask you to pitch in with their work, provide training, or help out with something else. Their request may start as a quick favor, but they continue to rely on you to help as the session is beginning.

Method(s): Contextual inquiry
Frequency: Rare
Pattern(s) to apply: Clarify the task/question; Disengage with the participant

What to do

➤ Clarify your purpose for being onsite and what you want to get out of the contextual inquiry. Emphasize that you wouldn't typically be there to help, so you would rather see how the participant handles his work on his own.

➤ The participant and your other contacts may perceive your session to be something informal, especially if you have a preexisting work relationship with them. If this is the case, disengage slightly and adapt to a more formal moderating style. For example, you may want to take a less social tone, and let them know that you need to start/resume your planned session goals.

➤ If you have the resources available, offer to help after the session is over (if there is time) and/or to find them more help.

What to say

➤ "I'm sorry, I would like to help—it actually looks fun/interesting. But my role is really to be a neutral outside observer here. If I'm helping, I won't be able to focus on all that I need to."

➤ "If I helped you, you'd be dividing up labor that you usually do yourself, so I wouldn't get an accurate depiction of your day-to-day work. I'd rather see what you'd do if I wasn't here."

➤ "I wish I could be of help, but I can't really leave to do <*favor asked of you*>. My role is to sit here and watch <*the participant's*> end-to-end workflow. I'm happy to help after, though."

If asked to train:

➤ "I'm sorry, my role is not to train. It's just the opposite—I don't want to show you what to do! I'm here to sit back and observe the way you naturally do things on your own. If we have time at the end, I can try to answer any questions for you then."

What not to do or say

➤ Don't be offensive or condescending about not helping. Remain professional and just explain your viewpoint.

➤ Avoid helping participants do their work, especially in a business environment. Doing so may create liability issues if you give them bad advice and they lose or corrupt data. If you're an expert in the systems used by the participant, you may offer some basic tips like shortcuts or ways to be more efficient at the end of the session. However, keep in mind that you don't know all the details about their systems, so it may be better to direct the participant to someone who is in a better position to help.

How to avoid

➤ While preparing for your field visit, set expectations that you're there to watch what the participants do. Reiterate this point when you brief the participants at the beginning of a session.

See also

➤ 5.1 Participant thinks that she is participating in a focus group

➤ 5.5 Participant treats a contextual inquiry like an interview

SURVIVAL STORY: "AN UNEXPECTED PICTURE STARTED TO EMERGE"
ANONYMOUS

In mid-2012, I was one of the user experience researchers for an interview-based study designed to inform new personas we were building. The main research goal of this exercise was to determine our customers' emotional relationships with their money.

The day had been going well; I was viewing sessions remotely, taking notes for the moderator. At the beginning of the next session, the male participant who entered seemed "normal" enough—around 30 years old, informally, yet neatly dressed, and pretty articulate. As my colleague warmed him up during the background interview, an unexpected picture started to emerge.

"You just told me that the economic downturn necessitated moving back in with your family, is that right?" (Sadly, this was not an infrequently heard fact—even worse were stories of participants who didn't have a "home" to go back to as they were on the brink of losing their houses and honestly did not know where they would turn next.)

"Well, yes, but I got kind of tired of that. So I moved after a few months. Into my … car."

My colleague could not have handled this startling news with more grace. The participant went on to detail his grooming rituals, which included using baby wipes, mouthwash, and powder.

For the personas we were building, it was clear that his input would be excluded as an outlier within our target customer base. After a few minutes, our colleague pricked up her ears, saying she thought he heard a knock on the interview room door. She left the room for 30 seconds (which seemed an eternity over the phone) and returned with regret in her voice to tell the participant that the team was experiencing "technical difficulties with the recording apparatus" and would need to end early. The participant seemed to take it in stride.

What surprised and impressed me about the moderator's reaction was how, once she had determined that the participant no longer qualified, she took a few minutes to gain composure and figure out what she would do next. She waited long enough past the critical moment to put his suspicion at bay, especially given her lack of reaction when she was listening to him.

CHAPTER 5

Participant Misconceptions:
Not What the Participant was Expecting

When there is a mismatch between the participant's expectations for the session and what you have planned, you need to clarify your expectations before continuing. If the participant brought someone or something else with her to the session, you also need to tactfully and quickly figure out if, and how, to proceed. These situations require you to immediately take responsibility for any misunderstanding and figure out the best way to move forward.

5.1 Participant thinks that she is participating in a focus group

When the participant arrives, it becomes clear that she is expecting to be in a focus group with other people. She may ask where everyone else is, or talk about her previous experience participating in focus groups. Or, she may arrive late because she assumes that the group won't be delayed or affected by one person not being there on time.

Method(s): In-person usability study
Frequency: Frequent
Pattern(s) to apply: Clarify the task/question; Reassure the participant; Build engagement

What to do

➤ Most people are familiar with focus groups but not with usability studies, so this is a common misperception. Let the participant know that what she'll be doing is similar to a focus group, but that she'll be the only person in the room with you and you'll be asking her to interact with a product directly rather than having a group discussion.

➤ Ask if the participant has been in a focus group before. This approach provides a lightweight way to get her talking, and may also reveal if the participant has actually participated in any kind of research before or if she has just heard of focus groups.

➤ If the participant assumed she signed up to participate in a focus group where she could hide behind a crowd, she may be shyer about performing tasks and thinking aloud. She may not be a personality type who would have signed up for a usability study. Because of this, you may need to adjust your style to be comforting and engaging until she feels more comfortable. You may also need to reiterate the kind of feedback you're looking to receive from her throughout the session.

What to say

➤ "What you'll be helping us with today is similar to a focus group, but you'll be the only person in the room with me and you'll be working with a product. I'm going to ask you to try to use the product to accomplish some tasks while thinking aloud about your experience. This will give us feedback on how the product works—both what works well and what should be improved. Let me tell you a bit more about how our session will work...."

➤ "It sounds like you're familiar with focus groups. Have you participated in any kind of research, like a focus group or usability study before?"

5.1 Participant thinks that she is participating in a focus group (cont.)

What not to do or say

➤ Don't disparage focus groups. Many user experience practitioners see focus groups as a technique that produces misleading results, but someone who has been in a focus group and had a great time doesn't need to hear your take on the methodology. Instead, focus (no pun intended) on the more practical aspects of how the research you're doing today will be different than a focus group. For example, the session is one-on-one, and the participant will be interacting with a product.

How to avoid

➤ In your recruiting screener and confirmation letter, be explicit about the type of research you're doing and that the session will be one-on-one between the participant and a moderator (you). However, be aware that no matter how explicit you are during the recruiting process, you'll still get participants who assume they're there for a focus group.

See also

➤ 4.6 Participant or others ask you to help
➤ 5.4 Participant brings you to a conference room or other space
➤ 5.5 Participant treats a contextual inquiry like an interview
➤ 5.7 Participant thinks the session is a job interview

5.2 Participant doesn't want to be recorded or has other concerns

> The participant was recruited with the understanding that the session will be recorded. However, once she arrives and reads through the consent form, she decides that she is uncomfortable with being recorded and will not proceed unless you refrain from recording the session. If she is remote, she may change her mind about being recorded once she is in the session, even if she already sent you back a signed copy of the consent form. Or, the participant may have other concerns about the consent form and refuses to sign it unless you make changes.

Method(s): Any
Frequency: Occasional
Pattern(s) to apply: Reassure the participant

What to do

➤ See if there is a level of recording that the participant is comfortable with. For example, instead of recording picture-in-picture, offer to remove the capture of the participant's face while still recording the screen and audio. However, don't press the point. The participant is under no obligation to be recorded if she doesn't want to be, and a recording is usually nice to have instead of a necessity for the session.

➤ If the participant has issues with video/audio altogether, ask if it would be okay for you to just take detailed notes or have another person in the room to help take notes. If she agrees to having another person take notes, ask your colleague to join you and sit behind you quietly with a notepad or note-taking device.

➤ If you're providing session recordings to stakeholders, be explicit about their storage and deletion responsibilities. You can share those responsibilities with the participant if she is nervous about how the recordings will be used and reassure her that her video will not end up on YouTube!

➤ If the participant is concerned about any other clause in the consent form, ask her to explain her concern. Do your best to address her concern, but if she is still uncomfortable, offer to cancel the session and let her leave with her full compensation.

➤ Be sure the participant signs the consent form before the session begins. If she refuses to be recorded but is willing to continue, mark up the consent form to reflect the change. Barring legal advice otherwise (see "How to avoid"), use a permanent pen or marker of a different color to make the edits required for the participant to continue. Make sure the edits are obvious. If a participant doesn't want to be recorded, for example, cross out the line regarding recording and write in big letters at the bottom, "NO RECORDING." For recognition purposes, it may help if you place your initials next to the change, and have the participant add her initials next to yours.

5.2 Participant doesn't want to be recorded or has other concerns (cont.)

What to say

➤ "I know you're concerned about the recording. Let me explain what would actually be recorded if you agree to it. The recording is a picture-in-picture showing the computer screen in the big window, and a small inset of your face in the corner. If you prefer, we can set it up so we do not capture your face, only your voice. The recording will only be used to make sure that we have an accurate record of your feedback. It will only be shared with the team working on this project, for this project—not for any other purpose. Does that make sense?"

➤ "Would it be okay if we adjusted what is being recorded so we're only capturing *<what's being recorded, e.g., just your voice and what you're interacting with, without capturing your face>*?"

➤ "If you don't mind, tell me what's concerning you about *<topic of concern>*."

What not to do or say

➤ Don't dismiss the participant's concerns. The prevalence of platforms such as YouTube and Vimeo have shown how easy it is to share video, so a participant's concerns regarding what will happen with her recording is warranted.

How to avoid

➤ Be explicit about the recording and how it will be used. Have whoever is handling the recruit share this information with the participant during the recruitment process and in her confirmation letter. Make sure that the participant knows the recording is optional, which it usually should be. Also share your consent form with the recruiter so she can answer participant questions ahead of time. If you work with the same recruiter multiple times, highlight anything unique or different that will be included in your study's consent form that hasn't been in previous forms.

➤ When a participant arrives, explain the consent form rather than just handing it to her. If you explain the clauses in plain terms upfront, she is less likely to panic when trying to read and interpret the text on her own.

➤ Ensure that your consent form is written in plain language that clearly explains what will be happening during the session and what will happen with the recording. This is often challenging in commercial environments, but is well worth the effort. Keep in mind that the consent form is a legal contract and work with your legal team to craft something that is both legal and clear. See Appendix C for user research method books that go into more detail about consent forms.

➤ If you have access to legal representatives at your organization, discuss with them how much leverage you have in adjusting consent forms on-the-fly. For example, you may be allowed to use a pen to make a change to the form, put your initials next to the change, and have the participant put her initials next to yours.

5.2 Participant doesn't want to be recorded or has other concerns (cont.)

➤ Expect that some participants will prefer not to be recorded, and plan accordingly. Have a note-taker to support your session or the materials with you to take your own notes.

See also

➤ 5.3 Participant has different expectations for the compensation

5.3 Participant has different expectations for the compensation

The participant thought that she was receiving either a different amount for her compensation (e.g., $100 instead of $75) or a different format (e.g., cash instead of a gift card). She may get very upset about this misunderstanding and feel like she was lied to.

Method(s): Any
Frequency: Occasional
Pattern(s) to apply: Take responsibility

What to do

➤ Address this issue as soon as it comes up. Ideally, a participant will notice the discrepancy at the beginning of the session when she signs the consent form (which should explicitly state the compensation she'll receive for participating). But, if it comes up later in the session, address it right away instead of waiting until the very end.

➤ If there is a way to provide the compensation in a different format, and the participant is insistent on receiving it that way, go ahead and make the adjustment if you can (and if there are no issues from a legal perspective for your organization—some organizations require that compensation be handled in very specific ways).

➤ If the participant is insistent that the recruiter promised her a different amount, apologize for the misunderstanding and ask if she has something documenting that amount, such as a confirmation letter, email, or voicemail. If there was indeed a mistaken promise, find a way to give her the promised amount even if it's different than what you compensated everyone else. Then, immediately follow up with the recruiter (if applicable) to see if this was a mistake that happened with other participants as well. If the participant can't document the misunderstanding, follow the earlier recommendations for what to do.

➤ If the participant is expecting a different amount because she knows other people who participated who received that amount, go ahead and make the adjustment if the inconsistency is an oversight on your part. If the other participants were doing something distinct from this session (e.g., had 1.5-hour sessions instead of 1-hour sessions), apologize and explain the discrepancy to the participant.

➤ Be prepared to explain any compensation formats that a participant may be unfamiliar with. For example, when we've provided participants with American Express cash cards, we also spend a few minutes explaining how those cards work and can be used.

5.3 Participant has different expectations for the compensation (cont.)

What to say

If you're trying to understand where the misconception came from:

➤ "Do you have a copy of your confirmation letter, or a voicemail from *<recruiter>*? I believe that she specified your compensation amount in there."

If you're able to accommodate the different amount or format:

➤ "I'm sorry for the misunderstanding. Please give me just a couple of extra minutes so I can make this adjustment for you."

If you're unable to accommodate the different expectation:

➤ "I apologize for any confusion about this. Your confirmation letter for the session specified the amount that we can provide and the format that we can offer. If you're unwilling to continue, let me know."

➤ "I'm so sorry about this. We're unable to offer compensation in a different format due to company restrictions."

What not to do or say

➤ Don't criticize or blame your recruiter in front of the participant, even if you see proof that she provided the participant with incorrect information. Be professional and apologetic about the mistake, keeping in mind that the participant may not see a distinction between your organization and the one that recruited her (if different).

➤ Try to be consistent with compensation amounts among participants, as participants sometimes encounter and talk to each other and may be unhappy at discovering that someone else is getting paid a different amount for the same amount of time.

How to avoid

➤ Be explicit in the confirmation letter about the promised compensation, its delivery mechanism, and any other reimbursement being offered (e.g., if you'll reimburse up to a certain amount for parking/transportation expenses).

See also

➤ 5.2 Participant doesn't want to be recorded or has other concerns

➤ Survival Story: "He refuses to leave"

5.4 Participant brings you to a conference room or other space

> You've scheduled a contextual inquiry at a participant's work location with the goal of watching her in her own environment. However, when you arrive, the participant brings you to a conference room instead, explaining that it will be quieter and easier to talk there.

Method(s): Contextual inquiry
Frequency: Occasional
Pattern(s) to apply: Take responsibility

What to do

➤ The participant may not understand why you want to see her in her workspace, and assumes that she is being helpful by providing a conference room or other space instead. Thank her for reserving the space, but explain that one of your goals is to understand how she works when you're not there, and that seeing her environment and what she does within that environment will provide the information that you need.

➤ The participant may feel like she doesn't have space for someone to join her in her workspace, or that her space is too messy for visitors. Let her know that you don't need a lot of space, and that it doesn't matter how it looks—you're interested in her day-to-day reality, not the tidied-up version of her work.

➤ If the participant has a crowded or open workspace, offer to chat in private with the participant at the end of the session. This private conversation may be an opportunity for her to give any feedback that she doesn't want her coworkers or manager to overhear in her work environment.

What to say

➤ "I realize I may not have been clear enough <*in the confirmation letter/when we talked earlier*>. It's really important for us to be in the environment that you're normally working in. Could we move there instead? It's okay if it's noisy or cramped. We can come back to this conference room at the end of the session to wrap up."

➤ "I'd like to watch you work in your own environment, so that I can witness your day-to-day tasks. But after that, we can debrief back in a conference room. Does that sound okay to you?"

What not to do or say

➤ Don't blame the participant for misunderstanding—take responsibility for not being clear enough about what you're doing or what you need.

5.4 Participant brings you to a conference room or other space (cont.)

How to avoid

➤ When setting up the session, specify that you want to be with the participant in her workspace, even if it's noisy. Explain that because your focus is on seeing how she actually works, it's important to be in her own environment. If the participant seems reluctant to have you in that space (e.g., because she sits right next to her manager), offer to split the session between her space and a conference room so you can get the best of both worlds.

 Watch Video 6 to see an example of a participant who is expecting an interview instead of a contextual inquiry. The moderator clarifies her expectations, but has to repeat them a couple of times as the session progresses.

Visit our website (http://www.modsurvivalguide.org/videos) or use your QR reader to scan this code.

See also

➤ 5.1 Participant thinks that she is participating in a focus group

➤ 5.5 Participant treats a contextual inquiry like an interview

5.5 Participant treats a contextual inquiry like an interview

You arrive onsite to perform a contextual inquiry but the participant expects that she just needs to talk to you about what she does with a product and what she thinks of it. For example, a call center representative anticipates an interview and schedules special time off from her phone queue to chat with you. Your goal was actually to watch her take calls and ask her questions in between calls. If you're doing the session remotely, the participant may just talk about her workflow instead of showing it to you through the screen-sharing software.

Method(s): Contextual inquiry
Frequency: Occasional
Pattern(s) to apply: Take responsibility; Clarify the task/question; Shift the focus

What to do

This situation may happen because the participant was given vague details when recruited for the study, or made the wrong assumption when asked to participate. Most people are familiar with the idea of being interviewed, but a contextual inquiry is not a very common method outside of the user research community.

➤ Clarify your expectations as soon as you realize what is happening, and apologize for not being clear enough ahead of time about what you were planning. Hopefully the participant will be able to adapt and you can continue the session as planned. If you can't continue as planned, see if you can reschedule or shift the focus to some other way to get feedback.

➤ If she seems embarrassed or feels bad about the mix-up, take responsibility for the miscommunication (even if was someone else's fault).

➤ Prepare a list of questions for times when you can't watch the participant work. This may come up even without a misunderstanding. For example, the participant's system may be down, or she may have completed a project early and have nothing to show you.

What to say

➤ "What I was actually looking to do today is watch you work in the way that you typically would if I weren't here. I may have some questions for you along the way, or things I ask you to show me, but in general, you should be working and my role is to mostly be a wallflower and watch quietly."

➤ "Are you able to get set up so that I can quietly just watch you while you work?"

➤ "I'm so sorry for the mix-up—I must not have clearly communicated my intent for this session. If it isn't too much trouble, could you go ahead and show me what you're describing?"

5.5 Participant treats a contextual inquiry like an interview (cont.)

What not to do or say

➤ Don't end the session, if you can help it. Try to find a way to have the participant get set up to work. If that is not possible, shift the focus of the research if turning it into an interview would provide some useful information. As a last resort, find a time to reschedule if possible and end the session. Since site visits usually take a lot of effort and time to plan, you should do your best to get some feedback out of the session.

How to avoid

➤ During the recruit, specify the exact setup of the session and what it involves. For example, include in your recruiting script and confirmation letter that you need to watch the participant at her work computer using a specific application.

 Watch Video 6 to see an example of a participant who is expecting an interview instead of a contextual inquiry. The moderator clarifies her expectations, but has to repeat them a couple of times as the session progresses.

Visit our website (http://www.modsurvivalguide.org/videos) or use your QR reader to scan this code.

See also

➤ 4.6 Participant or others ask you to help

➤ 5.1 Participant thinks that she is participating in a focus group

➤ 5.4 Participant brings you to a conference room or other space

➤ 6.6 Participant not approaching workflow naturally

5.6 Participant brings someone else to participate with her

> You have scheduled a participant for a one-on-one session. However, when she arrives (or when you call her if she is remote), she has brought one or more additional people with her to participate as well. This other person may be a coworker, her manager, or a friend who she thinks would be interested as well.

Method(s): Any
Frequency: Rare
Pattern(s) to apply: Take responsibility

What to do

When you're running a study within an organization, this misunderstanding may occur because participants (or the people recruiting the participants) don't understand the purpose of your research and assume that it's a training or sales session. Or, the other attendees may just be really interested in what you're doing and want a chance to provide their own feedback. The best thing to do in this situation depends on who the other attendees are.

If the other attendees have similar roles/responsibilities (or fit the original recruit criteria) as the participant:

➤ Schedule additional sessions to talk to the other attendees, and proceed one-on-one with the original participant. This technique may be appropriate if you have additional time slots available.

➤ Turn the session into a codiscovery session. This technique may be appropriate if there is only one additional attendee who cannot be scheduled for a separate session, and the session is a usability study or interview.

➤ Talk to each attendee separately, one-on-one, for a shorter period of time.

➤ Make sure to give or send consent forms to the additional participants and have them review and sign the form before continuing the session.

If the other attendees have very different roles/responsibilities (and do not fit the original recruit criteria) or are the participant's manager, family, or friends:

➤ Explain to the other attendees that your goal is to talk one-on-one with the original participant and that, while you're excited that they're so interested in giving feedback, you need them to leave the room. If they have a misconception that they'll be missing out on something, clarify that you're not providing any kind of training.

5.6 Participant brings someone else to participate with her (cont.)

➤ If they insist that they'll sit quietly during the session, politely decline. Their presence may change the behavior of the participant. Instead, explain that the session is really designed to be one-on-one with the participant with no one else present. If you ultimately decide to let them stay, give or send them consent forms to sign as soon as possible. This form may even be a deterrent to the additional attendees staying, since it may emphasize the session's level of formality.

➤ Take responsibility for not being clear enough about the purpose of the session and the need for it to be one-on-one.

What to say

➤ "It's great that you're both so enthusiastic about participating. Can you tell me why you're interested in participating?"

If the other attendees are trying to not miss out on a training opportunity:

➤ "I'm running this study to *<get early feedback from users on designs/observe the current experience of the product>*. I won't be providing any kind of training, just watching as *<participant>* uses the system."

If dismissing other person/people:

➤ "Because this session is designed for one-on-one feedback, unfortunately I can't have you stay in the room with us. I apologize for any misunderstanding about that. But we can provide you with a beverage if you want to stick around in our reception area and wait for *<participant>*."

What not to do or say

➤ Don't let the participant continue the session if her manager is in the room or observing the session, as you do not want any power issues to get in the way of your feedback.

➤ If you need to ask the additional attendees to leave, don't be rude about it. Be firm, but kind. You're representing your organization to anyone you come in contact with, even if they don't wind up as a participant. You don't want to create any grievances with a manager who has a lot of clout in your organization, or with an important customer.

How to avoid

➤ This situation often occurs because the participant is unclear about what will be happening during the session. Explain the setup of the session to the participant before she arrives (e.g., during the recruit and in the confirmation letter) and make sure the one-on-one aspect is

5.6 Participant brings someone else to participate with her (cont.)

clear. However, even if you're very explicit, you can expect to still run into this situation and should plan accordingly.

See also

➤ 5.8 Participant brings a child or pet to the session

5.7 Participant thinks the session is a job interview

The participant shows up in a polished suit and gives only positive feedback. At the end of the session, she hands you her resume and asks when she'll hear back about the job!

Method(s): In-person usability study; In-person interview
Frequency: Rare
Pattern(s) to apply: Take responsibility; Shift the focus; End the session early

What to do

This misunderstanding may happen if you're doing research for a well-known organization. If someone is unemployed and expecting calls for interviews, she may feasibly misinterpret a user research recruitment call for the *other* type of recruitment call. This can also happen accidentally if you have a main waiting area for lots of different people—site visitors, job interview candidates, customers, and user research participants. It's easy to bring in the wrong person and, believe us, things can get quite confusing and interesting after that.

➤ Be very clear and explicit in the briefing at the beginning of the session about why the participant is there and what she'll be doing. Hopefully any misunderstanding will surface at this time.

➤ If at *any point* you suspect that the participant is there for a job interview, try asking a couple of general questions. For example, ask what made her come in today, or if she has participated in a user research session before, and reconfirm the recruiting criteria. If it's still not clear, you might need to directly ask her if she is there for the session.

➤ If the miscommunication becomes clear at the start of the session (e.g., when asking background questions), spare the poor participant further embarrassment and explain the actual purpose of the session. Take responsibility for the miscommunication and offer to cancel the session while still providing her with the full compensation. If you realize that you brought in the wrong person from the waiting area, quickly find the participant!

➤ If you've offered to end the session but the participant seems legitimately interested in participating, consider letting her continue (unless your actual participant is waiting for you). If she doesn't fully meet the recruiting criteria, you could see if there is a way to let her stay and feel useful rather than that she wasted the travel time and a perfectly nice interview outfit. You may want to:

■ Run the session anyway if she is able to get through the tasks and questions without needing specialized knowledge or skills. Just make note in your findings how this participant deviated from the recruiting criteria.

5.7 Participant thinks the session is a job interview (cont.)

■ If the participant can't continue the tasks without key skills, consider shifting the focus of the session to something that better suits her. For instance, turn a usability study into an interview, or refocus interview questions on topics that you can still make use of and that she understands.

➤ If the participant asks you to connect her with someone specific at the organization, or wants you to take her resume and "pass it along," do what makes you feel comfortable. Don't do anything out of obligation or to just placate her. If you don't want to be involved, try to find a gentle way to let her down and point her in a more helpful direction. For example, you may say that you're a consultant (if that is true), so you don't really have any connection with the other parts of the organization but know that the corporate website has a section for job applicants.

What to say

If unclear about why the participant is there:

➤ *Start general:* "What made you decide to participate today?"

➤ *More specific:* "You're <*name*>, correct? And you're here for the research study?"

At the beginning of session, if you realize there is a misunderstanding:

➤ "<*Participant*>, I'm really sorry but I think there was a misunderstanding. This is not a job interview but rather a research study. It's completely our fault for not being clear. If you'd like, I can just give you the promised compensation and we'll cancel the session."

➤ "I completely understand if you want to leave, but if you're still interested in the study, I could tell you about it."

If the participant asks for a connection or interview and you don't want to be involved:

➤ "I'm sorry. I wish I could help but I'm just here to run the session today. If you want, I can provide you the link to the careers web page."

➤ "I am really just involved in user research, so I can't help you with that. I can walk you to the front desk if you'd like, and they may be able to put you in touch with someone in HR."

What not to do or say

➤ Don't let the participant leave thinking that the session was a job interview.

How to avoid

➤ Provide your recruiter with a script that is explicit about recruiting for a research session. If someone within an organization is doing the recruit for you, provide her with an explanation of the session that can be shared with potential participants to alleviate any confusion. We recommend talking with your recruiter about it as well so she is very clear that the session is for research, not an interview.

➤ When you greet the participant, greet her by name and confirm that she is the right person before bringing her into your research space.

See also

➤ 5.1 Participant thinks that she is participating in a focus group

➤ Survival Story: "She was desperate for work"

5.8 Participant brings a child or pet to the session

The participant arrives with a child (or children!) or animal in tow. The animal isn't a service animal, but is just a pet. The participant may expect you or your team to provide childcare, or may indicate that the child or pet can "quietly" stay in the room with you.

Method(s): Any in-person method
Frequency: Rare
Pattern(s) to apply: Take responsibility; End the session early

What to do

➤ Confirm that the participant is aware of how long the session will last and what you'll be asking her to do. You can also show her the space that you'll be in, as that may change her mind about continuing (in which case, you can offer to reschedule her or just offer the compensation for coming in).

➤ If the participant has brought a child, ideally she came prepared with items to keep her child occupied during the session. If not, take a deep breath and get creative! Depending on the child's age, you can volunteer to bring in some paper and markers for her to use, or some other set of (safe!) materials for the child to play with, such as a deck of cards or a tablet.

➤ While we haven't seen participants bring pets other than dogs to usability sessions (unless they're service animals), we're sure it can happen. In that case, raise any potential concerns with the pet being there. For example, you need to limit future participants' exposure to allergens, and make sure the pet's behavior and "calls to nature" can be controlled without interfering with your session.

➤ If the child or pet is being excessively and/or consistently disruptive after an initial period of time, try to be patient and understanding if the participant seems eager to continue anyway. But if there are constant disruptions, you might want to end the session early. Do so delicately, without blaming the child or pet. If you need to use a pretext, you can blame technical difficulties or explain that you made it through all your questions faster than anticipated. Offer again to reschedule for a time when the participant can come on her own. If she is unable to reschedule, we recommend still giving her the full compensation.

What to say

When the participant arrives:

➤ "This is meant to be a focused one-on-one session. Will your <child/pet> be okay in the room with us? Our setup may not be comfortable for <child/pet>, so we're happy to reschedule you for a time when you can come by yourself."

If concerned about a pet, blame allergies:

➤ "I'm sorry, we try to keep this room allergen-free since we have so many people coming through here. Are you able to reschedule for a time when you can come by yourself?"

If child/pet is being excessively disruptive and you need to end early:

➤ "It looks like we made it through everything faster than I expected, so you'll have a bit of extra time in your day. Thank you so much for your feedback, and here is your compensation."

What not to do or say

➤ Do not allow team members to babysit or petsit during the session, even from within the research room. Doing so would potentially leave your organization vulnerable if something happened to the child or pet while they were out of the participant's view. Also, you don't want to risk the possibility of your colleague being bitten (by a child *or* pet!). If the participant asks for this service, let her know that you're not equipped to do so and offer to reschedule at a more convenient time when she can come in on her own.

How to avoid

Explain the setup of the session to the participant before she arrives (e.g., during the recruit and in the confirmation letter) and make sure the one-on-one aspect is clear.

See also

➤ 5.6 Participant brings someone else to participate with her

➤ 12.8 Participant has an unexpected disability or service animal

➤ Survival Story: "I know what she needs" in Chapter 2

PARTICIPANT MISCONCEPTIONS: NOT WHAT THE PARTICIPANT WAS EXPECTING

PARTICIPANT MISCONCEPTIONS: NOT WHAT THE PARTICIPANT WAS EXPECTING

SURVIVAL STORY: "SHE WAS DESPERATE FOR WORK"
ADRIAN HOWARD

I was moderating in-person usability sessions that compared a number of websites designed for people seeking work.

The sessions were run at the client's site and we had a *lot* of participants. I helped set up the screening parameters, but the recruitment of the participants was managed by the client.

We ended up organizing a testing production line. While I was moderating one session, the next participant was being prepared in a different room by a coworker. The people who handled the recruitment managed the meet-and-greet as participants arrived.

Toward the end of a long day, a participant walked into the test room under a major misapprehension. A few minutes into the session it became very clear she thought this was an actual job interview.

Oh dear.

Obviously I stopped the session immediately. It would have been unethical to continue. Once I explained, the participant became upset almost to the point of tears. She was desperate for work and had used time and money to attend that she could ill afford to waste. All because she thought it could lead to full-time employment.

We went to a private office to talk in more comfort and I emphasized the situation wasn't her fault but ours. I immediately reassured her that she would not be out of pocket for the day and gave her time to compose herself while I fetched coffee.

We ended up providing a taxi home along with some additional compensation to cover her costs in attending. She would never have participated if she had understood it was just a usability session.

When we looked to the underlying causes of this failure we discovered three main factors: poor communication, poor screening, and time pressure.

The lack of communication was the biggest issue. The recruiters didn't raise problems they encountered when people arrived. The person briefing the participants assumed that

Survival Story (cont.)

they had had the process explained to them. I assumed that the participant was ready for the test. Our innocent victim fell between the gaps.

Better communication would have helped us spot the poor screening questions. The language used could be misinterpreted by somebody in a job-seeking context (e.g., the word "interview"). It became obvious our participant had verbally okayed things in the screening and briefing that she hadn't fully understood in the vain hope that this rather strange job interview process would soon make sense! I should have been more involved with the recruiters and ensured that the screening questions were working well.

Finally, at the end of a long day, everybody involved was tired and not paying as much attention as they should have been. Tight time constraints cause problems. We need to give ourselves the time to pay full attention to every participant we work with. If we hadn't been running a production line to try and jam as many sessions as possible into a tight schedule, we would have caught this participant much earlier.

SURVIVAL STORY: "HE REFUSES TO LEAVE"
CLIFF ANDERSON

I was at my desk when I got a call from the lab (another usability engineer was running a study that week). It was from our lab assistant, who seemed more than a little excited. "Cliff, there is a man here, and he refuses to leave, and he is threatening us, and we don't know what to do." After calming her down, I learned that he had expected to get his $100 compensation in cash, but was balking because we were offering Visa gift cards—something that was new for us and for our regular recruiting agency.

I told her "I'll be right down," then hit the stairs to get to the lab. When I got there, I found our assistant, the usability engineer who was running our test, and the user. Things seemed pretty under control, but I did notice that the user seemed a little perturbed.

I went right up to him, introduced myself, shook his hand, and asked him what was the matter. He went into his story, and I did my best job at active and empathetic listening, using all the tricks and tropes that I had learned over the years working with users and doing research.

I could tell he was calming down, but I still hadn't come up with a way to address his problem. So, I put my hand on my chin, knotted my brows, and it came to me! "Why don't you give me that gift card, and we can go to the ATM in the lobby downstairs, and I can withdraw your $100?"

He agreed, we withdrew the $100, shook hands, and parted amicably. I went back upstairs shaking my head, but giving myself credit for keeping cool under pressure (in general, one of the best skills a usability engineer can have) and also making sure that our screener (and recruiting agency) made sure to mention this new form of compensation ahead of time.

CHAPTER 6

Some Guidance Required: Participants in Need of Shepherding

Sometimes you need to give participants a little nudge. This nudge may take the form of an assist in a usability study or reassurance that they won't get in trouble or hurt anyone's feelings if they provide honest feedback. Approach the situation thoughtfully and gently to avoid embarrassing the participant while encouraging him to provide the feedback you need.

6.1 Participant is reluctant to say anything negative

> The participant hesitates before answering questions and his answers are vague. You get the feeling that he may be reluctant to say anything negative about a product or process.

Method(s): Any
Frequency: Frequent
Pattern(s) to apply: Reassure the participant

What to do

We see this sometimes when the participants are internal employees of your organization (also discussed in section 15.1). The participant may not want to offend the manager who taught him the process you're watching as part of a contextual inquiry, the team who developed the procedures that he is following as part of a usability study, or the in-house developers who wrote the software that you're interviewing him about.

➤ If the participant is overly diplomatic in his responses, you may be able to see right through his sugar-coating. But less tactful participants may seem to be lying or avoiding a question, and it's usually because they know they're being observed or out of fear that their feedback may not remain confidential.

➤ If you suspect that the participant is lying or avoiding a question to spare someone's feelings, try to gently coax the truth out of him. Remind him that his feedback will benefit future users and help improve the product. For example, you could say, "I just want to assure you that any feedback you provide will be used to make improvements to the product that will help other users. Your name will not be associated with any of our results."

➤ If you know a question will be particularly controversial or sensitive for a participant, consider prefacing it with something that will make him feel better about being candid. For example, if you're interviewing a call center representative about his call procedures and sense that he is worried about getting in trouble for not following them, consider saying something like, "I know that there is a certain way you're trained to do things, however, I'd like to understand more about when you have to do something that is different from your training. Please know that any feedback you share will be kept confidential."

➤ Talk to your observers after the session and remind them to respect the participant's feedback and anonymity, even (and especially) if his feedback was controversial.

What to say

To the participant:

➤ "I know that this is a product you're required to use in your job, but tell me candidly.…"

➤ "Please know that your honesty is appreciated. Nothing you say will hurt anyone's feelings. You're here to help us make the product better for yourself and future users."

To observers:

➤ "I got the sense that this participant was worried about offending someone with his feedback. So I just want to remind all of you, for him and our other participants, please respect the participant's confidentiality and feedback. Don't approach the participant to discuss his participation or talk to one another about his participation since he is an employee here."

What not to do or say

➤ Avoid making the participants feel like you don't believe them. If you suspect a participant is not being entirely honest, don't say, "It's okay, you can tell the truth," or "Could you tell me how you *really* feel?"

How to avoid

➤ Set expectations with the participant that his data will be kept confidential, and that his superiors or team members are not observing the session and will not have access to the raw identifiable data from the study.

See also

➤ 6.7 Participant does not have any negative feedback

➤ 8.3 Participant looks or sounds uncomfortable and/or nervous

➤ 10.5 Participant gives vague responses to questions

6.2 Participant does something you don't understand

The participant starts sharing feedback of a highly specialized nature in a domain that you don't fully understand. Perhaps you're a consultant who is new to the content or the participant is an expert in a field that you don't know much about. Either way, you aren't able to follow everything that he is saying or can't determine what pieces of his feedback are important or relevant. Similarly, in a contextual inquiry, you may observe the participant doing something you're unable to understand or follow.

Method(s): Any
Frequency: Frequent
Pattern(s) to apply: Clarify the task/question

What to do

If the participant is *saying* something you don't understand:

➤ If you have observers who are subject-matter experts or if the session is being recorded, you can capture the feedback and continue with your study plan. After the session, verify with observers what the participant was talking about. This will move the session along smoothly, but you may lose opportunities for immediate follow-up.

➤ If you know enough about the domain that what the participant says is within reach of your understanding, ask him to clarify what he means. Be honest—tell him that you're not a subject-matter expert and would appreciate hearing his thoughts in more common terms.

➤ In some cases it helps to have an in-room observer (or on-phone observer for remote sessions) who is a domain expert but is also trained in talking to users and knows the ground rules of moderating user research. Allow that observer to ask follow-up questions at times where you might have missed the opportunity due to lack of understanding. Be sure to coordinate with the observer ahead of time how this will work.

➤ Alternatively, you might have another way to communicate with observers (e.g., through an instant message program) where domain experts can answer your questions in real time or can help you pose follow-up questions. Keep in mind that this type of multitasking can be challenging and may take some practice, but it can be incredibly valuable.

If the participant is *doing* something you don't understand:

➤ If there is time for interruption during the participant's workflow, ask him to explain what he's doing in laymen's terms and why he's doing it.

➤ If it would be too disruptive to his workflow to ask for clarification, make sure to capture the exact process/steps with your notes and/or recording equipment. If possible, have domain

6.2 Participant does something you don't understand (cont.)

experts observing or share your notes with them later. If there is time after he's completed the workflow, ask the participant about what he was doing.

What to say

➤ "I'm not a subject-matter expert here, so bear with me for a second—can you explain in plain terms what you mean by that?"

➤ "I'm not sure I understand. Could you rephrase that for me?"

➤ "<*Trained observer*>, do you have any follow-up questions about that for <*participant*>?"

Post-observation of participant's workflow during contextual inquiry:

➤ "I noticed you doing something that I couldn't quite follow. Could you help me understand better what you were doing and why? It was when you <*did thing*>."

What not to do or say

➤ Don't make the participant feel like he was being inarticulate or supercilious with his feedback. Be humble yet professional when asking for clarification.

➤ Don't ignore the feedback altogether just because you don't understand it. Try to seek clarification either during the session with the participant or afterwards with a domain expert. You may actually learn a few things!

How to avoid

➤ A good practice when performing research in an unfamiliar domain is to gain a basic level of familiarity with the domain and product before you start your sessions. Having even a shallow foundation will help you filter relevant information from the participant and ask more targeted questions. You don't have to become an expert—in fact, some user researchers argue that it is actually helpful if you're not too immersed in the subject matter so that you can maintain a neutral and objective perspective. However, if your research is with expert users, you'll find that a bit of additional knowledge will help you come up with meaningful follow-up questions. Some evidence of understanding on your part will help establish your credibility with the participant and may even encourage his feedback.

➤ Tell the participant at the beginning of the session that you're not a domain expert. Stress that your role is to get his feedback and report it back to the team. Tell him that you may not be able to answer his questions, and that you may ask him for clarification at times when you don't understand something.

See also

➤ 10.3 Participant does something very unexpected

6.3 Participant is not thinking aloud

Even though you asked him to think out loud, the participant is very quiet and forgets to share his thoughts or expectations with you as he interacts with the product being evaluated.

Method(s): Usability study
Frequency: Frequent
Pattern(s) to apply: Clarify the task/question; Build engagement; Shift the focus

What to do

This behavior may not be a problem for summative studies, when you're capturing usability metrics such as time on task. But in formative or more exploratory studies, thinking aloud is usually an important part of the process, so you may need to gently draw the participant out of his comfort zone.

➤ Give the participant another moment or two before prompting him. He may need to process what he is seeing on the screen before verbalizing his reaction to it. As discussed in section 2.1, taking this moment may be enough for this situation to resolve itself.

➤ After a few moments ask the participant what he is thinking. This cue is usually enough to get him to think aloud for the rest of the session.

➤ If the participant is persistently silent, remind him to try to think out loud as he continues.

➤ If the participant still doesn't give much feedback, try to build engagement; draw him out with more general questions about what he is doing or what his experience is like. For example, you may ask him to compare his experience to other products he has used.

➤ If the participant is remote, encourage him to think aloud by describing what you see him doing. Use the excuse of not being beside him as motivation to keep him talking, For example, "Since I'm not able to see you as you use this product, it's helpful if you tell me what you're trying to do and whether what you're seeing is working for you." This will get him used to being verbal on the call, and will lead to more feedback.

What to say

➤ "What's going through your mind right now?"

➤ "What are your thoughts on this?"

➤ "I'd like to remind you to try to think out loud as you go through these tasks. I know it may feel uncomfortable at first, but it helps us understand more about how you're approaching the tasks."

6.3 Participant is not thinking aloud (cont.)

If the participant is remote:

➤ "*<Participant>*, since I'm not there beside you to see when you're doing certain things like clicking, I'll ask you to just explain to me what you're doing as you're doing it. If there is anything along the way that you particularly like or don't like about what you're seeing, let me know that too."

➤ "I can't see you, so it will be hard to know what's going on when you fall silent. So please remember to think out loud for me as you're going through the tasks. If you're too quiet, I'll remind you to think aloud!"

➤ "It looks like you tried to *<click or do something>*. What were you expecting to happen?"

What not to do or say

➤ Try not to be machine-like when asking participants to think aloud. Paralanguage (how you say something) matters. "What are you thinking?" may not roll off your tongue comfortably and you may feel (and sound) awkward saying it. Try to use a friendly tone and play with wording to find something that sounds more natural for you. For example, "What is going through your mind right now?"

How to avoid

➤ Explain the value of thinking aloud in the introduction to the test, specifying what you're interested in hearing. For example, "What I mean by thinking aloud is, tell me what steps you're taking, what you're looking for, what you're trying to do, what you expect to happen, and whether or not what happens meets your expectations."

➤ Partway through the study, thank the participant for thinking aloud to confirm that he is doing what you asked and encourage him to continue.

See also

➤ 6.5 Participant ignores or pretends to understand your question

➤ 8.6 Participant is unwilling or unsure

6.4 Participant is not able to complete a necessary task

You're conducting a usability study where tasks are interdependent—that is, one task needs to be accomplished before moving forward with the other tasks. Or, within a particular task, the participant must find or do something to reach the other areas you need feedback on. The participant is not successful at one of the dependent parts, which means that you need to provide a way to get him to those areas.

Method(s): Usability study
Frequency: Frequent
Pattern(s) to apply: Clarify the task/question; Redirect the participant

What to do

➤ Decide how and when to give the participant an assist. Time permitting, try to allow the participant to keep working on his own for a bit to see if he self-corrects. Then, if the participant has not self-corrected, give him a broad or vague assist, followed by more specific ones if needed. Think of it as a funnel slowly leading the participant to the desired location if he can't get there on his own. For example, say the participant is using a mobile device to look for a place to change a setting for his email account. He keeps overlooking the Settings screen and navigating elsewhere to do it. When he is ready to give up, you might say, "What if I were to tell you that there is a way to do that from the Settings screen?" It gives him broad direction but isn't pointing out anything specific. If he still can't find it, you might then point him toward a specific area of the Settings screen. Ultimately, you could point out the particular link that you need him to select.

➤ When you need to point out a specific area to the participant, find a way to do it that doesn't make the participant feel stupid or embarrassed. In the previous example, if you finally have to point out the "Email Settings" button, you might say something like, "This has been helpful seeing where you were expecting to find that option. I'll just point out this button here. What do you think about where it's located?" By providing this direct assist:

■ You acknowledge that what he did up until this point was not wasteful.

■ You allow the session to proceed.

■ You reassure the participant that he is there to help evaluate the design.

➤ Be careful with the feedback you get immediately following a direct assist—participants will often say something snarky like, "Well, obviously I didn't find it so it's not intuitive," or become overly accommodating and say, "Now that I know it's there, that is fine." Asking for the participant's feedback here more about his emotional well-being than your data collection.

6.4 Participant is not able to complete a necessary task (cont.)

➤ We also like to use a stealthier tactic in situations like this. For a detailed description, see the Chapter 3 sidebar "The Diversionary Assist."

➤ Another option is to set the product to the necessary state yourself while the participant's not looking. For example, you can pause the screen-sharing with a remote participant, or have an in-person participant look away briefly so that you can do whatever needs to be done. While this avoids the complications of a direct assist, it can be awkward to do, especially if you need to ask the participant to look away. Some gentle humor and a smile can make this less awkward, for example, "I know this sounds strange, but I need you to look away for a few seconds while I reset the prototype for our next task"

What to say

For an initial vague assist:

➤ "What if I were to tell you that…."

➤ "I'll just let you know that there is a way from here to do that…."

For a direct assist:

➤ "Let me draw your attention to this area. What are your thoughts on it being here?"

➤ "I'll point out that you can find that functionality here. Talk to me about this versus your expectations."

➤ "It's good to see your thought process in doing that. I will just let you know that there is actually a *different* way of doing that task. I'm curious to know what you think of it" *<point him to correct way>*.

For a redirect as part of a diversionary assist:

➤ "Let's move on for now. I wanted to ask you about what you did earlier."

➤ "Why don't we stop this task here, because I wanted to ask you about…."

➤ "Let's stop this here and we can come back to it later. Read the next scenario…."

What not to do or say

➤ Try to avoid asking, "Did you notice this link?" when the participant obviously hadn't. It can work in a pinch with nothing else to say, but it often makes the participant feel a little uncomfortable.

➤ Avoid saying anything implying there is a correct answer. For example, "What you're looking for is here" or "This is the right answer."

How to avoid

➤ The nature of usability studies is to discover usability problems so, unfortunately, there is no way to avoid this. Just be prepared for it!

See also

➤ 4.2 Participant either refuses to or can't do a key task

➤ 6.8 Participant believes he has successfully completed a task

➤ Chapter 3 sidebar: "The Diversionary Assist"

6.5 Participant ignores or pretends to understand your question

The participant seems to be pretending to understand your questions and is giving you vague (e.g., "sort of" or "I don't know") or convoluted responses. Alternately, the participant may blatantly ignore your question and start talking about other topics. If you're asking him to show you something specific or attempt a task, he may ignore what you ask him to focus on and instead show you something else that he is obviously good at or knowledgeable about.

Method(s): Any
Frequency: Occasional
Pattern(s) to apply: Take responsibility; Clarify the task/question; Redirect the participant

What to do

➤ Blame yourself as the moderator for not being clear with a question/task. For example, "I'm sorry, I didn't explain this very well. What I'd like to hear from you is...." This technique reassures the participant that he is not being evaluated and that he is not stupid for failing to understand your question.

➤ Rephrase the question/task to make it easier for the participant to understand, or break down your question into a set of smaller questions that will lead to your goal.

➤ If the participant is watching your lips closely or tilting his head to be closer to yours, he may be having trouble hearing you. Move your chair a bit closer to his, speak a little louder, and use short, direct sentences.

➤ If the participant still doesn't understand you or is still being vague, move on to your next task or question.

What to say

➤ "If anything I ask doesn't seem to make sense, please let me know."

➤ "I know this may not be what you typically work on, so please let me know if I'm not being clear about what I'm asking you to <do/talk about>."

➤ "I'm sorry, I don't think I'm being clear with my question. Let me rephrase...."

➤ "Would it help if I rephrased the question?"

➤ "Let me back up a little, and first ask you this...."

What not to do or say

➤ Don't ask the same question over and over in hopes of getting different responses. This will just exacerbate the problem and further frustrate the participant.

6.5 Participant ignores or pretends to understand your question (cont.)

➤ Try not to say anything that may be perceived as blaming the participant. For example, "Did you not understand my question?"

How to avoid

➤ At the beginning of the session, reassure the participant that he is an important part in your research. For example, "I will be asking you some questions during this session, but if anything I ask isn't clear, please don't hesitate to tell me." Another example might be, "I'm not a subject-matter expert here, so if I'm not asking a question that makes sense, please let me know that."

➤ If the participant is an internal employee, provide reassurance about how his feedback will be used to help alleviate any concerns about looking bad in front of his fellow employees. For more information, see section 15.1.

See also

➤ 6.3 Participant is not thinking aloud

➤ 8.6 Participant is unwilling or unsure

➤ 10.5 Participant gives vague responses to questions

➤ Survival Story: "I would have trusted my gut" in Chapter 11

SOME GUIDANCE REQUIRED: PARTICIPANTS IN NEED OF SHEPHERDING

6.6 Participant not approaching workflow naturally

The participant demonstrates the "correct" way of going through his workflow. Perhaps he highlights the fastest way to accomplish his workflow, demonstrating his competence rather than how he usually gets things done.

Method(s): Usability study; Contextual inquiry
Frequency: Occasional
Pattern(s) to apply: Clarify the task/question; Reassure the participant

What to do

Because he is being observed, the participant may feel like he is being evaluated even if you've assured him that he is not. He may want to look competent, fast, or smart. He may not want to get into trouble for failing to follow procedures. These factors may keep the participant from behaving naturally.

➤ Since it can be difficult to tell if a participant is approaching something naturally or not, look for these signs:

- ■ He seems to struggle a lot with a task that he supposedly does on a regular basis.
- ■ He uses descriptions like, "we do …" or "we then have to do …" rather than "I do. …"
- ■ He seems nervous, looks at you frequently, and/or otherwise acts like he is being evaluated. For example, he asks, "Are you going to grade me on this?"
- ■ Instead of showing you the workflow, he just describes the process, even after you prompt him otherwise.

➤ When you notice these things happening, clarify with the participant that you want to see what he *actually* does, even if it's not official procedure or the most efficient way to do things.

➤ If the participant seems afraid of getting into trouble because of what he shows or tells you, talk to him about how the collected data will be used (e.g., the data are kept confidential and aggregated before they're shared with the project team). Reassure him that he is not being evaluated in any way.

What to say

➤ "In a normal work week, how often would you do this?"
➤ "Is this how you typically do this task day-to-day?"
➤ "About what percentage of the time would you say that you do it this way?"

➤ "What are some other ways you've tried approaching this task before?"

➤ "I am here to watch how you work so that I understand what does and doesn't work well for you. We then take this information and use it to design a better experience. Just to be clear, I am not here to evaluate your skills or how you do your job."

➤ "Please know that anything you say or do will not be associated with your name."

What not to do or say

➤ Don't joke about evaluating the participant.

➤ Don't tell the participant that he is doing a good or bad job.

➤ Don't act entitled to watch the participant work, especially if someone else signed him up for it. Instead be appreciative that you're able to watch him and behave as if he is doing you a favor.

How to avoid

➤ In the recruiting communication to the participant, try to make it clear what your role is, why you're there, and how the information will be shared/used.

➤ If you're doing a contextual inquiry onsite, try to provide a short general briefing to all the participants you'll be talking with when you arrive. This briefing can help set context for what you'll be doing, how you'll collect data, and what you'll do with the results.

See also

➤ 5.5 Participant treats a contextual inquiry like an interview

6.7 Participant does not have any negative feedback

The participant seems to be a "yes-man," with one or more of the following characteristics:

➤ Seems to be trying to please you or the observers.

➤ Likes everything and dislikes nothing about the design.

➤ In a usability study, completes everything without experiencing any problems.

Method(s): Usability study
Frequency: Occasional
Pattern(s) to apply: Take responsibility; Reassure the participant

What to do

➤ If a usability study participant completes his tasks without experiencing any difficulties, don't panic! Receiving all or mostly positive feedback is unusual but not unprecedented. Do not pressure the participant to come up with negative feedback. Remember that it is useful to know what works well in a design so you can make sure it doesn't get changed.

➤ If the participant seems to have contradictory reactions (e.g., struggles excessively with tasks or usage of the product but loves everything about the design), think about what may be in play:

■ Did you forget to mention at the start of the session that participants should be candid and provide both positive and negative feedback? If so, find a way to sneak that into discussion, even if you need to take responsibility and admit that you forgot to say it.

■ Does the participant think or know that you worked on the design, or that the team who designed the product is observing? If so, make it clear that everyone wants to hear both positive and negative feedback so they can keep what is working and fix what isn't.

➤ Is the participant a die-hard fan or early adopter of the product and feels that it can do no wrong? If this seems likely, try to specifically draw out things that he *does not like* about the product since he may not mention those things on his own. For example, "If you could wave a magic wand and change one thing about this product, what would it be?"

What to say

If the participant seems to have had a genuinely positive experience:

➤ "If you could wave a magic wand and improve any one thing about this product, what would it be? Why?"

6.7 Participant does not have any negative feedback (cont.)

If you suspect he is reluctant to give negative feedback:

➤ "<*Participant*>, I'm sorry! I forgot one point to tell you when I was going through the introductory information. I didn't introduce myself properly—I'm a user researcher, which means I'm a neutral observer here—and anything you have to say, positive or negative, will not praise me or hurt my feelings."

➤ "Thank you for this feedback—it is all very helpful to hear. The project team is really excited to get all feedback—both positive and negative. So just continue to let me know anything you want to tell me, good or bad. Let's move on to...."

➤ "This has been very useful feedback, so thank you. Let's think about this <*task/topic/area*> for a moment. What did you like most about it? What did you like least? What would you want to improve first if you were using this at work or home?"

What not to do or say

➤ Try not to call out the participant for giving only positive feedback, or pressure him to come up with negative feedback. Doing so may unnaturally bias the participant's approach to the product during the session, and might ostracize your stakeholders.

How to avoid

➤ Make sure that participants know upfront that you want them to provide both positive and negative feedback.

See also

➤ 6.1 Participant is reluctant to say anything negative

6.8 Participant believes he has successfully completed a task

> The participant is confident that he has successfully completed a task, and that it was easy. However, you know that he was not successful.

Method(s): Usability study
Frequency: Occasional
Pattern(s) to apply: Clarify the task/question; Redirect the participant; Reassure the participant

What to do

This situation is closely related to the situation described in section 6.4 except that, in this case, the participant doesn't even realize that he was unsuccessful. What to do in this situation depends on:

➤ Does the participant actually need to know that he did not complete the task? As a moderator, you shouldn't tell him when the task was "successful" or not. Instead, let the participant decide for himself when he is done. If he happens to do something wrong, you usually don't need to point anything out and can simply move on. Just remember that if he gives subjective feedback or ratings, his performance may not be correlated with his rated experiences. Because he doesn't know that he wasn't successful, the participant may think everything is great and rate his experience very highly.

➤ If the participant does need to know that he wasn't successful (e.g., if tasks are interdependent in such a way that requires a task to be completed before attempting the next one, or the participant never got to a key area of focus for your research), follow the recommendations in section 6.4 to provide an assist.

What to say

If the participant doesn't need to know or see the correct path:

➤ "Okay, why don't we move onto the next task?"

What not to do or say

➤ Don't make the participant feel like he did anything wrong or is being tested. Avoid saying things like "This task isn't yet complete" or "Let me show you the correct way."

6.8 Participant believes he has successfully completed a task (cont.)

How to avoid

➤ Participants will do this from time to time, so there is no way to avoid it! Remember that this type of feedback is just as valuable as seeing participants struggle to complete a task.

See also

➤ 6.4 Participant is not able to complete a necessary task

6.9 Observers are not engaged in the session

The observers are obviously not engaged in the session you're running. They may be checking their email, working on other projects, or having side conversations. When you ask for their feedback on an issue (outside of the participant room), or check to see if they have any questions, they're so disengaged that they're unable to provide anything helpful.

Method(s): Any
Frequency: Occasional
Pattern(s) to apply: Take responsibility

What to do

➤ If the observers are in the same room as you and the participant, you may need to take a short break so that you can ask them to pay more attention to the session. Remind them that the participant's feedback is valuable and he needs to feel comfortable to provide it. A disengaged observer in the room distracts from this.

➤ Provide ways for observers to take ownership over the session results. Ask them to track the usability issues that they see during the sessions, and review their findings with them after each session. Post the list as they create it so that it is constantly visible for all the observers. For more ideas on how to involve your stakeholders, refer to *It's Our Research* (Sharon, 2012).

➤ Encouraging engagement from remote observers can be more challenging. However, you can do something similar to the previous recommendation by asking each observer to keep track of the issues that they observe during sessions, and then running quick debriefs after each session so the observers can share their findings. If some of the remote observers are in the same location, recommend that they get a conference room so they can watch the sessions together and create a unified list of their findings.

What to say

➤ "How do you think the sessions are going so far? Have you seen or heard anything that was surprising?"

➤ "During this next session, I'd like you to keep track of any issues that you see, both positive and negative. We can then compare that list with mine and discuss further after the session."

What not to do or say

➤ Don't lash out at the observers. While it can be very frustrating to know that your hard work is not being observed (or actively appreciated), recognize that most people are very busy and that it can be difficult to get enough time to commit to a whole session. Instead, try to make it as easy as possible for observers to become, and remain, engaged.

How to avoid

➤ If the observers will be in the same room with you and the participant, provide them with guidelines for their expected behavior prior to the sessions. See section 15.4 for more on this and providing ground rules to observers in general. For example, you may want to ask the observers to track issues that they see during sessions to encourage them to pay attention, and then you can review and compile results with them.

➤ Reach out to individual stakeholders before the sessions and personally invite them to attend. This can help get them excited and engaged in the research.

See also

➤ 9.2 Observers are loud and distracting

SURVIVAL STORY: "SHE WAS SO APPRECIATIVE"
KAYCEE A. COLLINS

I was conducting an in-person usability study for a newly conceptualized investment tool. For client-facing designs, I used a third-party vendor to complete the recruiting process. I would provide a screener and client list for the recruiters to use and they would provide the scheduled participants. At the time, I was not meticulous about double-checking the scheduled participants to verify that they matched the type of user I was looking for. Walking into the lobby, I met my first participant of the day and started small talk, nothing out of the norm, but simple questions like "Did you find the facility okay?" and "How is your day going?" This is when I learned that the recruiter scheduled two people for consecutive sessions who were not only living in the same household, but had just filed for divorce.

The woman continued to talk about her soon-to-be ex-husband and the emotional abuse she had endeavored. After listening to her for about 10 minutes and acting as a pseudo-psychologist, we were able to focus on the study. The remainder of the session she was so appreciative to have had someone listen to her, she returned the favor by concentrating on the prototypes without the distractions of the stressful situation running through her mind. Every question was answered honestly and without hesitation. In the end, I received great feedback that positively impacted the design due to her openness. Sometimes it just takes letting participants get things off their chest before buckling down and focusing on the task at hand. When participants have other thoughts on their mind, it can be hard to get focused on providing feedback on a design because they're preoccupied. I always greet participants with a warm smile and small chat to break the ice and hopefully put them in the right mindset to provide feedback. In this case, the participant and I had already built a rapport and trust before even starting the session.

As for the husband, he was waiting when I walked his wife to the door after the session. I thanked him for coming and told him we overbooked, not because of the conversation I had with his wife, but to avoid having more than one person per household to negate any sample error, especially when testing with only a handful of users. I then took the floater for the next session.

I learned a lot from this experience. First, double-check my scheduled participants sheet to validate I have the right users. Second, have a close relationship with vendors. The vendor I was working with had no idea having two participants from the same household would have a negative impact on the study; they were more than happy to keep a lookout for this situation in the future. Third, when participants need to talk, let them get it off their chest. It will be beneficial in the end.

CHAPTER 7

Make it Work:
Handling Technical Obstacles

A technical problem can stop your session in its tracks. Whether you're encountering broken equipment or difficulties with your remote session setup, you need to reassure the participant that the problems are not her fault and find a way to resolve the issues so you can get back to your study plan.

7.1 Technical issues arise with your setup and/or equipment

Something goes wrong, or stops working, with your technical setup. Your audio recorder may stop working, your camera may run out of battery power, or your screen recording software may decide to stop recording. The mobile device that you're using for your study may receive an (unrelated) call in the middle of the session, or the product breaks while the participant is using it.

Method(s): Any
Frequency: Frequent
Pattern(s) to apply: Take responsibility; Take a break; Shift the focus

What to do

➤ Figure out if the problem can be easily resolved. Batteries can be replaced or charged, cables can be tightened, device volumes can be lowered, and computers can be restarted (restarting a computer often corrects a multitude of issues).

➤ If the problem can't be resolved, decide whether you're able to proceed. In most cases, you should be able to proceed with slight modifications (e.g., you may not be able to record the session, but you can still take detailed notes of what the participant says and does).

➤ If you have observers who can help fix a more complicated problem with a product, you can ask them for an estimate for how long a fix would take. Based on that, you can either steer the session in a different direction with the participant while the item is being fixed (e.g., ask a series of interview questions) or end the session.

➤ If you plan to fix a technical issue with a product in front of the participant during a usability study, first think about what the participant might see. If by fixing the product, the participant will discover parts of the design that you hadn't intended her to see yet or that might bias later tasks, consider asking her to turn away or take a short break. If the participant is remote, pause or stop the screen-sharing application first so that the participant doesn't see what you're doing.

➤ If someone needs to enter your research space to fix the technical issue, ask her to not interact more than necessary with the participant. Then, warn the participant and let her know exactly who is coming into the space and why. Offer to let the participant leave the room to get a drink or go to the restroom while the work is being performed, or just sit in a corner and use her phone or mobile device. Be sure the recording equipment is turned off while the work is doing done, and remember to turn it back on when the session resumes.

7.1 Technical issues arise with your setup and/or equipment (cont.)

What to say

➤ "Excuse me for just a moment, but I just noticed that there is something wrong with our equipment. Let's take a short break so I can get it working again."

➤ "Please bear with me as I try to get this working again. Sorry about this!"

➤ "We're having a technical problem and I need to get one of our technical experts to come in and fix this. She'll need to use *<the product>*, and it may take a few minutes, so let's take a break. *<Technical expert>*, please come on in."

What not to do or say

➤ Don't freak out or panic!

➤ Try not to badmouth the makers of the equipment or software that you're using. While you're probably frustrated by this situation, maintain a professional demeanor around the participant.

➤ Don't blame the participant for anything that happened, even if the technical issue was caused by something she did.

How to avoid

➤ Test the technical setup beforehand. If the setup is complex, write a checklist of everything that needs to happen. That way, if you need to restart or change something in the middle of the session, you can reference the checklist to make sure you haven't forgotten something. This checklist should also include any URLs, user names, or passwords necessary. For more tips and discussion, refer to section 15.3.

➤ Verify the status of all your equipment before the session. Make sure any devices and rechargeable batteries are charged. Also, be sure you have additional batteries or battery packs.

➤ In cases where you have equipment or software problems that will take time resolve, it helps to have a generic questionnaire prepared to give to participants. For example, you could put together a survey asking the participant additional background questions about her usage of the product and her experiences.

➤ If you're using a screen-sharing application for observers to watch the session, consider having a backup account with a different service so if you have technical problems with one, you can quickly set up a new meeting using your backup service. Be sure to include information about this backup service on your checklist.

See also

➤ 7.2 Remote participant experiences difficulty joining

➤ 7.3 Facility loses its Internet connection

➤ 7.4 Remote participant drops off the call

➤ Chapter 15 sidebar: "Troubleshooting Skills Are a Lifesaver"

➤ Survival Story: "The lights seemed dimmer than normal"

7.2 Remote participant experiences difficulty joining

As you try to get the remote participant set up in the session, you run into a number of technical difficulties. The most common are difficulties accessing screen-sharing software (e.g., trouble downloading software or any necessary extensions).

Method(s): Any remote methods
Frequency: Frequent
Pattern(s) to apply: Take responsibility; Shift the focus; End the session early

What to do

Because screen-sharing software is usually vital for doing any kind of remote research, these difficulties may reduce the amount of time you can spend actually getting the feedback you need for the study. You may feel extra stressed if you have observers, as time spent troubleshooting means less time spent on what they care about.

➤ Ask the participant to describe exactly what is happening on her computer. If you've created a step-by-step guide (see "How to avoid" section), have this in front of you so you can match up what the participant is seeing with what she is supposed to see.

➤ Ask the participant to verify what kind of computer (e.g., Mac or PC) and web browser (e.g., Internet Explorer or Chrome) she is using. You can then verify this information against the screen-sharing software's system requirements. Keep in mind that even if a browser meets the official requirements, there may be missing or degraded functionality for older versions of browsers. Try another browser (if the participant has multiple ones installed or can install a different one) and see if that solves the problem. If the participant's setup still doesn't work with the screen-sharing software, ask if she has access to another computer that does meet the requirements.

➤ If possible, try to follow along with what the participant is doing using the same browser as her (e.g., if you're already connected to screen-sharing using Firefox, open Internet Explorer). By doing this, you can check on exactly what the participant is, and should be, seeing, at various points in the process even if you don't have a step-by-step guide.

➤ If you have access to another screen-sharing application, consider using it instead. If you have a team member available, ask her to send out the new observation information to any remote observers while you try to get the participant set up on the new application.

➤ If none of these solutions work and you were intending to run a usability study or contextual inquiry, consider changing the focus of the research to more of an interview approach that only requires a conference call.

➤ As a last resort, ask the participant if you can reschedule her session, and follow up with her separately to work out any troubleshooting issues.

7.2 Remote participant experiences difficulty joining (cont.)

What not to do or say

➤ When giving troubleshooting directions to the participant, avoid using user interface jargon (e.g., status bar, dialog box), as she may not understand what you're talking about. Instead, reference areas of the screen based on their location and physical characteristics.

➤ Be very careful about suggesting something that may cause harm to the participant's computer. For example, you might not want to have the person go into the Windows registry to delete a file or disable features or devices.

What to say

➤ "Can you tell me exactly what you're seeing on the screen right now? I'll do my best to get this sorted out for you."

➤ "Please bear with me while I try to follow along. Thank you for your patience!"

How to avoid

➤ Meet with the participant before your scheduled session to do a five-minute dry run of the technology. This dry run will let you verify that the participant has the correct system requirements to support your screen-sharing software, and gives you additional time to troubleshoot any problems that come up.

➤ Research any restrictions that either your organization or the participant's organization (if she is at work) have on networking. We've found some pretty funky issues in the past with screen-sharing applications due to a company's firewall/security settings, virtual private network (VPN) access, platform and browser support, or a combination thereof. For example, we've discovered cases in which internal employees of a company attempting to use WebEx through their VPN could only join if they used the Chrome browser on a PC or the Safari browser on a Mac. We don't make this stuff up!

➤ Create a step-by-step guide for joining your screen-sharing application, with screenshots, and have it printed out in front of you as you ask the participant to join the session. You can also create an abbreviated version to send to participants ahead of time.

➤ If you have observers who are only available at certain times, consider scheduling backup or floater participants in case you need to cancel a participant due to technical difficulties. See section 15.1 for more on making this decision.

See also

➤ 7.1 Technical issues arise with your setup and/or equipment

➤ 7.4 Remote participant drops off the call

➤ Chapter 15 sidebar: "Troubleshooting Skills Are a Lifesaver"

7.3 Facility loses its Internet connection

At some point during your research, the facility you're in loses its Internet connectivity. The Internet is required for your research, either because the product targeted by your research requires access or because you have remote observers or participants. This situation can happen at your location, at a participant's site, or anywhere in the field.

Method(s): Any
Frequency: Occasional
Pattern(s) to apply: Take responsibility; Take a break; Shift the focus

What to do

➤ If you're using a conference call to share audio of the session with observers, let them know that you're experiencing Internet problems and that you're trying to resolve them. Place them on hold or mute while you're trying to figure it out.

➤ Verify (or ask the participant to, if you're in her environment) that the Internet connection is down and that it is not a problem with the product or prototype. A quick way to check is to open a web browser and try opening any website. If you're in an organization with an intranet, try both an intranet website and an external website to narrow down the problem. If you're able to see both an internal and external website, you know that the problem is likely specific to your product or prototype rather than something wrong with the internal or external network.

➤ If you're in your facility, check to make sure your network cable is still plugged in (if using a wired connection) or that the wireless network is still visible. If the machine is wireless and the wireless network is not visible, make sure that the wireless feature is turned on and connected to the correct access point. If that still doesn't help, reboot the computer and try again. Be aware that if you were the host of a screen-sharing meeting before experiencing the Internet difficulties, that hosting role may get assigned to someone else in your absence. You may need to reclaim that role once you're able to return to the meeting, which may either happen automatically or you may need to do it manually from within the meeting (the specifics of how to do this varies depending on which tool you're using).

➤ If the Internet is still unavailable after a few minutes, move to a part of the session that doesn't involve using the Internet. For example, you could move to questions that are more interview-based, or ask the participant to complete a paper survey (as discussed in section 15.2).

What to say

➤ "It looks like we have lost our Internet connection. Please bear with me as I try to get the connection working again as quickly as I can."

What not to do or say

➤ Don't badmouth the facility that you're using or the networking team. Even though you may just be trying to share your frustration, the participant and observers may take it the wrong way.

How to avoid

➤ If you're using a prototype, try to install it locally on the computer being used for the research instead of on a network. Another option is to have the prototype stored on a thumb drive or other portable storage disc or device. If you're asking the participant to use her computer (e.g., because you're in her location), you can ask her permission to install the prototype, but be sure to uninstall it after the session.

➤ Most screen-sharing applications provide a call-in number that can be used instead of a "call using computer" (voice over IP, or VoIP) option. Provide this call-in number to observers so if the screen-sharing portion goes down due Internet issues, they can still hear what is going on during the session.

➤ Identify a technical support person who can be contacted with any issues. Ideally, you can let her know when you're performing research so she can notify you of any planned outages or upgrades that may affect your session. If you're testing at a participant's facility or remote site, you can ask your host to introduce you to a technical support person who can help in a pinch.

See also

➤ 7.1 Technical issues arise with your setup and/or equipment

➤ Chapter 15 sidebar: "Troubleshooting Skills Are a Lifesaver"

7.4 Remote participant drops off the call

You're running a remote session using screen-sharing and audio-conference technology such as WebEx. Suddenly you realize that you can no longer hear the participant. She may also no longer be visible as an attendee in the screen-sharing application.

Method(s): Any remote session
Frequency: Occasional
Pattern(s) to apply: Take a break

What to do

➤ First check to see whether you have a visual representation of who is in the audio conference, either via your screen-sharing application (if using VoIP) or your phone interface. If you do, check to see if the participant is still listed there. If she is listed, you may be able to send her a chat message from within the application to see if she is still on the call.

➤ If you do not have a visual indicator of everyone on your conference call, first verify whether the participant is really gone or just accidentally muted. Ask her if she is still on the call, and to check to make sure she is not accidentally on mute.

➤ Assuming the participant really is gone, the best thing to do depends on how the participant was brought into the call. If she dialed in on her own, wait a few minutes for her to call back in. If you called her or conferenced her in (i.e., she doesn't have a number to call to rejoin the conference), you'll need to replicate the initial steps you took to bring her in to the audio portion of the session.

➤ If you're having trouble getting hold of the participant or if she has not yet dialed back in on her own, take a break for a moment to provide the observers with an update. Let them know that you'll continue trying to get in touch with the participant.

➤ Send the participant an email with your contact information so she can reach out to you if she is experiencing technical problems that are keeping her from rejoining the session.

What to say

To participant:

➤ "*<Participant>*, I can no longer hear you. Are you still there? If you can hear me, please check to make sure you're not on mute."

To observers on call:

➤ "I believe that we've lost our participant. Please stay on the line, and I'll attempt to get in touch with her."

7.4 Remote participant drops off the call (cont.)

What not to do or say

➤ Don't say anything negative about the participant, as she may not really have been dropped from the call (e.g., she may just be having audio problems) or may be dialing back in. You may not want to allow observers to speak on the call for the same reason.

How to avoid

➤ Provide the participant with instructions ahead of time on what to do if she gets dropped. For example, "I will call you again at this number."

See also

➤ 7.1 Technical issues arise with your setup and/or equipment
➤ 7.2 Remote participant experiences difficulty joining
➤ Chapter 15 sidebar: "Troubleshooting Skills Are a Lifesaver"

7.5 Prototype or product changes unexpectedly

During a usability study session, you notice that something in the prototype has been changed since the prior session or even since earlier in the same session. The change may be something like a new label for a link or a button, updated content, or different color choices for graphical elements. Something similar may occur if you're asking participants to use a live product. If the product development isn't frozen during your research, you may notice subtle or not-so-subtle design changes!

Method(s): Usability study
Frequency: Occasional
Pattern(s) to apply: Take responsibility; Take a break

What to do

➤ Play it cool. Remember that you're in charge of the session, and it won't help the participant if you act startled or surprised by something that she is giving feedback on.

➤ If you see more than one change (or are very concerned about the one change you see), excuse yourself from the room and talk with the designers/developers to identify what has been changed, and why. Explain that you need to know because the questions in your study plan are carefully calculated to not be leading or use any of the terms from the product's user interface, and you may need to readjust your plan accordingly.

➤ If you feel that the changes made were not helpful or unnecessary, ask if there is a way to "roll back" to the earlier version of the prototype or product. Changes in the middle of a study may ruin the integrity of your data if the goal of the study is to gather summative (quantitative data) that measures the experience. But, you might also consider changes unhelpful or unnecessary if:

■ The change was only based on the feedback of one or two participants (assuming that you're testing with a larger number than that).

■ The change violates design and usability best practices.

What to say

If the participant notices the change (because the change happened after she had already interacted with the product):

➤ "Yes, it looks like the team was eager to start adjusting the design based on your feedback. What do you think about this change?"

7.5 Prototype or product changes unexpectedly (cont.)

If you need to leave the room to talk to designer/developers:

➤ "I'm sorry, I'm noticing a technical issue we're having with the prototype. Please excuse me a minute while I consult someone on the team. You're welcome to check your phone or take a break as well, but please don't click around in the prototype while we work on this issue."

If you're using a live product and unable to guarantee a design freeze:

➤ "You're going to be giving feedback on a live *<product>* today. Because it's live, some things may change as you're using it. This shouldn't get in the way of your tasks, but if you see anything that doesn't make sense or that you have a question about, please let me know."

What not to do or say

➤ Don't point out a change if the participant hasn't noticed it on her own.
➤ Avoid badmouthing the designers/developers for making the change.

How to avoid

➤ Discuss your rules ahead of time with the designers/developers. We typically ask our teams not to make any changes to the prototype or product without consulting us ahead of time (and even then, we may not agree that the change should be made). It's also important to insist that no changes be made to the prototype during a session, not only to prevent the surprise factor but also so that nothing breaks the prototype. Often a "quick" change has unexpected consequences elsewhere. See section 15.3 for more on this topic.

➤ If using a website for the study, find out if any A/B testing is done on the website and, if so, see if there is a way for you to either have that functionality turned off during your research or for you to consistently see the same version of pages (e.g., always the A design).

➤ As part of your participant briefing, let the participant know that she'll be using a live product so she might notice changes as she proceeds with the session. This warning can be especially useful if you're unable to guarantee a design freeze.

See also

➤ 7.1 Technical issues arise with your setup and/or equipment
➤ Chapter 15 sidebar: "Troubleshooting Skills Are a Lifesaver"

SURVIVAL STORY: "THE LIGHTS SEEMED DIMMER THAN NORMAL"
CAROL SMITH

Usability studies always have challenges, but the biggest one I've faced came when the building I was conducting the study in lost power!

I was contracting to a large company in a big suburban office park. Driving in, everything had seemed okay despite the bad weather, but as I came into the building I noticed that the lights seemed dimmer than normal. I hurried to the testing lab and when I got there found that the lights were not working. Luckily there was a lot of natural light from large windows across one side of the room.

It was too late to contact participants as this was a relatively large city and participants were most likely in route and were to arrive fairly soon.

Luckily all of the consent forms and other supporting documentation were ready to go. The study was to test a clickable prototype on a desktop computer running Morae. Someone had either planned for such an instance or we got very lucky, as the testing machines were all plugged into outlets connected to the backup power generator.

As participants arrived, I explained the situation to them and told them that if it made them uncomfortable we could try to reschedule. I was especially concerned because I needed to walk them down a very dark hallway prior to entering the testing room. I cannot think of a more stressful way to enter a study if the dark makes you nervous.

This situation only affected a few participants and they were very understanding. I was careful to make sure the participants felt safe before beginning each session. By the third participant that day the power came back on and I continued the study without further issues.

Having the necessary documents prepared ahead of time was a lifesaver. As much as possible I try to continue to plan for each day's testing the day before. Regardless, it was pleasantly surprising how much we could do without electricity!

CHAPTER 8

Is This Right?
Responding to Uncertain Participants

The artificial situation created by user research may cause participants to be nervous or worried about not being a "good" participant. Even if you tell a participant that he's not being tested, a usability lab setting or the presence of recording equipment and observers may be intimidating. You need a set of responses and comforting steps that can help reassure the participant and make him more comfortable with the session.

The participant seems unsure about what he i's saying or doing, and looks to you for affirmation. He may ask direct questions (e.g., "Am I doing this right?") or use passive statements (e.g., "I hope this is helping").

Method(s): Any
Frequency: Frequent
Pattern(s) to apply: Redirect the participant; Reassure the participant

What to do

This situation is similar to one where participants blame themselves and apologize (see section 8.4), except in this case they're more explicitly looking for feedback from you to direct them.

➤ Assure the participant that he is providing the kind of feedback you need (which is different than assuring him he is doing anything "right"), and reiterate that anything he does or says is helpful for the research team.

➤ Check your body language and see if anything you've done during the session may have caused the participant to think that he is doing something wrong. For example, if you're taking notes, make sure that you're taking notes both when the participant is being successful and when he isn't, instead of just when the participant encounters an issue.

➤ Rather than letting the participant dwell on his desire for affirmation, follow your reassurance with an immediate redirect to another follow-up question or task related to the research goals. For example, you may say, "This is just the kind of feedback we want to hear. Now, earlier you mentioned...."

What to say

➤ "This is just the kind of feedback we want to hear."

➤ "All of this has been very helpful to hear and see. Thank you for your continual feedback."

➤ "Don't worry about how you're doing—we're not looking at it that way. We're just here to see/hear how you'd approach it, and get your feedback on the process."

What not to do or say

➤ Avoid agreeing (or disagreeing) with a participant about his feedback. For example, don't say, "Yeah, this is obviously a big problem we never thought about."

8.1 Participant looks for affirmation (cont.)

➤ In a usability study, avoid letting the participant know whether he is doing a task correctly or not.

➤ Avoid using leading phrases like "You've completed this task" or "This task is complete" because it implies correct and incorrect ways of approaching tasks. Similarly, avoid leading questions that imply or suggest an expected answer. For example, "So you do this every day, right?"

How to avoid

➤ Keep your body language consistent throughout the session so participants, who may be extra sensitive due to being observed, don't feel like you're being affected by their performance. For example, avoid leaning forward when the participant is taking an unexpected path during a usability study if you've been leaning back throughout the rest of the session. Similarly, avoid frowning or shaking your head if you disagree with feedback provided during an interview.

➤ Encourage the participant by periodically telling him that his feedback is helpful. If you take this approach, be sure to not just provide this encouragement after the participant provides certain types of feedback (for more on this technique, see Chapter 3 sidebar "Should You Tell a Participant That Her Feedback Is Helpful?").

 Watch Video 1 to see an example of a moderator interacting with a self-blaming participant during a usability study. The participant is very nervous about the session and is looking for affirmation.

Visit our website (http://www.modsurvivalguide.org/videos) or use your QR reader to scan this code.

See also

➤ 8.2 Participant asks for your opinion

➤ 8.4 Participant is self-blaming

➤ 8.5 Participant asks, "Did other people have trouble with this?"

8.2 Participant asks for your opinion

The participant answers a question or completes a task and then asks you for your opinion. His query may be very pointed (e.g., "What do you think is the best brand?") or more general (e.g., "What do you think about it?").

Method(s): Any
Frequency: Frequent
Pattern(s) to apply: Redirect the participant; Disengage from the participant

What to do

The participant may be using these questions to engage you in a conversation like he would if you were talking in a more casual setting. A conversation may feel more natural to him than being asked to just respond to your questions.

➤ Redirect the question by reminding the participant that you're interested in what he thinks. Explain that you want to stay neutral.

➤ If you find that the participant is being overly friendly or conversational with you, and his friendliness is leading to these types of questions, adapt your moderating style (as we discussed in sections 1.5 and 1.6) away from a more informal disposition. For example, if your style was similar to the Friendly Face, you could shift to the more formal Down to Business. In conjunction with this change, you may need to disengage slightly from the participant by subtly changing your tone and body language/positioning as discussed in section 3.6.

What to say

➤ "My opinion isn't important to the team—we're here to talk about yours. What do *you* think?"

➤ "I want to stay neutral here, so I'm going to turn that back on you. What are your thoughts on this?"

What not to do or say

➤ This one is easy—do *not* give your opinion!

➤ Don't ignore the participant's question, as your avoidance may come off as rude.

➤ Also try not to sound inconsiderate by saying something like, "I'm not going to answer you." Participants are already in a vulnerable position, so don't make them feel worse!

IS THIS RIGHT? RESPONDING TO UNCERTAIN PARTICIPANTS

8.2 Participant asks for your opinion (cont.)

How to avoid

➤ Use language at the start of the session to let the participant know that you're trying to be a neutral observer, which means that you may not answer his questions directly. Even though this won't prevent the question from ever coming up, it's important to set the expectation at the beginning so you can refer back to what you said if the participant keeps pressing you for an answer.

See also

➤ 8.1 Participant looks for affirmation

8.3 Participant looks or sounds uncomfortable and/or nervous

The participant looks or sounds uncomfortable and/or nervous. If you're in a usability lab, you may notice that he is looking around the room and at the cameras, his arms are crossed, and he is very quiet.

Method(s): Any
Frequency: Frequent
Pattern(s) to apply: Reassure the participant; Build engagement; Take a break

What to do

Usability participants often are nervous and uncomfortable at the start of the session. They may be surprised that it's a one-on-one situation rather than a focus group, or feel nervous about being watched. And, of course, as much as we tell participants they're not being tested, sometimes they still feel like they are. Similarly, contextual inquiries are all about being watched, so a participant may feel awkward or nervous about your presence.

➤ If a participant seems nervous at the beginning of the session, try to ease his discomfort so that he doesn't get even more nervous. Spend a few minutes asking how he is, if he had any difficulty getting to your location (if applicable), and/or other niceties like the weather or (noncontroversial) news of the day. Ask if he has participated in any kind of research before to get a sense of any prior experience. Then, proceed to your normal participant briefing.

➤ If the participant seems nervous about being observed, explain at a high level who the observers are and why they're watching. You can also reassure him that while it may feel strange at first to be watched, you'll be the only person interacting with him and after a while he'll probably forget about the observers.

➤ Remember to check if there is anything you're doing to contribute to the situation, as we discussed in section 2.3. Check your body language and see if anything you've done during the session may be contributing to the participant's nervousness. For example, ensure that you're not sitting too close to the participant, or doing anything uncomfortable like staring intently at him.

➤ Tone of voice can go a long way toward calming a participant's nerves. Be genuinely interested in what he says, which will help keep your tone kind and gentle, while still neutral and nonpatronizing. This is a tricky balance to achieve but an effective one.

➤ Provide occasional reassurance that the participant's feedback is helpful. For more on how to provide this reassurance, see the Chapter 3 sidebar "Should You Tell a Participant That Her Feedback Is Helpful?"

➤ If a participant seems extremely nervous or uncomfortable, and is not responding to the previous suggestions, take a short break. After the participant has had a few minutes to himself, you can then ask him, in private (e.g., outside of the research room), if he is okay to continue with the session.

What to say

Before the session:

➤ "Please know that we're not at all testing you or your abilities; you're here to help us *<evaluate the product/learn more about your process>*."

➤ "Anything you do or say is useful for us to know; there are no wrong answers."

If disclosing observers:

➤ "Any observers who may be watching are all on the team for this project, and want a chance to see feedback firsthand from their *<current/potential>* users—both positive and negative."

➤ "Even though there may be observers, you'll only be interacting with me. After a while, you may even forget that anyone else is watching."

During the session:

➤ "This is just the kind of feedback we want to hear."

➤ "All of this has been very helpful to hear and see. Thank you for your continual feedback."

What not to do or say

➤ If your moderating style is similar to the Down to Business style described in section 1.5, you may find that such a hands-off approach makes a participant's natural nervousness even worse. Instead, try adapting your style to be a bit more reassuring and gentle with your questions and instructions.

➤ Don't ignore a participant's nervousness, as this may make him even more nervous or uncomfortable.

How to avoid

➤ Nervousness can't usually be avoided but it can be tempered by some of the techniques discussed—adapting to a more gentle style, assuring a participant upfront that he is not being tested, and reassuring him throughout the session that what he is doing is helpful. Also, follow the tips described in section 2.3 to ensure that you don't contribute to a participant's nervousness.

8.3 Participant looks or sounds uncomfortable and/or nervous (cont.)

 Watch Video 1 to see an example of a moderator interacting with a self-blaming participant during a usability study. The participant is very nervous about the session and is looking for affirmation.

Visit our website (http://www.modsurvivalguide.org/videos) or use your QR reader to scan this code.

See also

➤ 6.1 Participant is reluctant to say anything negative

➤ 8.4 Participant is self-blaming

➤ 8.6 Participant is unwilling or unsure

➤ 12.7 Participant seems upset

➤ Chapter 3 sidebar: "Should You Tell a Participant That Her Feedback Is Helpful?"

➤ Survival Story: "She looked agitated"

8.4 Participant is self-blaming

The participant blames himself for not understanding something or for performing a task wrong. He may apologize for what he perceives as his poor performance or lack of knowledge, or explain that if he wasn't so nervous he'd be doing a better job. In a contextual inquiry, the participant may discount his abilities and say that you may be better off watching someone who has received better training or who has more experience than he does.

Method(s): Usability study; Contextual inquiry
Frequency: Frequent
Pattern(s) to apply: Redirect the participant; Reassure the participant

What to do

➤ Refer back to what you told the participant during the briefing at the beginning of the session—that he is not being tested, and that his feedback is appreciated.

➤ If the participant doesn't think he has the experience level necessary or is otherwise unqualified, reassure him that you're interested in hearing from users with all types of experience.

➤ Rather than letting the participant dwell on his self-blaming, follow your reassurance with an immediate redirect to another follow-up question or task related to the research goals. For example, you may say, "Remember what I said earlier—if we don't see what areas work well and not so well, we wouldn't learn anything. Tell me more about what you were expecting.…"

What to say

➤ "Please don't feel badly. Remember that we're evaluating the product, not you."

➤ "If we didn't see what areas work well or not so well for you, we wouldn't learn anything."

➤ "You're here to partner with us to evaluate the design, so all of this is really helpful for us to see and hear."

➤ "There are no wrongs here; you're here to help us."

➤ "It's important for us to bring in users with all levels and types of experience because we want this product to be easy to use for everyone."

What not to do or say

➤ Do not dismiss the participant's comments by saying something like, "It's okay," or "No problem," as it may be perceived as confirming that he is not doing a good job.

144

8.4 Participant is self-blaming (cont.)

➤ Try to avoid phrases like "Everyone else hasn't been able to figure that out," or "You're not the only person who's had difficulty with this" because (a) you're acknowledging that he is doing something wrong and (b) by stating that others have had problems, you're empathizing too much and not remaining unbiased.

How to avoid

➤ Making a participant feel as comfortable as possible in the beginning of the session will help avoid this. As part of your participant briefing, let the participant know that anything he says or does will be useful to the team, and that any problems he experiences are a reflection on the product, not on him; those problems are an opportunity for improvement. Say this as sincerely and empathetically as possible; we've found that just racing through this section of your study plan often results in information going in one ear and out the other.

 Watch Video 1 to see an example of a moderator interacting with a self-blaming participant during a usability study. The participant is very nervous about the session and is looking for affirmation.

Visit our website (http://www.modsurvivalguide.org/videos) or use your QR reader to scan this code.

See also

➤ 8.1 Participant looks for affirmation
➤ 8.3 Participant looks or sounds uncomfortable and/or nervous

8.5 Participant asks, "Did other people have trouble with this?"

> The participant struggles with the product and asks you if other people also had difficulty. Or, he may ask a similar question about his performance or the experience of your other participants.

> **Method(s):** Usability study
> **Frequency:** Frequent
> **Pattern(s) to apply:** Redirect the participant; Reassure the participant

What to do

Participants often want to know if they're the only ones who can't understand or do something. If a participant knows that others have had trouble too, he thinks that he'll feel better about any problems he's having. Because the question is asked so directly, you may feel on-the-spot to answer or address it.

➤ Avoid answering the question, even if you want to say "yes" to make the participant feel better.

➤ Try to turn the question into an affirmation that his individual approach and feedback is what really matters, and then redirect the conversation to close the subject.

➤ If it feels too disingenuous and you feel the need to give some kind of answer, tell the participant that you can't remember or are not sure, and quickly redirect to another question or task.

What to say

➤ "What matters is *your* experience, which we can learn from. Tell me more about what you're experiencing here…."

➤ "I'm not sure, but tell me more about what you're thinking here…."

What not to do or say

➤ Do not respond "yes" or "no." Saying "yes" to a participant has an inherent bias because he may change his approach and reaction to the product given the new piece of information. Saying "yes" also may come across as agreeing with him, which breaks your neutrality. Saying "no" may make him feel inadequate or insecure about his abilities.

How to avoid

➤ There is no good way to prevent this question from coming up. However, you can reduce the odds by telling the participant at the beginning of the session that you're trying to be a neutral

IS THIS RIGHT? RESPONDING TO UNCERTAIN PARTICIPANTS

8.5 Participant asks, "Did other people have trouble with this?" (cont.)

observer, which means that you may not answer his questions. Even though this won't prevent the question from ever coming up, it's important to set the expectation at the beginning so you can refer back to what you said if the participant keeps pressing you for an answer.

See also

➤ 8.1 Participant looks for affirmation

8.6 Participant is unwilling or unsure

When you ask the participant, "How was that experience for you?" or "What would you expect to happen there?" he answers, "I don't know." He may be giving one or two word answers—for example, "sure" or "I guess"—and not responding to your efforts to follow up or get him to go into more detail.

Method(s): Any
Frequency: Occasional
Pattern(s) to apply: Reassure the participant; Build engagement

What to do

While sometimes participants really just *don't know*, if they give one- or two-word responses repeatedly it usually indicates a problem. Two common causes are that participants are either unwilling to put in effort or are unsure about how to articulate their thoughts. The former tend to be either people who were forced to participate (e.g., by managers) or are just participating for the compensation. The latter can be anyone, but you can sometimes tell that they're struggling to find words. The signs of a nervous/uncomfortable participant described in section 2.4 might also accompany these responses.

➤ Try to address this situation at the very beginning of the session or, if it appears later in the session, as soon as you notice it. Thank the participant for joining the session and tell him how much his feedback will help.

➤ Keep encouraging the participant throughout the session. Without interrupting his workflow or train of thought, continually ask for the participant's feedback so he knows that his opinion matters.

➤ If the participant seems to have trouble articulating his thoughts, be sure not to rush him. Sometimes a little bit of extra time is all that is needed. If the time doesn't seem to help, you can try asking a question a different way or try to narrow the range of possible answers. For example, instead of, "How was your experience using this vacuum?" ask "Was your experience with this vacuum the same, better, or worse than the experience with other vacuums you've used?"

➤ If the participant's reticence seems to stem from nervousness, use some of the techniques outlined in section 8.3 to alleviate his nerves.

➤ If your session is being held remotely, the participant may be distracted and doing other things, which may make him seem unwilling to put in any effort. See section 11.1 for more discussion on this situation.

➤ If despite your best efforts, the participant still seems distracted or frazzled and unwilling to put in a good effort, don't lose hope. Instead of being annoyed at him, change your perspective and see the situation as a challenge. Try to get him engaged in the session by making your task/question more personal. One of the most satisfying things for a moderator is watching a participant go from moody or annoyed to calm and engaged during the course of a session.

What to say

Before the session:

➤ "Thanks so much for participating. I know that we're taking time out of your busy day, but I want you to know that your feedback is extremely important to us. You're helping us make the product better."

➤ "Hopefully this session will be a fun break from your typical work."

During the session:

➤ "This is just the kind of feedback we want to hear."

➤ "All of this has been very helpful to hear and see. Thank you for your continual feedback."

➤ *To try to personalize:* "Have you ever tried to do this, or anything like this, before? Tell me about your experience."

What not to do or say

➤ Try not to get frustrated with the participant, as it may lead him to be more closed down and resentful.

How to avoid

➤ Participants should never be forced to participate. Sometimes we leave recruiting to others who have access to the right people, like call center managers or representatives at a target organization. But they don't always know the ins and outs of user research, and don't know the trickle-down effect that their decisions can have on the quality of the research. If they're not positioning the research as something valuable, or worse, are coercing participants to take part, you'll end up with participants who may not be interested in putting forth the effort.

➤ We suggest working closely with those recruiting for you to make sure they're finding people to participate voluntarily and that the participants know ahead of time what to expect. Refer to section 15.1 for more discussion.

See also

➤ 6.3 Participant is not thinking aloud

➤ 6.5 Participant ignores or pretends to understand your question

➤ 8.3 Participant looks or sounds uncomfortable and/or nervous

➤ 10.5 Participant gives vague responses to questions

➤ 11.1 Remote participant is obviously distracted

IS THIS RIGHT? RESPONDING TO UNCERTAIN PARTICIPANTS

SURVIVAL STORY: "SHE LOOKED AGITATED"
CAROL PETERSON

My colleagues and I were doing onsite testing of Windows-based search and retrieval software in the early 1990s. Our users were librarians, not all of whom had experience with Windows since a lot of catalogs were still on text-based mainframe systems. We had told our recruiter we wanted participants with at least some Windows experience.

Our participant arrived, and I welcomed her and explained she would be trying to do some search tasks on the computer we had brought. I told her she could start the first task so she turned to the computer … and just sat there, not saying or doing anything. After a bit, I asked her what she was thinking. She didn't answer me and she looked agitated. After another silence that seemed interminable, she suddenly got up, said "excuse me," and quickly left the room.

My colleagues (who were acting as observers) and I looked at each other in confusion. Several minutes passed, during which we wondered what had happened and if she was going to come back—we had no idea where she had gone or why.

Finally, after about 10 minutes she did return, still looking nervous. She told me she had been very anxious about the test to begin with, and when she saw the computer screen, she didn't know what to do since she had never used a mouse—she had needed to leave to compose herself.

Of course I immediately reassured her, apologized for causing her angst, etc., while inside my head I was frantically thinking of ways I could salvage something from the study. Fortunately, at that time Windows was new enough it included mini-tutorials on how to use a mouse and work with the desktop. And even more fortunate, I actually remembered this. I asked her if she wanted to try one of the tutorials to learn the mouse, and she was willing. After completing the tutorial, she had calmed down and felt competent enough to try some of the tasks.

We didn't get a lot feedback on the software, but I learned some valuable lessons:

➤ Ensure your recruiter understands which criteria are "make or break"—they must understand not only what will qualify a participant, but what will disqualify one.

Survival Story (cont.)

> ➤ Get to know the participant. When the participant first arrives, before I talk about the tasks I want them to perform, I ask them to briefly describe their background and their current job. Talking about a known topic helps relax the participant, plus it gives me a chance to judge whether there are any potential gaps in their knowledge that will affect the test.
>
> ➤ Stay flexible during the test. If I hadn't been able to adapt, not only would we have missed a chance to get data, but we would have left the participant feeling awful, which in my mind is even worse.

CHAPTER 9

What's Going On?
Recovering from External Interruptions

Your session is going smoothly until something or someone interrupts the flow. Or, your session time may have started but the participant is nowhere to be found. These situations involve regaining control, limiting the possibility of future interruptions, and moving forward with a recovery plan.

9.1 Participant is running late

The session was scheduled to start 20 minutes ago. You have a room full of observers, some of whom flew into town just to watch your research. You have no idea whether or not the participant is stuck in traffic or just decided not to show up. You need to try to track down the participant while also managing any observers or stakeholders, prioritizing your study plan for a truncated session, and preparing for the possibility of a no-show.

Method(s): Any
Frequency: Frequent
Pattern(s) to apply: Take responsibility; Shift the focus

What to do

This situation is especially challenging due to its unpredictability. You may have no idea whether the participant is going to be slightly late, extremely late, or a no-show. If your study is in an urban area, the participant may be stuck in traffic or on a broken-down train—sometimes even the most conscientious participants fall victim to a big city's transportation hazards.

➤ If you're using a recruiter, reach out to her to see if the participant has contacted her. If the participant hasn't been in touch, ask the recruiter to call the participant (or give you the participant's phone number) to check her status—is she late, or not coming?

➤ While waiting for the participant, identify how you can adjust the study plan or method based on when she arrives. For example, if you're doing a summative study, you may want a very late participant to attempt at least a few tasks so you have more data, whereas for a more formative study, you might decide to do a product walkthrough instead where you bring the participant to specific areas rather than asking her to get there on her own.

  ■ Consider putting together a quick survey or written version of your background questions that you can ask the participant to quickly fill out on her own. For more on this idea, see section 15.2.

  ■ If you have a floater or backup participant available, consider starting with her instead. If your scheduled participant arrives later, you can step outside to thank her for coming in, provide her with her compensation, and let her know that she can leave early.

➤ Update all your observers on the session's status, especially if you have remote observers who may be wondering what's happening as you're talking to the in-facility observers. A good solution, if applicable, is to enter text on the computer or device being shared with the observers, letting them know that the participant hasn't arrived yet (or any other status update necessary).

9.1 Participant is running late (cont.)

➤ If you have remote participants who you're trying to get in touch with, leave a status message for observers. For example, "9:05 a.m.: Tried calling participant, but no answer. Will try again in five minutes." We suggest not using a screen-sharing program's chat feature to do this, as the participant may see the entire conversation later. Something like a document or text file works icely. If you get in touch with the participant, close the document before you bring her in to the remote session.

➤ If the participant arrives late, be gracious and sincerely thank her for coming in.

➤ If the participant arrives extremely late and even a little bit of feedback will be helpful, consider running an abbreviated session.

   ■ If she is willing to stay later, and your schedule allows for spilling over, continue with the session past the scheduled end time. Just make sure not to go beyond the total number of minutes for which the participant was promised compensation.

   ■ If she is unwilling or unable to stay late to make up for the lost time, bring her through as much of the prioritized parts of the session as time permits.

➤ If she is so late that even this isn't possible, let her know that you're unable to run the session with her. If she asks for her compensation, provide it to her unless you specified that the compensation was contingent on arriving by a certain time. For more on this decision, see section 15.2.

What to say

To observers (in the example of shifting session focus to a product walkthrough):

➤ "I'd like to use the 20 minutes we have with the participant to do just a quick walkthrough of the design. So for this session only, I'll be showing her things and asking for feedback, rather than having her attempt tasks on her own. I think this is the best way to obtain feedback on all the important parts of the design in a short amount of time. Does that sound okay to you?"

When the participant arrives/starts:

➤ "Because we're getting started later than planned, are you able to stay after your scheduled time so we can get as much of your feedback as possible? About how long can you stay?"

If you need to dismiss the participant:

➤ "I'm sorry, *<we won't have enough time to run the session/we've started the session with another participant>*. I know that you did your best getting here, so we'd still like to compensate you and give you some time back in your day."

What not to do or say

➤ Don't blame the participant for being late, no matter how frustrated or irritated you are.

➤ Avoid making veiled comments about how much more you had planned to get through if the participant had been on time.

How to avoid

➤ Ask the recruiter to ensure that participants arrive 15 minutes early to fill out forms or to "check in." If there are typically traffic or parking issues in a particular area, or a known event or construction is happening, have the recruiter warn participants about scheduling extra travel time and suggest alternative methods of transportation.

➤ Obtain the participants' cell phone numbers so you can call them directly if they're running late. Ensure that the participants also have a contact phone number for you and your recruiter in case they're running late.

➤ Schedule backup or floater participants for sessions when it's extremely important to not have a late or no-show participant (discussed more in section 15.1).

➤ If budget is a concern for your study, consider working out an arrangement with the recruiter where, if the participant is not at your location within a certain number of minutes of her scheduled time, she'll not receive her compensation. If you do explore this option, we definitely recommend having a backup or floater system so you don't end up with empty timeslots. Include the use of floaters in your proposal to the stakeholders who manage your research budget, although keep in mind that this system probably won't reduce your compensation costs.

See also

➤ 9.4 Participant cancels or is a no-show

9.2 Observers are loud and distracting

You have a number of observers for your session, all watching from a room near where you and the participant are working. You (and the participant) can hear the observers laughing, yelling, or just talking loudly. The participant may ask you if the observers are laughing because of something she did.

Method(s): Any in-person method
Frequency: Frequent
Pattern(s) to apply: Take responsibility; Reassure the participant; Take a break

What to do

As we saw in the opening survival story in Chapter 1, hearing observers laugh, snicker, sigh, or otherwise react can be an awkward and humiliating experience for both you and the participant.

➤ If the observers are loud, but not laughing, take responsibility for their rudeness and apologize to the participant for the interruption. Then, excuse yourself to ask the observers to quiet down for the remainder of the session.

■ If the observers are in another room, remind them that you're able to hear them through the walls and that the participant is also able to hear them.

■ If the observers are in the room with you and causing the distraction, take them outside the room for a brief chat and ask them to stay quiet for the remainder of the session.

■ Regardless of where they're located, let the observers know that even if they're laughing at something unrelated to the participant or the session, the participant may feel like she is being laughed at, which will affect her behavior and her comfort.

➤ If the observers were laughing, reassure the participant that she is not being laughed at, even if you think that is what the observers were doing. Try to make her feel comfortable, even if you have to use a pretext for the observers' behavior, such as:

■ *(If it's not obvious where the sound is coming from):* "There's another meeting space next door and there might be another meeting going on."

■ "The observers often get into intense conversations about the product and stop paying attention to the session, so you're probably just hearing part of their discussion."

What to say

To excuse yourself so you can go ask the observers to be quiet:

➤ "*<Participant>*, I apologize for the noise. Please excuse me while I go ask the people next door to be quiet."

To the observers:

➤ "I just want to let you know that the participant and I are able to hear you. This is making the participant feel very uncomfortable, and that is my number-one priority, so forgive me for being direct—if you aren't able to be quiet in here, please go to another part of the building. Remember that our participant is giving her time to us today and deserves to be treated with respect."

If participant asks whether she was being laughed at:

➤ "No, the observers are definitely not laughing at you. Right now they're probably discussing the best way to address the issues you've uncovered today. I'm going to go remind them to keep their voices down."

➤ "No, absolutely not. Everyone observing today is really grateful for your feedback. They just sometimes stop watching the session and become distracted by other conversations, and get loud about it. I'll go talk to them to make sure they pay attention!"

➤ "I think that was actually sound coming from another conference room on the other side of this area, and they may not know we have a study going on. Excuse me for a moment while I go let them know."

What not to do or say

➤ Don't let the participant think she is being laughed at, or that the loudness coming from the next room has anything to do with her or her actions.

How to avoid

➤ Provide ground rules for observers ahead of time that include remaining quiet during a session, and let them know that they're required to take them seriously. See section 15.4 for more about these ground rules.

See also

➤ 6.9 Observers are not engaged in the session

➤ 9.5 Observer unexpectedly interacts with the participant

➤ 9.6 Session interrupted accidentally by an observer or someone else

➤ Survival Story: "Are they laughing at me?" at the start of Chapter 1

9.3 Participant receives a call during the session

During your session, the participant receives a call on her mobile phone. Ideally, the participant immediately turns off the phone or ringer so this doesn't happen again. However, sometimes the participant answers the call and proceeds to have a conversation with the caller. She may forget that the session is being recorded and that she is being observed.

Method(s): Any
Frequency: Frequent
Pattern(s) to apply: Take a break

What to do

➤ Let the participant chat for a few seconds, as she may immediately tell the caller that she'll call them back later.

If the participant talks on the phone for more than 15 or 20 seconds, take the following steps:

➤ Remind her that she is still being recorded, or just pause/turn off the recording if you have an easy way to do so. The reminder may encourage her to get off the call quickly.

➤ If the participant is remote (e.g., she is on her office speakerphone with you but you hear her answer her mobile phone):

■ Ask the participant to mute herself and unmute when she is free.

■ If the participant is gone for a long period of time, speak up on the call to try to get her attention, or contact her through the screen-sharing chat feature or email to gauge when she'll be able to resume the session.

➤ If the participant is in-person:

■ Mute the audio for observers. If you don't have a quick and easy way to cut off the sound (e.g., because your observers are in an observation room as part of a usability lab setup), remind the participant that she can still be heard in another room.

■ If the participant continues to talk and the conversation doesn't seem to be ending soon, stop the recording and take a break.

■ If it seems like an important phone call, you can also offer to bring the participant to a more private room.

■ Once taking a break, check back in with the participant after five minutes or so and ask how much longer she'll be so you can plan accordingly.

9.3 Participant receives a call during the session (cont.)

- When you resume the session, consider asking the participant to mute or put her phone on a silent mode for the remainder of the session. If the participant says she needs to keep the phone on and/or says she is dealing with an important situation, be understanding, but prepare yourself for subsequent interruptions.

- If it seems like the participant is distracted and/or upset by the phone call, you may need to take some additional care to keep the participant comfortable and reevaluate the plan for the session. See section 12.3 for additional tips about this situation.

What to say

➤ "Sorry to interrupt, but I just wanted to remind you that you're still being recorded. Should I pause the recording?"

➤ "Let's take a short break so you can finish this conversation. *<I'm going to turn off the sound/ you might want to step outside/let me bring you to another room, because others can hear you right now.>*"

If the participant is remote:

➤ "*<Participant>*, there are some observers on the line and we want to be respectful of your privacy. Can you go ahead and mute this conference call and unmute when you're done?"

What not to do or say

➤ Even if you want to, do not snap at the participant. Give her the benefit of the doubt—even if you think she is dealing with a frivolous situation, you don't truly know what is going on.

How to avoid

➤ Ask participants to turn off or at least mute their phone at the beginning of the session.

See also

➤ 9.7 Session interrupted by someone the participant knows

9.4 Participant cancels or is a no-show

> Your session's scheduled start time has come and gone, and you find out that the scheduled participant can no longer make her timeslot. Or, you've waited for a while and the participant does not show up and you consider her a no-show.

Method(s): Any
Frequency: Occasional
Pattern(s) to apply: Take responsibility; Shift the focus

What to do

➤ If the participant canceled, let any observers know that the scheduled participant will not make it. If the observers are upset, try to absorb the responsibility as much as possible rather than blaming the participant or recruiter, which can come across as unprofessional. If the observers include stakeholders, use this opportunity to refocus the conversation and discuss the best use of the session time moving forward.

➤ If you have scheduled a backup or floater participant (as discussed in section 15.1), you can start the session with her. Keep in mind that if you're starting the session late, you may need to shift the focus of the session by adjusting your method or study plan to accommodate a shortened session duration.

➤ If you don't have a scheduled backup or floater participant, decide if it would be appropriate to find someone onsite who is either qualified for the study on her own or could act as a surrogate user. This technique is most appropriate when you have a very general set of recruit criteria. If you do leverage a surrogate user, make sure to manage expectations and appropriately weigh that person's feedback when discussing results with stakeholders.

What to say

To let observers know about the cancelation or no-show:

➤ "It looks like the participant isn't coming. Would you like me to look for a replacement in this office as a surrogate user? It won't be an actual end user so we'd have to weigh the results carefully, but we have the timeslot and may get some insightful feedback."

If the observers are upset about the no-show:

➤ "I know you *<flew out here/cleared time in your busy day/etc.>* specifically to see these sessions! I'm sorry that we're unable to secure a participant for this session; we'll make sure to confirm again for the other participants. Let's talk about what the best use of this time may be...."

What not to do or say

➤ Don't badmouth or otherwise disparage the no-show or canceled participant, even if you're frustrated over the situation. Remember to stay professional.

How to avoid

➤ Make sure that the recruiter is clear with scheduled participants that they will be participating in a one-on-one session. Participants may not feel guilty about canceling if they assume that they're in a focus group and will be covered by other people.

➤ Set expectations with observers that no-shows and cancelations happen, and work with them to establish appropriate backup plans for the best use of time when it does.

➤ Schedule backup or floater participants for sessions when it's extremely important to not have a late or no-show participant (e.g., if you have observers flying in from out of town to observe your research, or know that important stakeholders will be watching a particular couple of sessions).

See also

➤ 9.1 Participant is running late

9.5 Observer unexpectedly interacts with the participant

Before the session, you asked an observer to sit in the room with you and quietly watch the session. If the session is remote, you may have an observer listening on the call with you. You asked your observer to hold any questions until the end. However, while you're moderating, she interrupts and begins to interact directly with the participant. Or, if the observer is watching from another room (like a usability study's control or observation room), she may come into the research room to talk to (or at) the participant.

Method(s): Any
Frequency: Occasional
Pattern(s) to apply: Take responsibility; Reassure the participant

What to do

➤ First, quickly try to figure out why the observer felt the need to interrupt, and what tone she is taking with the participant. Is she probing for more detail based on something the participant said or did? Or is she being defensive about the product or topic being discussed, and is trying to clarify an assumption or constraint? Or worse, is she verbally attacking the participant for not understanding a concept or for doing something that she didn't agree with?

➤ If the observer is following up on something that the participant said and is not being emotional or argumentative, you might let the participant answer the question as long as it won't take you too far off track from the study plan and the research goals. However, you also need to ask the observer to go back to quietly observing (and if she is remote, to also mute her phone) and hold off on additional questions until the agreed-upon time.

➤ If the observer is asking a question that comes across as defensive, gently reword her question for the participant so it sounds more neutral.

➤ If the observer is remote:

■ Remind everyone listening to keep their phones muted. If you're leaving time at the end of the session for questions from the observers, remind them of that as well.

■ If your remote observer is being argumentative or accusatory and you're using a screen-sharing application, use any available options for muting an attendee's audio (e.g., in WebEx right-click/contextual-click on the observer's name to mute her). While extreme, keep in mind that your first responsibility is to provide a safe and comfortable environment for the participant and that the observer is violating that rule.

➤ If the observer is onsite and has entered your research space, get the observer to return to the observation space and stay there for the remainder of the session. You may need to get up and walk her out of the room with you.

9.5 Observer unexpectedly interacts with the participant (cont.)

➤ If the observer continues to be argumentative or problematic, take a quick break so you can talk with her privately. Pay careful attention to how the participant reacts to the interruption and adjust accordingly. If the participant seems nervous or scattered, adjust your tone to be calm, focused, and reassuring. Reset the context for what you were doing before the interruption. For example, you can ask the participant to re-read the task or summarize what the participant had been talking about. Take a quick break if the participant seems especially rattled.

What to say

At beginning of a remote session to observers, before calling the participant:

➤ "I'm about to call the participant. Just a reminder to everyone listening to keep your phones on mute for the duration of the session. Please check to make sure you're on mute now."

If the observer is asking questions:

➤ "*<Observer>*, I appreciate your perspective on this. *<Participant>*, let us know what you think, and then, for the sake of time, I'd like to get back to our planned questions. If we have time at the end of the session, we can pursue this topic further."

➤ "I'd like to bring us back to the *<task/question>*. Let's come back to this issue at the end of the session."

➤ *(For a remote session)* "Just a reminder that all observers should keep their phones on mute. There may be a chance for additional questions at the end of the session, but for now we need to return to our planned questions."

If the observer asks innocent questions that were inadvertently leading or accusatory:

➤ "*<Participant>* , what *<observer>* meant to ask was *<rephrase neutrally>*."

If the observer is being defensive, threatening, or confrontational:

➤ "*<Observer>*, please keep in mind that *<participant>* is here to help us improve the product. It's good for us to see how she thinks about and approaches this. There are no wrong answers here. Now, I'd like to bring us back to *<task/question>*...."

➤ "*<Observer>*, let's step outside for a moment." *(Once outside):* "This session is meant to be one-on-one between me and the participant. Your interactions with the participant seem to be making her uncomfortable. I don't want her to feel evaluated, and I'm worried we won't be able to accomplish the goals of this session if you continue. It would help if you could just observe and remain quiet for the rest of the session. Does that sound okay to you?"

9.5 Observer unexpectedly interacts with the participant (cont.)

What not to do or say

➤ Don't let the observer take over the session.

➤ Don't enter a verbal altercation with the observer in front of the participant. If the conversation gets heated, bring the observer outside of the research space and out of the participant's earshot.

How to avoid

➤ Provide explicit ground rules to your observers ahead of time to remind them to be respectful of the participant and the goals for the research (see section 15.4 for more about this). These rules should also specify what kind of interaction (if any) they're allowed to have with the participant. Stress the importance of you maintaining control of the session so the participant always knows who to talk to. Here are some examples of ways that observers can get you their questions:

  ■ Ask observers to write down their questions for you to ask at the end of the session (or for them to ask, if you're comfortable letting them do so). We typically recommend this approach as it is the easiest and least distracting to implement.

  ■ When an observer is in the room, have her pass notes with questions to you. Let the participant know about this ahead of time so she is not surprised or distracted.

  ■ When observers are remote or located in another room, have them use an instant-message program to communicate with you in the middle of the session.

➤ If your session is remote:

  ■ At the beginning of the session, before the participant is on the call, let remote observers know that the session is about to begin and to please mute their phones.

  ■ Take advantage of any available options within your remote testing application and/or conference calling system to automatically mute all observers. Tell observers ahead of time that they should mute their phones when they join the call—you can't be too careful!

 Watch Video 5 to see an example of a moderator dealing with an interrupting observer during a contextual inquiry. The moderator pulls the observer out of the room to reiterate the session ground rules.

Visit our website (http://www.modsurvivalguide.org/videos) to use your QR reader to scan this code.

9.5 Observer unexpectedly interacts with the participant (cont.)

See also

➤ 9.2 The observers are loud and distracting

➤ 9.6 Session interrupted accidentally by an observer or someone else

➤ 9.7 Session interrupted by someone the participant knows

➤ Survival Story: "'Too dumb' to yield meaningful results"

9.6 Session interrupted accidentally by an observer or someone else

> At some point during the session, someone accidentally intrudes in the study space. The intrusion may be in person (e.g., someone coming into your research space without realizing that it's occupied) or remote (e.g., an observer doesn't realize that her phone is not muted, or puts you and the other observers on hold and now everyone hears hold music).

Method(s): Any
Frequency: Occasional
Pattern(s) to apply: Take responsibility; Reassure the participant

What to do

For an in-person interruption:

➤ Get the interrupter out of the room as quickly as possible. If the interrupter is lost or looking for something in particular, take a moment to help her or direct her to someone who can.

➤ Apologize to the participant for the interruption, and let her know that you don't anticipate any more interruptions going forward (then hope for the best).

If the interruption is during a remote session:

➤ Remind all observers to put their phones on mute.

➤ If you're using screen-sharing software that has an embedded conference call, you should be able to manually mute the offending observer (e.g., in WebEx, by right-clicking/contextual-clicking on the observer's name and choosing Mute). If you can't find this functionality, you should be able to eject the observer from the meeting, which will disconnect her audio. Conference calling systems sometimes have a similar ability to mute everyone or eject certain attendees.

➤ If you can still hear the observer (e.g., if she has stepped away from her phone and you can hear background conversation), ask a colleague to send an email reminding all observers to mute their phones. You may also need to pause the session for a few minutes, especially if the noise is very loud. This pause may give the disruptive observer a chance to get back to her desk and realize what is happening.

➤ If you have access to another conference call number, you can ask everyone to join a new call instead. If the participant is remote as well, be sure to give the new information to her, or let her know that you'll call her directly to conference her in (depending on your setup).

➤ If you don't have the time or means to set up another conference call, you can simply just call the participant directly and not let any remote observers listen to the remainder of the session. If you do so, send out a message to the observers (or have someone do so on your behalf) so they understand why you made the change and offer to share any recordings.

➤ If none of these options are possible solutions for you, you can try to continue the session and tolerate the distracting sounds. If the noise from the offending observer is too loud for this to be a viable option, ask the participant to wait until the noise issues get resolved. While this may mean that you have to end the session earlier than planned, hopefully all the steps you've taken in the meantime will prevent this from happening again—with this group of observers, at least.

What to say

If there is an in-person disruption, to the person who interrupted:

➤ "I'm sorry, this room is being used for a research session. It will be available *<later/at X time>*."

If on the phone:

➤ "*<Participant>*, please hold on for just a moment; we're getting some background noise. Could everyone on the call please make sure that your phone is muted?"

If you're not able to get the attention of a remote observer who is typing or otherwise making a lot of noise unknowingly:

➤ "*<Participant>*, please bear with me while I work with my team to try to get in touch with the person making the noise. I am going to mute my phone and step away for a few minutes. Please stay on the line."

What not to do or say

➤ If you think you know who the offending remote observer is, try not to call her out by name unless it's the last resort in getting her attention. Make a generic announcement about everyone needing to mute their phones and attempt to get in touch with the observer some other way, like email, instant message, or through the screen-sharing application with a private chat message.

How to avoid

➤ If your session is in person, put a sign on the door of your study space to let passersby know that they should not enter the space.

➤ If your session has remote observers, take advantage of options within your screen-sharing application or conference call system to automatically mute all attendees from the start (except for the participant, of course; you may need to call her separately if she is remote). Also, tell observers ahead of time that they should mute their phones when they join the call—you can't be too careful!

See also

➤ 9.2 The observers are loud and distracting
➤ 9.5 Observer unexpectedly interacts with the participant
➤ 9.7 Session interrupted by someone the participant knows

9.7 Session interrupted by someone the participant knows

During an onsite session, there is an interruption by someone the participant knows. This interruption may come from the participant's spouse or kids if you're at her home, or a coworker or manager if you're at her office. The participant may tell the interrupter that she is in the middle of something, but the interrupter is insistent that she needs the participant's attention immediately.

Method(s): Any in-person method
Frequency: Occasional
Pattern(s) to apply: Take responsibility; Take a break; End the session early

What to do

➤ If you're in the middle of something critical or time-sensitive with the participant, let the interrupter and participant know how much more time you need to get out of that critical process, and see if she is able to wait that long.

➤ If not, offer to take a break so the participant can deal with the interruption immediately. Set a time limit for the break, although accept that the participant may need more time than you'd like.

➤ If the person interrupting the session seems angry or forceful toward the participant, minimize your presence and step out of the situation as much as possible. If your presence is making the situation worse and is creating the conflict, apologize, thank the participant for her feedback, give her the agreed-on compensation, and end the session early.

What to say

➤ "We'll be done in just *<number of>* minutes. If it's okay with *<whoever is interrupting>*, would you be able to wait until then?"

➤ "*<Participant>*, why don't we take a quick break so you can handle this? Let's plan to resume in 10 minutes."

What not to do or say

➤ Don't be inflexible and insist that the participant continue the session with you. Letting the participant deal with the situation will keep her from being distracted and/or irritated.

How to avoid

➤ These situations are difficult to avoid in a participant's environment, and you may not want to avoid them. Interruptions may be a regular part of the participant's life and you can learn a lot about whether these interruptions are typical, and how her workflow or approach to tasks is affected. You may be able to follow up with the participant about the interruption and gather feedback that you might have missed otherwise.

➤ However, if you're less interested in the specifics of a participant's environment (e.g., you're just performing an interview), ask the participant when arranging the session if she can schedule a conference room or some other private space that may minimize the potential for interruptions.

See also

➤ 9.3 Participant receives a call during the session

➤ 9.5 Observer unexpectedly interacts with the participant

➤ 9.6 Session interrupted accidentally by an observer or someone else

SURVIVAL STORY: "'TOO DUMB' TO YIELD MEANINGFUL RESULTS"
CHARLOTTE SCHWENDEMAN

At the conclusion of a session during the first usability study I ever facilitated, a developer who watched the session from an observation room approached me in a slightly confrontational manner. He put his hands on his hips, stomped his foot, and asked, "Where did you get these stupid users?" I didn't expect to hear participants called "stupid" again during my career, but, alas, I did.

My team was in the process of creating and iteratively usability testing paper prototypes for a web-based solution for a new concept. The company itself was new and its existence depended on the success of the solution. I was working for a small consulting firm at the time and my client consisted of the group of senior marketing executives who originated the idea for the concept.

I sold the client team on the value of observing the sessions and we all flew to the city where my team would facilitate the first round of usability studies. Since our client had never seen a usability study before, I sat with them in the observation room, explaining what was happening and why, while another member of my team facilitated the first session. About 20 minutes into the session the client began making noises that the participant was just "not normal." After a few more minutes the client became quite angry and vocal, stating the participant was "too dumb" to yield meaningful, valid results. The client team wanted me to end the session prematurely and move on to the next participant because they didn't think they were "getting enough" from the session. I attempted to calm the client and explain in as many ways as I could that the participant was a good match and that what they were seeing was very typical. The client team was persistent and, in the end, got its way.

As I write about it now, long after the fact, it doesn't seem any more unusual than other oddities that occur during usability studies; however, at the time, the client was so angry about it that it created a very volatile situation. It changed the relationship between the client and my team going forward. They feared their concept would fail and my team feared the marketing team would insist on cherry-picking participants for the remainder of the project, thereby rendering our usability studies useless. If I had a "do-over," I think I would have paid more time and attention upfront to explaining to the client that participants who fit the profile can run a fairly wide gamut. The biggest lesson I learned was to take the time before a test to explain in detail to stakeholders what they will see and why, and the type of results they can expect.

CHAPTER 10

Get on Track:
Overcoming Momentum Blockers

Momentum blockers slow the progress of the session, sometimes all the way to a full stop. Whether you're having difficulty understanding the participant, or you're running out of time to accomplish your tasks, this chapter will help you figure out the best way to move forward and bring the session back on track.

10.1 Participant starts going on a tangent

While answering a question, the participant goes off on a tangent that is not directly connected to or relevant to the research you're doing. Similarly, if you're running a usability study or contextual inquiry, he may start exploring an area in the product that's outside the scope of your study plan.

Method(s): Any
Frequency: Frequent
Pattern(s) to apply: Clarify the task/question; Redirect the participant

What to do

The participant's tangent may be irrelevant to your research for a variety of reasons. Perhaps the functionality or processes he's using or discussing are out of scope, you already have enough data about the subject matter, or it has nothing to do with what you're researching. However, the participant doesn't know this, and the information he's providing may be important to him.

➤ Ask the participant to tell you in his own words what he's trying to do. His answer will help you figure out if he misunderstood you or is pursuing the tangent for other reasons. If he did misunderstand you, repeat or reword your question, or ask him to re-read the task.

➤ If you have time in the session, consider letting the participant pursue his tangent. It helps him feel heard, especially if it's on a topic he's been eager to talk about. You may be surprised at the relevant feedback that can surface from letting him do this.

➤ Set a time limit for how long you'll let the participant stay on a tangent before steering him back. The time limit depends on the length of your session, what else you need to cover, and whether it seems like the tangent may connect back to something that's relevant to your research. For example, let's say you're running a one-hour interview about how users think about retirement. If, just a few questions in to the session, the participant goes on a tangent about mobile applications he's had negative experiences with, you may want to politely rein him in after just a couple of minutes. However, if he goes on the same tangent 45 minutes in to the session when you only have one or two questions left, you may let him go closer to five minutes. If you see a way to connect the tangent back to your study goals—say if the goal of your research is to understand how users approach their smartphones compared to their tablets—you may let him go even longer, and maybe probe for more specifics about why those applications were so frustrating.

➤ If you're running a usability study:

■ Keep in mind that if you keep steering a participant back from his tangents to a specific area (the area that is the goal of your research), you're essentially telling him that the other ways are "wrong." This both clues him in on the "right" path, and also can make him feel more like he is being tested, and is failing. Using an apologetic tone and acknowledging what he was trying to do can help negate this. For example, "It's helpful to know that you would want to look in this area, and what you'd be trying to find. I would like to get your feedback on this other area as well…."

■ If the participant seems genuinely interested in exploring part of the product that's not part of your study plan, you can let him know that if time permits, you'll let him return to that area at the end of the session.

What to say

At the beginning of the session:

➤ "We have a lot to get through, so I may at times gently push you along so that we can make sure to cover everything."

➤ "If we wind up spending too much time on any one topic, please don't be offended if I ask us to move on, just to keep things on track."

During the session:

➤ "This is all very helpful to see and hear. Just for the sake of time, I'm going to ask you to go *<to the next task/go back to….>*"

➤ "I'm interested in hearing more about this. I do want to make sure we cover everything we have planned. So if there's time, let's come back to this at the end of the session."

If you need to interrupt and redirect:

➤ "I'm sorry, I just want to stop you here for a second. For the sake of time I'd like you to return to the *<task/question>*, but we can revisit this topic at the end of the session if time permits."

What not to do or say

➤ Do not zone out while a participant is talking about topics you don't care about. We've seen moderators stare into the distance, scratch their heads, look at their watches, and go on their mobile devices or computers. This behavior is disrespectful to participants. You should give the *impression* of your undivided attention at all times, no matter how irrelevant or tangential you consider their feedback. If you're a bad actor and need something to help you focus, try taking notes on what the participant is saying to help him feel heard. However, keep your ears peeled because you never know when the participant will move into something that *is* relevant to your research—you don't want to miss it!

How to avoid

➤ Warn participants at the beginning of the session that you may be moving them along if you need to keep on task or make it through all of your questions. In a usability study, you may also set the expectation that you may not get through every task, depending on time.

See also

➤ 10.2 Participant consistently focuses on irrelevant details

➤ 10.3 Participant does something very unexpected

10.2 Participant consistently focuses on irrelevant details

The participant keeps honing in on things that are irrelevant to what you're trying to research, even after you've asked him to do otherwise multiple times. This can come in a mild form such as only focusing on the colors of a design rather than the functionality. For example, a participant might reiterate how much he hates the shade of green used in a prototype. Or, this focus may be more disruptive such as continuing to use a search engine to attempt tasks that you've asked him to do on a particular website.

Method(s): Any
Frequency: Occasional
Pattern(s) to apply: Clarify the task/question; Redirect the participant

What to do

➤ Verify that the feedback provided by the participant really is irrelevant. The behaviors that participants keep coming back to during a session may represent their natural behavior and can be a valuable set of data for a research project. If there is a way to get value out of his behavior or answers, you can let him continue as long as time and your research agenda permits.

➤ Ask the participant to tell you in his own words what he is trying to do. His answer will help you figure out if he misunderstood you or if something else is at play. If he did misunderstand you, repeat or reword your question, or ask him to re-read the task.

➤ If you find yourself asking the participant to re-read the task or are repeating questions over and over again, acknowledge what he is trying to do and explain what you want to focus on instead. For example, if the participant keeps trying to use a search engine instead of the website you're evaluating, let him know that you understand that he would typically use a search engine to attempt these tasks, but you need him to stay on the website so you can find ways to make that experience better.

➤ If the participant seems to have an agenda regarding what he wants to provide feedback on, consider letting him vent for a few minutes and then redirecting him back to the task/question as described in section 11.7.

What to say

➤ "You've mentioned that *<feedback on irrelevant aspect of design>*. What do you think about *<relevant aspect of design>*?"

➤ "I've noticed that you have a lot of feedback on *<irrelevant topic>*. Due to our time constraints, we unfortunately can't focus on that in today's session. But, do you want to take a minute or two now to tell me your thoughts before we move to the other topics?"

In a usability study:

➤ "It's helpful to know that you would look for a lot of this information in *<area>*. While that might be one place to find that information, we don't want to focus on it today. Instead, I'll ask you to try these tasks another way."

What not to do or say

➤ Try not to be rude or abrupt about redirecting the participant. It can be easy to offend or embarrass the participant, especially if you tell him there are no right or wrong answers but keep steering him to a certain topic. Acknowledging what he is trying to do will go a long way.

How to avoid

➤ At the beginning of the session, set expectations about what the participant should try to focus on. However, avoid going into so much detail about the research goals that you bias him.

➤ Warn the participant that, for the sake of time, you may sometimes move him along to another topic just to make sure you cover everything you need.

➤ If your stakeholders are responsible for finding participants, remind them to avoid filling the schedule with their most vocal customers or ones who frequently volunteer their feedback. These types of participants often participate with a preset agenda and expect to talk about what they have on their mind. See section 15.1 for more on how to avoid this.

See also

➤ 10.1 Participant starts going on a tangent
➤ 11.7 Participant becomes insulting or has an agenda

10.3 Participant does something very unexpected

While attempting a task or answering a question, the participant does or says something very unexpected. This may be something that no other participants have done or mentioned, or that is radically different from what you expected. For example, you ask a participant in an interview how he uses a mobile application, and he begins talking about the stereo system in his car.

Method(s): Any
Frequency: Occasional
Pattern(s) to apply: Take responsibility; Clarify the task/question; Redirect the participant

What to do

➤ Let the participant continue down his path for a few minutes. If you're running a usability study, remind the participant to think aloud. With a little more information, you should be able to tell whether the participant misunderstood you or is instead revealing something interesting about your users and their potential behavior. Using the example of asking the participant about his mobile application, he may have assumed that "mobile" meant the systems he interacts with in his car rather than on his smartphone.

➤ If you're still not sure why the participant is doing this unexpected thing, repeat the question or task to verify that he didn't mishear you, but be careful with your tone so it doesn't sound like you're reprimanding him (see examples in Appendix A). You can also try rephrasing or adjusting the question or task slightly, and see if he does the same thing. For example, if you asked the participant to change his mailing address on an e-commerce website and he goes someplace that doesn't seem to make sense, ask where he would go to change his billing address.

➤ Similarly, ask the participant to tell you in his own words what question he is trying to answer, what he is trying to do, or what he is looking for.

➤ Verify that you're not using industry jargon or being overly verbose in your questions and tasks, and reword if necessary.

➤ If the participant is watching your lips closely or tilting his head to be closer to yours, he may be having trouble hearing you. Move your chair a bit closer to his, speak a little louder, and speak in short, direct sentences.

➤ If you're conducting a usability study and think the participant did something unexpected because he missed the correct path, and you need to get him back on the correct path due to dependencies in future tasks, bring him back to where the divergence happened and ask a general question about the purpose of that screen or the options available. Then, if necessary, you can direct him to where you need him to go using the technique described in the Chapter 3 sidebar "The Diversionary Assist."

10.3 Participant does something very unexpected (cont.)

What to say

For any method:

➤ "Please tell me what you're thinking."

➤ "I just want to make sure that I gave you the right *<task/question>*, so let me go over it again. Sorry if I've caused any confusion."

➤ "Let me know if you're having trouble hearing me—sometimes I don't speak loudly enough."

In a usability study:

➤ "What are you looking for here?"

➤ "So tell me in your own words, what are/were you trying to do?"

➤ "Just to make sure I understand what you just did, I asked you to *<task>*, and to accomplish this task, you would *<do unexpected thing>*."

What not to do or say

➤ Don't imply that the participant is doing anything wrong, especially in a usability study.

How to avoid

➤ Before your first session, hold a pilot session with a representative participant so you can get initial feedback on any tasks or questions that might be confusing.

➤ If your tasks are complex, consider printing out the tasks for participants to reference. This reduces potential misunderstandings and frees their working memory to focus on each task.

See slso

➤ 6.2 Participant does something you don't understand

➤ 10.1 Participant starts going on a tangent

➤ 10.5 Participant gives vague responses to questions

➤ Survival Story "The request caught me off-guard"

10.4 Participant is slow or thorough

The participant is taking a lot of time to read, think, respond, and elaborate. This behavior may simply be a result of a slow and careful personality, or the participant may not realize how much other content you've planned for the session. He may also feel the need to be thorough because he's being watched or out of perceived obligation because he's being paid for his time.

Method(s): Any
Frequency: Occasional
Pattern(s) to apply: Redirect the participant

What to do

➤ To see if the participant is just a naturally slow or thorough person, ask him whether what he's doing is similar to what he'd do on his own. For example, "If you were doing this on your own, would you read through these Terms and Conditions like you are now, or spend more time on them, less time on them …?"

➤ If the participant is being slow because that seems to be his natural approach, accept that there's not much you can do to change that. Rushing him might confuse him or provoke anxiety. Instead, go into prioritization mode. Think across all your upcoming questions or tasks and consider what can be dropped and skimmed over.

➤ If the participant is being slow because he feels like you want him to be thorough, reassure him that you want him to behave as he would be if he was doing this on his own without you watching. This cue should help speed him up. If it doesn't, use the same prioritization technique mentioned in the previous point to direct him to the next task/question with the highest priority.

➤ If the participant seems to feel bad that he didn't get through all your tasks or questions, assure him that you hadn't planned to get through everything in the allotted session time.

What to say

If you anticipate the participant being slow upfront, give background instructions:

➤ "We have a lot of *<questions/tasks>*, but we probably won't go through all of them. You may see me skipping around to make sure I make the most out of our time."

If you want to see whether the participant is behaving naturally or is being slow and thorough for your sake:

➤ "Please go at whatever pace you would if you were doing this on your own and I wasn't sitting here with you. Don't feel like you have to rush or be more thorough because I'm here."

10.4 Participant is slow or thorough (cont.)

➤ "You seem to be spending some time *<doing this task>*. Would you be doing that if you were on your own at *<place/home/work>*?"

If the participant needs some pushing along midsession:

➤ "This is all very helpful to see and hear. Just for the sake of time, I'm going to ask you to *<go to the next task/go back to....>*"

➤ "I'm interested in hearing more about this. I do want to make sure we cover everything we have planned, so if there's time, let's come back to this at the end of the session."

If the participant feels badly about not getting through everything:

➤ "Don't worry about that; I didn't expect us to get through everything. All of your feedback was very important and helpful. I'm glad we spent the time the way that we did."

What not to do or say

➤ Don't rush participants through tasks or questions for the sake of getting everything done. Be respectful of the participant's speed and level of detail, and adjust your questions/tasks accordingly.

➤ Don't panic. If you're concerned about time, try not to let it show. This, of course, comes with practice but it's good to be mindful of it.

How to avoid

➤ There is no way to avoid participants who are slow and deliberate. It's just a matter of being prepared! The best way to be prepared is to identify which questions/tasks are the highest priority as you put together your study plan. This will help you adapt the session if necessary as discussed in section 15.2.

See also

➤ 10.7 You don't have time to complete everything

GET ON TRACK: OVERCOMING MOMENTUM BLOCKERS

10.5 Participant gives vague responses to questions

The participant responds to your questions with vague answers. You may not be sure if he doesn't understand your questions, isn't articulate, is shy, or just wants to collect the promised compensation.

Method(s): Any
Frequency: Occasional
Pattern(s) to apply: Take responsibility; Clarify the task/question; Build engagement

What to do

➤ Try clarifying or rewording your questions in case the participant didn't understand what you're asking. If necessary, try to back up to broader, easier questions and then, once you've built up that foundation, lead into the harder questions. If he seems frazzled or confused, take responsibility for "not being clear" about your question.

➤ Ask "Why?" to help prompt the participant to dig deeper into his response. For example, if you ask a participant about his experience using a remote control and he says it was okay, you can follow up with, "Tell me more—why do you say it was 'okay'?" You can ask "Why?" multiple times until you feel like you've reached the level of detail needed.

➤ If the participant is being vague because he seems to be unfamiliar with the subject matter, move on to the next task/question that doesn't cover the topic. If familiarity with that topic is a deal-breaker, see section 4.1.

➤ If you sense that the participant is shy and reluctant to share feedback, try to adapt your moderating style as discussed in section 1.5 to a more informal and approachable one such as Friendly Face or Inquisitive Mind.

➤ If the participant just doesn't seem interested in the topic or seems eager to get through the session as quickly as possible, see section 8.6 for ideas on how to inspire his interest.

What to say

To clarify:

➤ "I'm sorry, I don't think I'm being clear with my question. Let me rephrase...."

➤ "Let me back up a little, and first ask you this...."

To build engagement:

➤ "Thanks so much for participating. I know this is taking time out of your busy day, but your feedback is very helpful."

10.5 Participant gives vague responses to questions (cont.)

➤ "Have you ever tried to do this before? Tell me about your experience."

What not to do or say

➤ Try not to get frustrated with the participant, as it may lead him to become closed down and resentful.

How to avoid

➤ Craft your questions to provoke a thoughtful, detailed response. A poorly worded question or a question that can be answered with a simple "yes/no" may generate a vague and uninteresting answer. For example, a participant may give a general response to "What do you think about your local bus service?" but will be more specific when asked "Describe the last time you used your local bus service."

See also

➤ 6.1 Participant is reluctant to say anything negative
➤ 6.5 Participant ignores or pretends to understand your question
➤ 8.6 Participant is unwilling or unsure
➤ 10.3 Participant does something very unexpected

10.6 Participant is difficult to hear or understand

When the participant talks, you have a difficult time hearing or understanding him. He may have a very soft voice, be a fast talker, or have a thick accent. If the session is remote, a poor-quality phone connection may make it even more difficult to hear or understand him.

Method(s): Any
Frequency: Occasional
Pattern(s) to apply: Take responsibility

What to do

➤ Make sure the session is recorded so you can go back and review the participant's feedback more closely.

➤ If you're running a usability study, ask the participant to use his mouse (or finger if the product does not have a screen) to indicate the areas that he's providing feedback on. This can also provide vital context that may help you better understand his feedback.

➤ If you're having difficulty hearing the participant:

■ Ask the participant to speak up. This situation is a good place to use a pretext of the recording equipment having difficulty capturing voices if the participant is too quiet or a poor phone connection that keeps cutting out.

■ If the participant is remote, ask him to move closer to his phone or microphone. Also check the volume on your phone's speakers or your screen-sharing software to ensure that it's turned up as high as possible.

➤ If you're having difficulty understanding the participant:

■ If the session is in person, look at the participant's face and maintain eye contact while he's talking, even if that means you're unable to take detailed notes. Sometimes maintaining eye contact and being able to see a participant's facial expressions can help you better understand what he is saying.

■ If the participant is remote, ask the participant to repeat what he said, using difficulties with the phone connection as a pretext. However, this tip may not be practical if the participant continues to be difficult to understand. In those situations, you can use this tip occasionally, but accept that you'll need to go back to the recordings later.

■ Ask the participant to read tasks aloud. This may help you "calibrate" to the participant's way of speaking as he'll be reading something that you know.

10.6 Participant is difficult to hear or understand (cont.)

What to say

➤ "Can I have you repeat that just a little bit louder? I want to make sure that our recording equipment is able to pick you up."

➤ "Would you mind repeating that for me, a little bit slower so I can write it down?"

➤ "Could you use the mouse to show me on the screen what area you're talking about?"

If the participant is remote:

➤ "Could you move a little closer to the phone? I'm having a bit of trouble hearing you."

➤ "I apologize, I think our phone line cut out for a moment and I missed part of what you said. Would you mind repeating that for me?"

What not to do or say

➤ Don't tell the participant that you can't understand him because his accent is too strong, he is too soft-spoken, or there's something strange about the way he talks.

How to avoid

➤ Ask whoever is handling the recruit to screen out potential participants who are difficult to understand. However, if you're recruiting internally or interviewing very targeted users, you may not have enough flexibility to screen someone out for this reason.

➤ Keep in mind that even if a participant is difficult to understand, he still has valuable feedback to offer!

See also

➤ 4.3 Participant has an unexpected physical feature

10.7 You don't have time to complete everything

At some point you realize that you're running out of time and won't able to get through everything that you'd intended. The participant might have arrived later than scheduled or taken more time than anticipated on tasks and questions. You may have been overzealous in your study plan about how much you'd get through in your session. Whatever the reason, you need to figure out what to do and what you'll be able to cover.

Method(s): Any
Frequency: Occasional
Pattern(s) to apply: Take responsibility; Redirect the participant; Disengage from the participant

What to do

➤ Go into prioritization mode. Think across all your questions or tasks and consider what can be dropped and skimmed over. Or resolve to go partway through your tasks or questions and let the session end where it ends.

➤ If your priority is going for breadth rather than depth (i.e., getting a small amount of feedback on each of the remaining tasks/questions instead of attempting fewer complete tasks), consider turning the rest of the session into a "gut-reaction" game where the participant shows or tells you his first inclination in response to a task or question. For example, instead of having the participant complete a task of finding a savings account that meets his needs on a banking website, bring him to the homepage and ask him where he would click first if he was going to attempt that task. This approach will quickly give you "first-click" information that, depending on your research goals, may be useful.

➤ When you've gathered the information you need from a question/task, gently push the participant along to your next item. If you plan to do this repeatedly, warn participants that due to time constraints, you may keep moving them along.

➤ Consider narrowing the focus of any remaining tasks/questions. For example, you may tell the participant to only focus on a certain part of the design or process rather than the full experience.

➤ If a participant seems to feel bad at the end of the session because he didn't get through all of your tasks/questions, assure him that you hadn't planned to get through everything, and take the blame for trying to fit too much into one session.

What to say

To gently bring the participant to the next task/question:

➤ "This is all very helpful to see and hear. Just for the sake of time, I'm going to ask you to <*go to the next task/go back to….*>"

➤ "I'm interested in hearing more about this. I do want to make sure we cover everything we have planned, so if there's time, let's come back to this at the end of the session."

If you know that you need to move quickly:

➤ "I just did a time check, and we're running a bit low on time. We have a lot of *<questions/tasks>* that I'd like to get your feedback on, so I may just push you along at times so that we can cover as much as possible."

➤ "For the remaining tasks, we're going to move faster than we have before. For each of the following tasks, show me where you would click first."

If the participant feels bad about not getting through everything at the end of session:

➤ "Don't worry about that; I didn't expect us to get through everything. All your feedback was very important and helpful. I'm glad we spent the time the way that we did."

What not to do or say

➤ Don't rush participants through tasks or questions for the sake of getting everything done. Adjust and prioritize what you need participants to do based on the time available so they don't leave the session feeling like they were rushed.

➤ Don't panic. If you're concerned about time, try not to let it show. This, of course, comes with practice but it's good to be mindful of it.

How to avoid

➤ Run a pilot session with a participant to make sure that you have an accurate sense of timing. Of course, you'll always get circumstances that result in a time crunch, but at least you can adjust the things that are under your control.

➤ As you put together your study plan, identify which questions/tasks are the highest priority. This will help you adapt the session if necessary as discussed in section 15.2.

See also

➤ 10.4 Participant is slow or thorough

10.8 Participant struggles excessively with a task

> The participant struggles with a task for longer than expected, possibly even longer than other participants. He may also be growing visibly upset, frustrated, and/or agitated.

Method(s): Usability study

Frequency: Occasional

Pattern(s) to apply: Take responsibility; Clarify the task/question; Redirect the participant; Reassure the participant; Take a break; End the session

What to do

Watching where and why participants struggle is a main purpose of performing usability studies. Discovering those pain points will help you improve the product for future users (Dumas and Loring, 2008). However, excessive struggling can take an emotional toll on the participant's well-being, or use up valuable session time that could be spent exploring other research questions.

➤ If the participant is struggling excessively to the point where it's taking too much time or no longer providing data that's relevant to your research goals, but the participant is *not* showing signs of being emotionally distraught, have him stop what he's doing and move onto the next question or task. If moving on requires that you give an assist (as discussed in section 6.4), go ahead and do so.

➤ If the participant is displaying minor emotional discomfort, such as frustration or annoyance with the product, or seems to be less engaged in what he is doing, take a short break. After giving him a few minutes, check in with him privately to make sure that he's comfortable continuing. When the break is over, reassure the participant that his feedback has been helpful and then move on to a different task or question. If he becomes more upset, see section 12.7 and end the session early if necessary.

What to say

To move on from the current task:

➤ "That's as far as we need to go with that. Why don't we...."

➤ "Just for the sake of time, I'm going to ask you to...."

To take a break:

➤ "This seems like a good stopping point. Why don't we take a quick five-minute break?"

➤ "I'm going to turn off our recording equipment, and give you a short break. I'm going to step out, but I'll be back in a few."

10.8 Participant struggles excessively with a task (cont.)

While talking in private:

➤ "I don't want you to continue the session if you're feeling uncomfortable. You've already given us very helpful feedback. Is there anything I can do to help, or would you like to end here?"

If ending the session, and the participant feels bad:

➤ "Don't worry about that; I didn't expect us to get through everything. All of your feedback was very important and helpful. I'm glad we spent the time the way that we did."

What not to do or say

➤ Avoid saying anything that implies the participant is taking longer than you expected, or that he's failing a task.

How to avoid

➤ This situation is not usually avoidable, but the tone you set at the beginning of the session can affect the emotional impact that struggling has on the participant. If he seems particularly sensitive or nervous at the start of the session, you may need to adapt your moderating style to be more approachable and reassuring, as discussed in section 1.6.

See Also

➤ 4.5 Participant has difficulty reading

➤ 11.8 Participant becomes agitated by a product's usability issues

SURVIVAL STORY: "THE REQUEST CAUGHT ME OFF–GUARD"
DANA DOUGLAS

We were conducting a usability study with international researchers for a collaborative research website. The sessions were conducted remotely from our lab in Maryland with participants located all around the world. One of the sessions was with a very pleasant man from Indonesia. At the beginning of the session as I was introducing the study, he asked permission to take a few-minute break when he heard the Islamic call to prayer, which he expected to sound during our session. While the request caught me off-guard, I knew that I wanted to respect him and make sure he felt comfortable with me, so I graciously agreed and we proceeded with the session. Then, in the middle of the session as he was completing a task, we both heard the call. At that point, he promptly excused himself and for the next few minutes I waited on the line for him to return. When he did, he thanked me and we picked up exactly where we left off.

Since the goals of the study were more qualitative than quantitative, the effect that the interruption had on the findings was insignificant. So, while the break was somewhat disruptive and caused the session to run a few minutes longer than planned, we were both able to smoothly transition in and out, and in doing so, I was able to respect his normal practices. This particular situation made it clear to me that, to get the most valuable feedback, the most important thing is to create an environment (even in a remote situation) in which the participant is comfortable.

Take the Wheel: Guiding Wayward Participants

If the participant becomes agitated, annoyed, or disparaging toward you or your organization, it's time for you to take the wheel of the session. These situations require you to diffuse the participant's frustration, and then monitor the session going forward to ensure the rest of her experience is not negatively affected.

11.1 Remote participant is obviously distracted

During a remote session, you hear the participant doing things that are obviously outside the realm of this study. Maybe you can hear her typing in a window that's not being shared or is on a different monitor. There may be muffled conversations or noises in the background, and the participant may be slow to respond or entirely miss your questions.

Method(s): Any remote method
Frequency: Frequent
Pattern(s) to apply: Clarify the task/question; Build engagement; Take a break; End the session early

What to do

➤ First, give the participant a subtle hint that you know something else is going on. Asking something like "Is this still a good time for you?" gives her an out in case she really does have something more important to deal with but is too polite to say so. It also gives the participant a chance to share any complications within her environment. For example, participants within corporate environments (if you're talking to employees who are participating from work) often find it impossible to truly shut out the rest of the world for your research, and may be multitasking as you're talking to them. The participant may tell you that she has to keep her email open during the session, or that it's a very busy time and she may need to stop occasionally to talk with coworkers. In this case, you can offer to reschedule but you may need to accept that even so, she may still experience similar distractions.

➤ If the participant is willing to continue and seems genuinely interested in providing feedback, but is dealing with distractions outside of her control, focus on the most important tasks/questions so you can make the most of her limited feedback.

➤ If the participant doesn't respond to your hint or you still get the sense that she is distracted, make a judgment call on whether or not to continue the session and, if you do continue, what you can adapt to fit these circumstances. If you think the session may be salvageable, consider asking the participant questions that are more directly targeted to what she does (e.g., how her process works today or what parts of the product she uses most often) instead of continuing with your preplanned tasks. Getting her to talk about herself may help increase her engagement in the session. If this works, you can then move back to your study plan, using the knowledge you've gained to tailor what comes next. However, if she still seems distracted, tell the participant that you've covered everything you'd planned, and then wrap it up early.

11.1 Remote participant is obviously distracted (cont.)

What to say

➤ "*<Participant>*, is now still a good time for you?"

➤ "It sounds like there's something else going on. Do you need to take a quick break before we continue with *<task/question>*?"

➤ "There seem to be a number of things competing for your attention right now. Are you able to continue with this study? If not, that's fine, and we can reschedule."

➤ "I know you're very busy, so I appreciate you taking the time to give us feedback."

What not to do or say

➤ Hide your frustration or annoyance with the participant. Be polite and respectful.

How to avoid

➤ Be upfront about your expectations for the session so the participant can reschedule any competing priorities and plan accordingly. But, recognize that even this may not be enough and that interruptions could still come up.

➤ During your recruiting process, ask the participant for the "best" time to conduct the session, and schedule her session for that time. Check with her the day before to ensure that the scheduled time still works.

 Watch Video 3 to see an example of a moderator interacting with a distracted participant during a remote usability study. The participant ends up sharing more than she intends.

Visit our website (http://www.modsurvivalguide.org/videos) or use your QR reader to scan this code.

See also

➤ 8.6 Participant is unwilling or unsure

➤ 12.2 Something personal, inappropriate, or confidential is visible

➤ 12.3 Participant is obviously distracted by external circumstances

11.2 Participant is distressed by a personal line of questioning

You've had to ask the participant some relatively personal questions and she starts to become uncomfortable and edgy. The tone of her voice changes, her voice gets louder or softer, and her answers become short and curt. She may tell you outright that she is not comfortable answering certain questions. The questions you're asking are part of your study plan and may be domain-specific, like online dating behaviors as part of a usability study for a dating website or the frequency that she shaves as part of an interview about disposable razors. Or, you may be asking some specific questions about her job (e.g., how a factory worker breaks rules to get something done more safely, easily, or efficiently).

Method(s): Any
Frequency: Occasional
Pattern(s) to apply: Reassure the participant; Take a break

What to do

➤ Think about the participant's expectations. If the participant was expecting to only talk in general about financial websites and is distressed by your questions about estate planning, try to make your questions broader and less personal to be more in line with her expectations. If this isn't possible, it's best to just drop the topic even if it means losing that data point. If the participant signed up to participate in an interview about online dating, then you can soften the personal nature of the questions you're asking, but she shouldn't be too surprised about the topic you're exploring.

➤ Let the participant know that if there are any questions that she's not comfortable answering, she should tell you.

➤ Reassure the participant about how her answers will be used. For example, tell her that her feedback will be aggregated with the answers of other participants, and her name will not be associated with it. This reassurance will help make the participant feel as comfortable as possible sharing what she is willing to disclose.

➤ If the participant seems afraid of getting in trouble because of her answers (e.g., because she is an internal employee and the research is for her organization), add to your reassurance a reminder that she's not being evaluated in any way on how she approaches her work or any other aspect of her life.

➤ If the participant is especially uncomfortable or agitated by your questions, offer to talk to her about it in private, with any recording equipment turned off. If she seems really rattled, take a break, and when the session resumes, soften the personal questions or move on to another area of your study plan. If the participant still seems upset or agitated, bring the session to an early end.

11.2 Participant is distressed by a personal line of questioning (cont.)

What to say

➤ "Let me know if you're uncomfortable answering any of my questions. While we want to learn as much as possible from you, I also want to respect your privacy and your comfort."

➤ "I'm sorry, I didn't mean to pry with that question. Let me rephrase...."

➤ "Please know that anything you say will be kept confidential."

➤ "Thank you for your feedback so far. I know these topics may be difficult to talk about, but your feedback will help us understand how to make the product better for you and others like you."

What not to do or say

➤ Don't ignore signs of the participant's agitation or discomfort! Even if it means having to adjust your planned tasks or questions, be empathetic toward the participant and do your best to make her more comfortable.

How to avoid

➤ Both during the recruiting process and at the beginning of the session, set appropriate expectations regarding the type of topics that will be covered during the session, especially if any of your topics are personal. This advanced warning should reduce a participant's surprise at your questions.

See also

➤ 8.3 Participant looks or sounds uncomfortable and/or nervous

11.3 Participant insists that she would never do something

When you ask the participant to show you how she does something or to complete a task, she tells you that it's not something she would ever do. Or, she tells you that the task doesn't fit into her current role or responsibilities.

Method(s): Usability study; Contextual inquiry
Frequency: Occasional
Pattern(s) to apply: Clarify the task/question

What to do

While this is similar to a participant who can't or won't do something that was a key condition of the recruit (see section 4.2), this participant does match your recruiting criteria.

➤ Take advantage of this opportunity to learn more about why this falls outside of what the participant does or would expect to do. You might learn something that will be incredibly valuable for your team about their users, especially if this task is a key component of the product. Ask her to clarify (and demonstrate if possible) her current involvement in the task or process. What are the steps that she takes, and the tools she uses? If the person who normally does the task isn't there, what would she do?

➤ In a contextual inquiry, if you need feedback specifically on this task or process, ask the participant if she can point you toward the person who actually does the task that you're interested in, and see if you can schedule time with that person. You may be able to adjust your study plan to get some other relevant information from the participant—especially since site visits can be tricky to coordinate—but even if you can't, be sure to provide her with the promised compensation!

➤ In a usability study:

■ Explain that while you understand that this task may not be something she does today, you'd still like her to attempt it so you can get feedback on the interface from the perspective of a new user.

■ If the participant pushes back (e.g., because she is more senior or more junior than the person who typically does this task), let her know that you understand, but her feedback would still be useful in making the product better by helping you understand what type of issues a new user may experience.

■ If she continues to push back or becomes obstinate about continuing, go ahead and skip to the next task. If time permits after you finish the rest of your study plan, you can ask the participant if she'd be willing to return to this task/process so you can get some feedback.

11.3 Participant insists that she would never do something (cont.)

What to say

➤ "Are you involved at all in *<task/process>*? If so, can you talk me through what you do, and what tools you use? Feel free to pull up any tools that you use as part of the process."

➤ "I understand that you don't typically do this. However, for the sake of today's study, I'd like you to play the role of someone who does *<task/process>* so we can understand what the experience would be like for a new user."

➤ "Okay, in that case, let's move on to our next task...."

What not to do or say

➤ Don't move on to another task right away. Take advantage of the moment to understand more about the participant's role, and how the task/process gets performed (and by whom).

➤ Don't push too hard if the participant is unwilling to play the role of a new user. Some participants have a harder time than others playing a role, and there may be political situations affecting her willingness to attempt this.

How to avoid

➤ During your recruit, ensure that your criteria are detailed enough about the responsibilities and roles participants must have, especially for your key tasks (see section 15.1 for more on this). Also, reinforce these criteria in your communications with scheduled participants so they know what kind of responsibilities you're expecting them to have. It's better to discover a mismatch between user types and tasks before you begin a research study!

See also

➤ 4.1 Participant does not seem to meet a key recruit criteria

➤ 4.2 Participant either refuses to or can't do a key task

11.4 Participant is frustrated by the prototype's limited functionality

The participant is using a prototype that isn't completely built out. As she tries to complete tasks, you have to let her know over and over again that the functionality she's trying to use isn't working. She's getting annoyed by this and may even make snarky comments like, "Oh, I bet this isn't working either," or "You ask me to give you feedback but the thing isn't even working. How am I supposed to comment on it?"

Method(s): Usability study
Frequency: Occasional
Pattern(s) to apply: Redirect the participant; Reassure the participant

What to do

➤ Refer back to what you told the participant in your briefing about her interacting with a prototype that has limited functionality instead of a finished product. Acknowledge that these limitations may be frustrating, especially if there are sections that she's really interested in seeing or being able to provide feedback for. Gather her expectations for those missing areas; even if it's outside the scope of your research, it will help the participant feel appreciated and may help reduce her frustration.

➤ If the participant seems concerned that the missing or broken functionality indicates quality concerns with the product, reassure her that the prototype is not the same as the finished product. The prototype is just showing a limited set of features so you can get feedback on those specific areas.

➤ Let the participant know that it's helpful for you to see where she is trying to go, even though the functionality isn't available. Emphasize that knowing her expectations for how an area of the prototype works is useful and ask for her to go into detail about how she would want those specific areas to behave.

➤ Be patient with the participant, even if she has complained about the lack of functionality multiple times. Use an appreciative, sincere tone.

What to say

➤ "I'm sorry that we couldn't get everything built out in this prototype for today. But your expectations for how it *should* work are important too. Knowing where you expect things to be and what you'd expect to see if those areas *were* working is very useful for us."

➤ "As you can see, not too much is working in the prototype today. But thank you for being patient and just keep showing me where you'd go for these tasks and describing your expectations."

11.4 Participant is frustrated by the prototype's limited functionality (cont.)

What not to do or say

➤ As much as you may want to snap back at the participant, don't! At the end of the day, the participant is "always right" and you need to try to diffuse any negative feelings she's having toward the study setup.

How to avoid

➤ Make your prototype as functional as possible given your available time and resources. For more discussion about how to build successful prototypes, see section 15.3.

➤ Set clear expectations with the participant at the beginning of the session about what she'll be using. A participant who is expecting a fully functional product may be horrified by a medium fidelity prototype with what she perceives as "broken" functionality. Reinforce those expectations when a participant tries to do something that isn't supported by the prototype by quickly acknowledging that the area isn't built out right now, but you'd like to hear what she expects to see/happen. By being proactive and redirecting her energy, you can limit the time that a participant spends wondering if the prototype is broken.

See also

➤ 11.8 Participant becomes agitated by a product's usability issues

11.5 Participant seems annoyed at your neutrality

The participant asks you tons of questions throughout the session, which you've responded to by deflecting the questions back to her and asking for her expectations. She seems to be getting more and more annoyed by your deflections and may even become snarky. For example, she might say, "You're not going to tell me, are you?"

Method(s): Usability study
Frequency: Occasional
Pattern(s) to apply: Take responsibility; Reassure the participant; Build engagement

What to do

This annoyance typically happens with first-time usability participants who may not understand the reasoning behind your moderating approach. Participants may feel annoyed, perhaps because they're genuinely looking for answers or help and aren't getting any. Or they may feel patronized or challenged by what they perceive as you avoiding their questions.

➤ Acknowledge the participant's frustration and the artificiality of the situation with a friendly and understanding tone.

➤ The next time you're asked a question:

■ Consider your words carefully before answering instead of immediately turning it around with "What do you think?" or "What were you expecting?"

■ With each question, subtly change the way you respond. For example, one time ask, "So —I'll turn that around on you again. What are you thinking?" and another time ask, "Tell me what you're expecting?" If you're not confident in your ability to rephrase on-the-fly, write down some responses ahead of time in your study plan that are similar in meaning but use different words.

■ Use paralanguage such as intonation to show that you're genuinely interested in an answer. If you're comfortable, you can use a bit of humor in your response. For example, "I know I sound like a broken record here! I really do want to understand your expectations though."

➤ If the participant is really annoyed, do one or both of the following things:

■ Reassure the participant that it's really valuable for you to hear her questions. Remind her that if she was attempting these tasks on her own you wouldn't be sitting next to her, so you'd like to see what she would do if you weren't there.

11.5 Participant seems annoyed at your neutrality (cont.)

■ Take responsibility by apologizing once for your constant neutral responses. Avoid apologizing more than once though, as that may create awkwardness and potentially bias the participant's feedback.

What to say

➤ "The feedback you're giving is really valuable for our team. We need to know what questions people will have when they try to use this, so the product can do a better job of providing those answers."

➤ "I know it's odd to have me keep turning the question around on you, but I really want to play a neutral role here and just understand your expectations. Thanks for being patient with me."

➤ "If you were doing this on your own and I wasn't sitting next to you, what would you do?"

What not to do or say

➤ Don't be defensive about being neutral, or apologize more than once for your responses.

How to avoid

➤ At the beginning of the session, set the expectation that you may not be able to answer questions during the session and that you may turn any questions back on the participant to gauge her expectations. Stress that even if you do so, you're genuinely interested in hearing her ongoing feedback and any questions she'd have while using the product.

See also

➤ 11.6 Participant does not seem to respect you or take you seriously
➤ 11.7 Participant becomes insulting or has an agenda

11.6 Participant does not seem to respect you or take you seriously

The participant does not seem to take you seriously. She seems to think that you're really young or inexperienced, old and out of touch, or are operating at a different (lower) level than she is. Participants who have a lot of authority in their jobs (e.g., doctors, high–net worth investors, executives) sometimes act this way, especially if they feel like the session may be a waste of their time. Their feelings may come across as condescension (e.g., "You wouldn't know the kind of things I have to go through") or rudeness (e.g., "You probably weren't even alive then").

Method(s): Any
Frequency: Rare
Pattern(s) to apply: Redirect the participant; Build engagement

What to do

➤ Be unfailingly polite. You can think of it as a challenge to get the participant to leave the session with a newfound respect (or at least a grudging acceptance) for you!

➤ If the participant pointedly asks you how old you are, or for any other personal information about yourself, try to avoid directly answering the question. For example, if she asks how old you are, you can say that you'd rather not answer and quickly redirect to another topic. Providing personal information shifts the balance of the session away from your control and may take the participant further off topic. However, if you do not answer the question it may be perceived as rude, so you should provide a quick answer followed immediately by a redirect back to the task or question at hand. If you're comfortable, you can also try using light humor. For example, if the participant asks what year you were born in, you can say, "I'm a baby boomer but that's neither here nor there! Can you tell me more about.…"

➤ Consider playing up the role that the participant seems to have cast you in by asking the participant to help explain things to you. For example, if the participant seems to think that you're too young or inexperienced to understand the kind of issues she's facing with retirement, respond immediately by asking her to tell you more about her situation and the challenges she's facing. This approach has the added advantage of flattering her ego, and may help her "buy in" to the session.

What to say

➤ "I'd rather not answer that question right now, but I would like you to tell me more about.…"

➤ "You alluded to some of the factors that you'd consider important when making this decision. Tell me more about those factors and how they would influence the choice you'd make."

➤ "It's really important for us to get the perspective from someone with your experience and expertise, so we're really grateful you found the time to come in. We want to make sure that this product will be designed to meet your needs."

What not to do or say

➤ Don't feel obliged to share personal information with the participant.

How to avoid

➤ Establish your credentials and your role at the beginning of the session. Let the participant know that you're a neutral observer, not a subject-matter expert.

➤ Treat the participant with respect by using her title (e.g., Dr. Smith) until she tells you otherwise.

➤ If the participant has a high-level role or a lot of authority in her job, acknowledge that the role she plays in her organization is a critical one so you'll make good use of her time.

See also

➤ 11.7 Participant becomes insulting or has an agenda

➤ Survival Story: "I would have trusted my gut"

11.7 Participant becomes insulting or has an agenda

During the session, the participant says something insulting or disparaging that's directed toward you, your stakeholders, or your organization. If the comment is directed toward your organization, she may be venting based on experiences she's had outside of the session. She may have come to the session with an agenda or to nurse a grudge, and wants to make sure her opinion gets heard. This kind of behavior can happen both with an organization's internal employees and its customers.

Method(s): Any
Frequency: Rare
Pattern(s) to use: Redirect the participant; Take a break; End the session early

What to do

➤ If the participant seems to be venting about your stakeholders or your organization, provide her with a focused outlet for her venting. For example, you can acknowledge that she seems to be upset about bad experiences she's had, and suggest taking the next few minutes to have her share what happened and then proceed with the rest of the session.

➤ If the participant insults you directly (e.g., "You're really bad at this"), take a moment before responding. You may be in shock but need to carefully think through your next step so you avoid escalating the situation. Try to either ignore the comment and move on without acknowledging it, or place that topic out of scope (e.g., "That's not relevant to our session today") before quickly moving on to another area of discussion.

➤ Try your best to not react, and maintain a neutral expression and tone. This may be difficult to do, especially if you feel personally attacked, but do your best. Take a deep breath, control your face, and imagine the participant's comments rolling off of you like water on a duck's back—don't let them stick.

➤ Take a short break if necessary so you can recover and maintain neutrality in front of the participant. Use the break to consider your options for what you can do to improve the session once you resume.

➤ If the participant's insult was in the context of what you're doing for the study (e.g., a derogatory remark when you ask her to use a website she strongly dislikes), clarify your role and responsibilities as a neutral observer and what your expectations are for what she'll be doing. Apologize for any misunderstandings and ask if she has any more questions about how the session will work.

➤ If the participant's comment seemed sparked by what you were asking her to do or talk about (e.g., "Only an idiot would even try to do that"), change the topic of conversation or redirect the participant to the next task or section of your study plan.

11.7 Participant becomes insulting or has an agenda (cont.)

➤ If the participant continues to be insulting or disparaging toward you or becomes confrontational, end the session early and pay her any promised compensation. Remember that you need to look out for your emotional well-being and that additional data point you'd gain by sticking with the session is not worth it.

What to say

For a venting participant:

➤ "You keep alluding to some really bad experiences with *<organization>*. Why don't we take the next few minutes for you to share your experiences? However, after about five minutes, we need to get back to my list of questions. Does that sound okay?"

➤ "Thank you for sharing that experience. Part of why this research is being performed is to help improve what users go through, so your feedback will hopefully keep others from going through bad experiences. So, let me ask you *<return to your study plan>*."

For a participant who deliberately insults you:

➤ "This topic is not relevant to our session today. Let's go back to our questions/tasks, unless you'd like to take a short break first?"

To redirect a participant:

➤ "I'd like to bring your attention now to *<next task or question>*."

What not to do or say

➤ Don't get pulled into the participant's agenda.

➤ Don't insult or get into an argument with the participant, even if you really want to! Remember to stay professional.

➤ If the participant insulted a group of people who you strongly identify with, don't bring up yourself as a counterpoint to whatever the participant said.

How to avoid

➤ Be upfront with participants about the purpose of the session. This may not filter out everyone who has an agenda, but may reduce the odds.

➤ Pay attention to the participant's emotional state throughout the session and diffuse any earlier discomfort before it escalates to insults or disparagement.

See also

➤ 10.2 Participant consistently focuses on irrelevant details

➤ 11.6 Participant does not seem to respect you or take you seriously

➤ 13.1 Participant curses or makes inappropriate comments

➤ 13.3 Participant knows an unexpected amount about you

11.8 Participant becomes agitated by a product's usability issues

The participant seems really upset by the product she's using. She may be frustrated at not being able to figure out how to accomplish a task or answer a question, and takes that anger out on the product or the people who created the product. While some agitation makes for powerful video clips, an extended period of anger ceases to be productive and could derail the session.

Method(s): Usability study; Contextual inquiry
Frequency: Rare
Pattern(s) to apply: Take responsibility; Redirect the participant; Take a break

What to do

➤ Maintain a calm, neutral demeanor, even if you're startled or nervous about the participant's agitation. Keep the tone of your voice neutral and calm, and avoid any sudden shifts in body language. Avoid anything that might increase the level of agitation.

➤ Acknowledge the participant's frustration, and thank her for sharing her feedback. Slowly adjust your position to angle toward her and make eye contact. Reassure her that even though you know she's irritated, it's helpful to hear about these issues so the product can be improved.

➤ Redirect her away from whatever is causing the extreme agitation. For example, if she's frustrated because she can't figure out how to accomplish a task, follow the recommendations in section 6.4 on giving the participant an assist to help her continue, or just move on to the next task/question that covers a different area of the product.

➤ If the participant continues to be agitated, take a short break so she has a chance to calm down. When you resume the session, move on to a task/question that covers a different area of the product.

What to say

➤ "It's really helpful for us to hear what areas are confusing or frustrating so they can be improved in future versions. So, we really appreciate you going through all this with us!"

➤ "Thank you for your feedback so far. Let's take a quick five-minute break so I can see if any of our observers have any questions for you."

What not to do or say

➤ Don't be impatient toward the participant or defensive about the product. Remember that the goal of your research is to understand a product's usability issues, which is exactly what the participant has discovered.

11.8 Participant becomes agitated by a product's usability issues (cont.)

How to avoid

➤ At the beginning of the session, tell the participant that if she finds anything confusing or frustrating, you want to hear about it so the product can be improved so others don't experience the same issues. Making sure the participant feels that she has permission to share her frustrations may reduce any agitation she feels later in the session.

See also

➤ 10.8 Participant struggles excessively with a task
➤ 11.4 Participant is frustrated by the prototype's limited functionality

SURVIVAL STORY: "I WOULD HAVE TRUSTED MY GUT"
CHRISTINA YORK

The first time I had an unqualified participant slip through our screener, I was pretty green. I was conducting in-person usability studies in our lab. The participants would meet us at our office and do the usability assessment in a little lab we had set up in an empty office. I was both moderator and notetaker, with only an audio recorder as backup.

The participant criteria were pretty specific. Participants did not have to be familiar with our product, but they did have to have at least one semester of college under their belt and be currently enrolled in a degree program.

The moment Bobby entered the room, I had a gut feeling he had fooled our screener. He walked in with way too much confidence but wouldn't look me in the eye. He had no paraphernalia that screamed, "I'm a student!"—no book bag, no computer, no notebook, no college colors, no case of acne. I didn't know enough to trust my gut instinct and find out if he really was a student, so I pushed on with the session. When I asked him what browser he usually used, he deflected easily: "Oh, any old browse [*sic*] you got." That is when I knew I was in trouble.

Bobby had difficulty with the tasks. He would ignore what I was asking him to do and dive into the website, gesturing with his hands at the screen, erratically moving the mouse (sometimes in midair), and all the while explaining why our website wasn't working. He took on the attitude of teacher, and started explaining to me how search works, or "how to use your computer to read books on." He confidently talked over any errors he was making or any confusion he had. He even explained to me how the mouse needed to be redesigned for "real people." I tried desperately to glean some insight into his behavior and prompted him with questions like, "Tell me what it is about the mouse that makes completing this task difficult." I didn't know what to do. I took notes, I asked questions, I thanked him, and I paid him.

Knowing what I know now, I would have trusted my gut and ended the session before it began. I've learned that you can't rely completely on any screener, and that confirming participant qualifications is necessary. I've also learned to have a retrospective on every study I conduct and examine my discomfort from situations like this so that I can plan how to handle future discomfort. Also, from that session on, I arranged for a "backup"—a person working nearby who will come into the lab to assist upon receiving my signal. That way, I would never feel like I was "on my own" conducting one-on-one research.

CHAPTER

A Delicate Touch:
Addressing Sensitive Situations

Sensitive situations involve matters that are personal, embarrassing, or emotional. These complexities mean that you need to be especially delicate with your approach to avoid making matters worse. These situations challenge both your empathy and your ability to tactfully and gracefully respond. Consider these a true test of your interpersonal skills.

12.1 Participant is extremely entertaining and friendly

> The participant seems to be enjoying both the session and your companionship. He may be trying to make you laugh or making casual side conversation. These efforts keep distracting him from what you're asking him to accomplish. You may find yourself distracted as well by how much fun you're having, or catch yourself starting to respond to his friendly conversation.

Method(s): Any
Frequency: Frequent
Pattern(s) to apply: Redirect the participant; Disengage from the participant; Take a break

What to do

➤ Remember that you're in a research situation, not a coffee shop! While you want to be a kind host and make the participant feel at ease, it can be a slippery slope from friendly banter to some other situations listed in this book—like a participant flirting with you, or starting to ask for your opinion. Plus, that constant friendly conversation can distract the participant from approaching his workflow in a natural way, which leads to potential biases in your results.

➤ Adapt your moderating style to help establish a more formal tone for the session. If you're being too friendly with your words, tone, and body language, try to disengage from the participant and move toward more of a Down to Business style (as discussed in section 1.5). Make slightly less eye contact, avoid laughing or smiling too much, and consciously try to listen instead of responding conversationally.

➤ As part of disengaging from the participant, consider changing where you moderate from. If you're running a usability study or contextual inquiry, and are sitting beside the participant, try moving slightly behind him so that it's harder for him to turn around and look at you. Or if you're in a lab with a separate control room that has a microphone, consider moderating from that room instead.

➤ Try to stick closely to your study plan, and use gentle redirection to more questions or tasks when the participant attempts to be friendly.

What to say

➤ "That sounds like an interesting story! I don't want to get us off task, though, so why don't we move on to...."

➤ "I'd like to hear more about that later. Let's go back to the point you made earlier here...."

➤ "I'm just going to scoot my chair behind you so that I can watch what you're doing."

12.1 Participant is extremely entertaining and friendly (cont.)

➤ "For the next few tasks, I'm going to run next door and facilitate from there so I don't distract you. I'll have a microphone so I can talk to you, and I will be able to hear you and see what you're doing."

What not to do or say

➤ Don't change your demeanor too abruptly, as this may make the participant uncomfortable. Try subtle changes instead. For example, don't change your tone and move your chair behind the participant at the same time—do one first, followed by the other a few minutes later.

➤ Don't be rude about redirecting the participant back to the task/questions. If it comes naturally to you, sometimes some gentle humor may help. For example, "I'm having a great time here but we'll never get anything done if we keep talking! I'm going to go into serious mode now so that we can stay focused."

How to avoid

➤ If you're not paying attention, it can feel like this situation sneaks up on you. So, if you get any indication that your participant is very friendly upon meeting him, start the session with a more serious, formal style to minimize the chances of having to adapt later.

See also

➤ 12.4 Participant tells you something personal

➤ 13.2 You know the participant, or the participant knows you

➤ 13.4 Participant flirts with you

12.2 Something personal, inappropriate, or confidential is visible

During a remote user research session, the participant is sharing his screen with you. He has acclimated so well to this setup that he forgets that others are watching, and begins doing something unrelated to your research (e.g., checking Facebook, typing in a chat window, responding to email) while you're watching. The session is being recorded and there are observers watching. In the worst-case situations, the information that the participant is unwittingly sharing is negative in some way toward you and your research, is inappropriate (e.g., lewd wallpaper), or confidential (e.g., a manager's list of employees and their salaries).

Method(s): Any remote method
Frequency: Frequent
Pattern(s) to apply: Take responsibility; Shift the focus

What to do

➤ For material that is mildly embarrassing but not confidential (e.g., a chat window or a browser window open to a nonwork-related website), ask the participant to hide or close out of anything that he doesn't want a wider audience to see. This subtle reminder is usually enough for the participant to realize what he's doing and close out of the problematic windows. Keep in mind that the participant will probably feel fairly embarrassed by the situation once he realizes what has happened, so don't draw any unnecessary attention to it.

➤ If the participant ignores your subtle reminder, be more explicit about what you're seeing without specifying the content. For example, you might say, "It looks like your email application is open. Could you close it to make sure we don't see anything we're not supposed to?"

➤ If you see material that's confidential (e.g., employee salary information or SSNs):

  ■ Consider immediately overriding the screen-sharing session to force him to stop sharing, or to eject him from the meeting (if your screen-sharing tool has that capability). Then, ask the participant to make sure that he closes anything on his computer that he doesn't want a wider audience to see. Once he has verified that he has done this, you can restart the screen sharing.

  ■ If you don't have the ability to override screen sharing, immediately ask the participant to close the window with the confidential information. Let the participant know how he can stop sharing his screen if you think he might need a few extra seconds to deal with the offending material.

➤ If, despite your reminders, the participant continues to share windows that he shouldn't, consider blaming technical difficulties with the screen sharing and then refocusing the research into an interview or other form of research that doesn't require screen sharing. If you have a way to easily continue the session without having the participant share his screen (e.g., by sharing your screen instead and giving the participant control of your applications), continue with the session that way.

➤ Any time you remind the participant to close out of sensitive materials, try to do so in a way that isn't scolding or embarrassing. Take the responsibility for not being clear enough about these precautions earlier in the session and remind him that it's for his own privacy.

➤ Remind your observers about maintaining participant confidentiality. Ask them not to laugh or discuss what they've seen with other observers or anyone outside of the test.

What to say

➤ "*<Participant>*, I just want to remind you that your screen is currently being shared, so please make sure you've closed anything you don't want us to see. Can I bring your attention back to…?"

➤ "Before we continue, would you mind closing the other applications and windows that are open on your computer (that aren't relevant to *<task/research>*)? Since you're sharing your screen, I want to be sensitive of your privacy and make sure you're only sharing what you intend to share with us. If you need a moment to close things that you don't want us to see, you can click Stop Sharing, and then Start Sharing again when you're ready."

➤ "*<Participant>*, I'm just going to stop the sharing for a second. Bear with me. I stopped the sharing because I noticed that there was potentially personal information on your screen. I should have warned you beforehand, sorry. We respect your privacy so I'll ask you to close or hide anything you wouldn't want a wider audience to see."

To refocus the research:

➤ "I'm sorry to have you start sharing and then stop it abruptly. What we're going to do now is switch modes slightly. I'm going to start by asking you some questions."

To observers:

➤ "I know this could make for a good story, but we take participant confidentiality and comfort seriously. So I'll ask you to try not to make fun of the participant or discuss what you saw, either in or outside of this room. Thanks for understanding."

What not to do or say

➤ Don't blame or accuse the participant of anything based on what you saw. It's best to pretend as if nothing happened.

➤ Don't come across as condescending or judgmental based on what you see. For example, if the participant has computer wallpaper that you would consider not safe for work, ask him to hide anything he doesn't want everyone to see, or if he needs more direction, ask him to change his wallpaper to something less distracting. Use directives more than descriptions—for example, don't say "your wallpaper is inappropriate."

12.2 Something personal, inappropriate, or confidential is visible (cont.)

➤ Avoid being snide. Even though your feelings may be hurt by a participant's lack of attention to your study goals, move past it and work on getting the participant back into the session.

How to avoid

➤ Before you have the participant share his screen, remind him that the session will be recorded and/or observed by others. Ask him to close or hide anything that he wouldn't want a wider audience to see.

➤ Explore your screen-sharing tool's capabilities so you know what options are available to you in case you need to stop a participant from sharing, or eject him (or an observer) from a meeting.

 Watch Video 3 to see an example of a moderator interacting with a distracted participant during a remote usability study. The participant ends up sharing more than she intends.

Visit our website (http://www.modsurvivalguide.org/videos) or use your QR reader to scan this code.

See also

➤ 11.1 Remote participant is obviously distracted

➤ 12.6 You have to point out something potentially embarrassing

➤ 14.8 Participant's environment contains dangerous items

12.3 Participant is obviously distracted by external circumstances

The participant seems to be frazzled or annoyed by something outside of the session. It may be something small scale that's distracting him (e.g., he has a lot to do today or couldn't find parking at your location) or something on a much larger scale (e.g., he just got into a car accident).

Method(s): Any
Frequency: Occasional
Pattern(s) to apply: Take responsibility; Clarify the task/question; Reassure the participant; Take a break; End the session early

What to do

It's not always easy to know why a participant seems distracted. Sometimes a participant will tell you outright the reason for his frazzled state (e.g., "Ugh, I need to wind down. I just got a huge speeding ticket!") while other times you might need to probe gently for a little more information so you can respond appropriately.

➤ If a participant is honest about why he's distracted, make a judgment call based on the severity of the issue. Once again we emphasize that comfort is your first priority.

➤ If something very big happened (e.g., he got into an accident, a family member is ill, he seems upset about something personal, etc.), offer him the compensation and let him leave to take care of the situation.

➤ If he insists on moving forward with the session, take a short break so he has a chance to cool off, and then start with the session. However, monitor him closely and plan to end early, especially if he still seems distraught. It's unethical to put a participant through an entire session when he's obviously in emotional distress.

➤ If the cause is on a smaller scale (e.g., he ran full speed to be there on time, he just came from a stressful meeting, etc.), offer to take a quick break before starting the session. If he refuses but obviously would benefit from a couple extra minutes, consider taking it into your own hands and tell him that you could use more time to get set up anyway. Offer him a beverage and a comfortable place to relax, away from observers. Let him unwind so that when he starts the session, he is ready to listen and concentrate.

➤ Once the participant starts the session, you might need to speak more slowly and deliberately so that he can absorb your information and questions. Reiterate or reword questions if it seems like he's not giving you undivided attention.

12.3 Participant is obviously distracted by external circumstances (cont.)

What to say

Before the session:

➤ "I'm sorry to hear that. If you aren't feeling up to the session, I completely understand and *<we can reschedule/you can leave if you need to>*."

➤ "It seems like you have a lot going on. We're not in an immediate rush. How about I get set up and you take about 5 or 10 minutes to relax? Would you like a beverage?"

➤ "I could actually use more time to set up, so why don't you take a few minutes to relax and get settled, and I'll be with you in a bit."

During the session:

➤ "I just wanted to check in quickly and make sure you're doing alright and are okay proceeding with the session? Remember that you can take a break or leave at any time."

What not to do or say

➤ Try not to invade a participant's privacy. Even if the participant tells you something of a personal nature, do not follow up with more detailed questions about his personal life. Respect his privacy and focus on getting information you need to decide whether and how to move forward.

How to avoid

➤ Just like we can't avoid distracting situations in our own life, we can't expect participants to avoid them in theirs.

Watch Video 2 to see an example of a moderator working with a participant who is distracted by external circumstances during a usability study. The participant is reluctant to leave the session early even though he is distracted and has trouble focusing.

Visit our website (http://www.modsurvivalguide.org/videos) or use your QR reader to scan this code.

See also

➤ 11.1 Remote participant is obviously distracted
➤ 12.4 Participant tells you something personal
➤ 12.7 Participant seems upset
➤ Survival Story: "She was so appreciative" in Chapter 6

12.4 Participant tells you something personal

The participant tells you something personal about himself or his situation. Maybe he apologizes for seeming distracted and lets you know that he's going through a very bitter divorce. Or, he starts telling you about his spouse's recent health problems and seems on the verge of tears. The information that the participant shares may be something that needs to be kept confidential, such as his social security number and personal financial details.

Method(s): Any
Frequency: Occasional
Pattern(s) to apply: Redirect the participant; Reassure the participant; Take a break

What to do

We've all experienced times when a participant shares personal information. Sometimes the participant is sharing because he knows that he's emotional and wants to give you a heads up in case something comes up later in the session. For example, "Sorry I'm not that focused. My mother died last week." Other times it comes up unexpectedly as an answer to one of your standard questions. Or, you may be starting the session with the expectation of hearing a participant's personal stories because a sensitive subject matter is the focus of your research.

➤ If the participant is unnecessarily giving away personal information such as financial information because he thinks it's necessary for the study (e.g., while interacting with a financial application), ask him immediately not to share any personal data. Go back to the notes and recording and make sure that any of that information is deleted or masked.

➤ If you're performing research in a sensitive subject area, you should be expecting to hear a participant's personal stories. Remember to remain empathetic as he answers your questions, and be sensitive if you probe on his answers or ask follow-up questions. Thank him sincerely for his feedback.

➤ If the feedback provided by the participant affects you deeply on a personal level (e.g., because you've had similar experiences), remember to keep the focus on the participant instead of sharing your story. You want the participant to feel safe and respected, and interjecting your experiences takes the focus away from the importance of his feedback.

➤ If the participant starts telling you a personal story that seems to be affecting him emotionally, let him finish the story, and then gently redirect him to the task at hand. For example, if you asked a participant to tell you how long ago he opened a checking account and he responds with a story about how he and his late wife chose it together, listen to him respectfully until he finishes the story. Thank him for his answer, and ask if he's okay continuing to the next section or if he'd like to take a short break.

12.4 Participant tells you something personal (cont.)

➤ Sometimes life just gets in the way, and a participant becomes distracted or upset over a personal situation. Handling this is a fine balance between comforting the participant and hijacking the session to listen to his issues. In these cases, start by taking a short break. Walk the participant out of the observed/recorded study area to see if he is okay and give him time to recover.

➤ If the participant is telling you something personal but doesn't seem emotionally fragile about it, consider its context and whether it becomes a recurring problem. For example, a participant may respond, "I watch a lot of pornography" in response to being asked about website usage. Although it is likely considered socially taboo, the participant was just answering a question and it was the only comment he made that was too much information (TMI!). In those cases, try not to react and just continue with the session. If, instead, the participant starts telling a longer personal story or goes into excessive amounts of detail, consider reminding him that he's being recorded or observed and redirect him back to the topic being discussed.

What to say

➤ "*<Participant>*, please use fake information rather than your own here. We want to respect your privacy."

In response to a personal comment where the participant does not seem emotionally affected:
➤ "Okay. Let's move on to…" or "Let me ask you about.…"

In response to a longer personal answer where the participant is emotionally affected:
➤ "Okay, thank you for that. Are you okay continuing to the next *<task/question>*?"

In response to a longer personal answer where the participant does not seem emotionally affected:
➤ "I'm sorry to interrupt. I just want to remind you that we're recording the session and there may be people listening in, so let's stay focused on the original topic. Unless there's anything else that you want us to know, let's move onto.…"
➤ "Why don't we take a little break and step outside for a couple of minutes."
➤ *(In private):* "I don't want you to continue the session if you're feeling uncomfortable. Why don't we end the session for today?"

What not to do or say

➤ Don't ignore any signs of emotional distress from the participant.
➤ Even if you're intrigued, avoid expressing interest in any stories that involve very personal information unless the story is relevant to your research goals. The participant may take your interest as license to overshare more and it may be harder to pull him back to your scripted questions.

12.4 Participant tells you something personal (cont.)

How to avoid

➤ For research involving sensitive topics, such as using a website about cancer, consider whether you need to recruit participants who have firsthand experience with the topic. In some cases it may make sense to do so, but in others you may want to actively screen out participants who are likely to experience distress because of the subject matter (e.g., family members of someone who has died of cancer).

See also

➤ 12.1 Participant is extremely entertaining and friendly
➤ 12.3 Participant is obviously distracted by external circumstances

12.5 Participant has a disconcerting or distracting physical attribute

The participant has some type of physical attribute that you find distracting or disconcerting. Many of these attributes may be relatively unconscious or uncontrollable (e.g., a participant who is sweating heavily, blinks constantly, or has a large birthmark). Or, the attribute may be a bad habit that you find disgusting or unsanitary (e.g., an intense nose picker).

Method(s): Any in-person method
Frequency: Occasional
Pattern(s) to apply: Take a break

What to do

➤ If the participant has a physical attribute that you find distracting (e.g., a birthmark or a very large mole), avoid staring at it. Remember to make eye contact with him!

➤ For a participant who is exhibiting a behavior such as sweating or nose picking, offer him something to alleviate his condition without calling direct attention to what he's doing. For example, if your participant is picking his nose, offer him a tissue. If you feel awkward doing even that, try taking a tissue yourself and using it to blow your nose. People tend to sometimes mirror behavior in those types of situations. If your participant is sweating heavily, ask him if the room is a comfortable temperature—if he says that he's warm, offer to open the door or lower the thermostat (if possible), and get him some water to drink.

➤ The participant may give you a reason for his attribute (e.g., he may have a medical condition, or a female participant may say she's experiencing hot flashes). When the participant gives you this information, maintain a neutral expression and tone, and offer to accommodate him however you're able.

➤ For behavior that you find unsanitary or distracting that continues throughout the session, do your best to avoid watching. If you become very uncomfortable by it, end the session early using a pretext such as technical difficulties.

➤ If the participant seems uncomfortable, even after you've done your best to accommodate him, take a break to see if that helps. If the break doesn't help, and the participant still seems too uncomfortable to provide useful feedback, gently end the session early.

What to say

➤ "Would you like a tissue?"

➤ "It feels a little warm in here. How is the temperature for you? I want to make sure that you're comfortable."

A DELICATE TOUCH: ADDRESSING SENSITIVE SITUATIONS

12.5 Participant has a disconcerting or distracting physical attribute (cont.)

What not to do or say

➤ Don't call direct attention to whatever you're finding distracting about the participant.

How to avoid

➤ There is no way to avoid this. Instead, be prepared to be respectful and empathetic toward your participants, no matter what they look or act like.

See also

➤ 4.3 Participant has an unexpected physical feature

➤ 12.6 You have to point out something potentially embarrassing

12.6 You have to point out something potentially embarrassing

> You notice something that the participant is doing, or that is happening to him, that may be embarrassing, especially if he finds out about it later on his own! For example, a button may have popped off a female participant's shirt, or a participant returned from a bathroom break with unzipped pants.

> **Method(s):** Any in-person method
> **Frequency:** Rare
> **Pattern(s) to apply:** Take a break

What to do

➤ Turn off your recording equipment, and if you have any observers, bring the participant into a more private space.

➤ Once in a private space where you and the participant cannot be overheard, kindly let him know about the embarrassing situation. Then, give him a private moment to address the situation, or direct him to the nearest restroom if he may need more privacy.

➤ If the participant seems embarrassed when he returns to the session, reassure him that it's okay, and make sure he's comfortable before resuming any recording or observing.

What to say

➤ "Excuse me, *<participant>*, I'm going to stop our recording equipment for just a moment. Could I ask you to step out into the hall with me?"

Once in a private location:

➤ "I just want to let you know that *<embarrassing situation>*, so you have a chance to address it before we continue the session."

What not to do or say

➤ Avoid pointing out the embarrassing item while on camera, or in front of observers.

How to avoid

➤ While there is no way to avoid this happening, try to do a quick check of yourself and the participant before you start recording.

See also

➤ 12.2 Something personal, inappropriate, or confidential is visible

12.7 Participant seems upset

The participant seemed nervous at the beginning of the session, but now seems more upset, even on the verge of tears. You've been sensitive and have been trying to help alleviate any nervousness and make him feel comfortable, but his emotions have escalated.

Method(s): Any
Frequency: Rare
Pattern(s) to apply: Take responsibility; Reassure the participant; Take a break; End the session early

What to do

➤ Immediately stop any recording of the session and let the participant know that you're putting the session on hold. For example, "I've turned off our recording equipment—let's take a short break from these questions."

➤ If you have in-room observers, quietly ask them to leave the room.

➤ Offer the participant a tissue if you have a box available—you can do this without speaking, just by sliding the box toward him. If there is a more private room available, offer to bring the participant there.

➤ Gently ask the participant if he'd like to leave the session early. Let him know that he is under no obligation to continue, that you appreciate the feedback he has provided so far, and that he'll still receive his full compensation. If he says he wants to continue, go ahead and resume but plan to end the session early.

➤ If the participant is too upset to answer your questions and leaves the building, do not follow him. Instead, make sure that he is able to get back in the building (e.g., depending on your setup you may have to notify a security desk that he may return). If he never returns, follow up with your recruiter to find a way to provide the participant with his compensation, and also to thank him for the feedback provided.

➤ If the participant offers a reason for being upset that has to do with the session setup (e.g., he's nervous about being observed by people in another room), immediately offer to resolve those issues, and ask him if he'd be comfortable continuing if those issues are resolved. For example, you may turn off your observation equipment for that session. However, as mentioned earlier, remind the participant that he's under no obligation to continue and that if he's more comfortable leaving the session early, he's free to do so.

➤ If the participant explains that he's upset about something outside of the session (e.g., a family situation), offer to reschedule the session for a different time.

12.7 Participant seems upset (cont.)

What to say

To talk in private:

➤ "*<Participant>*, why don't we take a few minutes and step into the room next door? It's more private in there."

➤ "I've turned off our recording equipment so no one is able to see or hear us right now. Let's take a break for a few minutes."

While talking in private:

➤ "I just want to remind you that you're under no obligation to continue with the session. You've given us very helpful feedback so far, and we really appreciate it. If you'd like to leave now or at any point, you'll still receive your full compensation. Please just let me know."

➤ "I don't want you to continue the session if you're feeling upset or uncomfortable. You can stop the session at any time, so just let me know. Is there anything I can do to help make you more comfortable?"

What not to do or say

➤ Do *not* ignore the participant's emotional state!

➤ Don't touch the participant, even if you think a pat on the shoulder or a hug would provide comfort! Touching a participant violates ethical boundaries and may make the situation worse since you don't know how a stranger will react to being touched.

➤ Don't directly say, "Why are you upset?" even if you're curious. This might make the participant feel like you called him out, which can make the situation worse.

➤ Try not to have the participant make a decision about continuing the session in front of observers.

How to avoid

➤ Situations like this rarely come from nowhere. Nervous or uncomfortable participants may become more so throughout the session if their concerns are not accommodated. Be responsive and aware of your participant's emotional state throughout the session and react quickly to any signs of emotional distress. This awareness and quick action will help keep a situation from deteriorating to tears.

➤ At the beginning of the session, genuinely reassure the participant that he's not being tested. This comfort can be effective even for a participant who's distracted by external circumstances.

A DELICATE TOUCH: ADDRESSING SENSITIVE SITUATIONS

12.7 Participant seems upset (cont.)

See also

➤ 8.3 Participant looks or sounds uncomfortable and/or nervous

➤ 12.3 Participant is obviously distracted by external circumstances

➤ 12.4 Participant tells you something personal

12.8 Participant has an unexpected disability or service animal

The participant has an unexpected physical disability such as visual or auditory impairment. He may also have brought a service animal with him. Because this situation is unexpected, your facility may not be set up to accommodate this kind of participant.

Method(s): Any in-person method
Frequency: Rare
Pattern(s) to apply: Take responsibility; Shift the focus

What to do

➤ First, assess whether the participant's limitation prevents him from participating as planned. With some types of visual impairment, the user can adjust a computer monitor's settings (e.g., font size and contrast) to accommodate his level of vision. A participant with an auditory impairment will probably have brought some kind of assistive hearing device, or can read lips. However, a legally blind participant who relies on a screen reader to use a computer won't able to use a computer that doesn't have a screen reader (e.g., Jaws) or magnifier (e.g., ZoomText).

➤ If you don't feel like you can proceed as planned with the participant, decide if it's appropriate to shift the focus of the research to still gain value from the session. For example, move to an interview instead of a usability study of a prototype. This shift will be most appropriate in formative studies, but depending on your client and your research goals, it may also work for other types of research. Sometimes just going into more depth with your normal background questions can yield valuable results.

➤ If the participant hasn't brought up his limitations, but you notice him squinting at a monitor or moving closer to the screen, gently let him know that you noticed him adjusting, and ask if there's anything that you can do to make the screen easier for him to read.

➤ If your participant brought a service animal, ask if there's anything specific that you should do or not do for the animal. Most animals are well trained and will quietly sit by the participant during the session.

➤ Likewise, ask the participant if there's anything you should or shouldn't do to accommodate his needs. For example, blind participants and others with walking challenges sometimes appreciate when they're offered an arm for them to hold onto while walking, whereas others prefer to rely on their walking stick or service animal.

➤ Keep in mind that users with physical impairments are often more difficult (and expensive) to recruit, so do your best to take advantage of the situation to provide your client team with feedback that they may not get otherwise.

➤ If you're unable to proceed with the participant and have to let him go (or end the session early), be sure to provide him with his full compensation.

12.8 Participant has an unexpected disability or service animal (cont.)

What to say

➤ "I see you have a service animal with you. Is there anything that you need me to do, or not do, for your animal during our session?"

➤ "You mentioned that you have some issues with your vision. Tell me about the issues you have, and about the setup you have at home to accommodate those issues."

➤ "I noticed that you seem to be squinting at the monitor. Is there anything I can adjust on it to make it easier for you to read? Feel free to move your chair closer to the monitor as well if that helps."

➤ "I want to be accommodating and respectful of your vision. Is there anything in particular you prefer that I help with or not help with while you're here?"

What not to do or say

➤ Don't make adjustments to your setup without checking with the participant first. You would just be making assumptions about what will work for him.

➤ Likewise, do not make assumptions about what the participant will need in terms of physical assistance. You don't want to come across as patronizing or make things more difficult. Just honestly ask him what he prefers that you help and don't help with.

➤ Don't pet or try to play with a service animal. They're on duty!

How to avoid

➤ Most participants with any kind of limitation will mention it during the screening process, so you'll usually have a heads up from the recruiter. However, if the participant doesn't mention it ahead of time and still meets your recruit criteria, there's a good chance he's still part of your target audience, so anything you can do to accommodate him will yield interesting results—that is, this may not be a situation you want to avoid.

➤ If there are very specific reasons why you can't have someone with a physical limitation (e.g., an eye-tracking study), include the criteria you need in the screener. For example, for eye-tracking studies, we include in our screener a question asking if the respondent uses bifocals, trifocals, or hard contact lenses—if he does, he is ineligible to participate. We recommend running your screener by an institutional review board (IRB) to ensure that your wording is nondiscriminatory.

➤ To learn more about conducting sessions with special populations, we recommend reviewing the "Interacting with Diverse Populations" chapter in Dumas and Loring (2008).

See also

➤ 4.3 Participant has an unexpected physical feature

➤ 5.8 Participant brings a child or pet to the session

SURVIVAL STORY: "MY BEST OPTION WAS TO SMILE"
DORIENNE ROSENBERG

One of my first moderating sessions was with a participant who was very jovial and frank with her remarks toward the website we were testing. The feedback she was providing was excellent and I felt the research team as well as the client was going to be able to learn a lot from her comments. Approximately three-quarters of the way through the one-on-one session, she made a racially inappropriate and offensive joke about users of the website we were testing. I was highly uncomfortable with her comment but was concerned that if I reacted instinctively, I would lose the rapport and trust I had built up with the participant. Further concerns I had were what the client and my observing colleagues would think if I did not express discomfort toward a derogatory comment. I figured that my best option was to smile to acknowledge the participant's attempt at humor and to make her feel comfortable, but not to verbally support or oppose her opinion. The participant did not seem affected by my response as the rest of the session went very smoothly.

I question if my choice to smile gave the participant the impression that I agreed with her, and if I could have chosen a different response that would have still kept the session on track, such as changing the subject. Looking back, I realize that my choice was the right one, for if I had been open about my distaste toward that participant's joke, I could have compromised the session, lost a data point, and wasted the client's time and money. I am pleased that my choice did not create tension between myself and the participant, but realize that the cost of suppressing your beliefs can be remorseful and unpleasant.

SURVIVAL STORY: "YOU SURE ARE PRETTY"
LORIE WHITAKER

I was conducting one-on-one usability sessions on a hospital website. To ensure we were testing the right demographic, my colleague and I traveled to three different cities in Texas that served the hospital district. The first two cities went smoothly—all participants showed up and were able to attempt/complete the tasks we asked of them. However, there was one incident that I still remember to this day.

We were in Round Rock, TX, outside of Austin and it was my turn to moderate. We had set up in a conference room at our hotel, with my colleague and client in a separate room watching the session via a projector and laptop with speakers. We relied on the receptionists at the hotel to meet and greet the participants but they were in no way obligated to turn anyone away—instead, they just had to let us know when the next person arrived.

I got the notification that the next participant had arrived so I went out to greet him. The man whom I greeted was older, overweight, and had a large 44-oz. mug with him. This isn't unusual for Texas, so I didn't think anything of it. I led him back to the session room, and as he walked, it appeared to me he was a bit drunk. Turns out, I was only a little right. As he made himself comfortable and I worked my way through my introduction, he was smiling at me. This wasn't out of the ordinary. However, the session took a turn when I asked if he had any questions and he began with the "Are you single?" line of questioning. I tried to deflect it, thinking (a) it's none of your business and (b) it's not about me—it's about you, the user. But he was undeterred and continued with "You sure are pretty" and "You have a nice smile."

This wasn't the first time this happened to me in a session, but I started to wonder what he was drinking in the 44-oz. mug! He then went on to tell me, rather proudly, while leering at me that he had attended the previous night's Dallas Cowboy's football game in Dallas (three hours away) and barely made it home before he had to come to the session. At this point I thought "This isn't going well" since I couldn't get him to focus on anything but me. So, I decided to fake a technical glitch and said I had to go in the back room and check on it. While I was in the back room, I told my male colleague that he needed to go out there and dismiss him. Pay him if he wanted to, but I wasn't going back out there until the guy was gone. My colleague agreed and went to dismiss the participant. I watched from the observation room and saw the participant never questioned the validity of the technology issue and left in a jovial mood.

From this experience, I learned you run in to all sorts of people when dealing with running usability tests because you're dealing with the public. While I used a tried-and-true method of getting a difficult participant back on track, I learned that when alcohol is involved, you have to use whatever you can think of to get the session back on track. When that fails, sometimes it's best to just end the session in a manner that leaves the participant feeling that it wasn't his fault. You may ask why you wouldn't just tell this particular participant that he is drunk and can't participate. One reason is that we all have bad days. We drink a little too much, we're a bit too cranky, or we didn't get enough sleep the night before. One method that has always worked for me is to blame the technology. If you can't steer the session back on track, pretend there is a technology issue and the session can't continue. This allows the participant to feel it was not his fault and also allows you to take a chance and bring him in again, if you can or want to.

CHAPTER 13

Uncomfortable Interactions: Responding to Awkward Situations

Any situation that makes you feel uncomfortable can be considered awkward. Addressing these situations requires a delicate touch to keep the participant from feeling embarrassed or insulted by your reaction. You also need to set appropriate expectations for her behavior throughout the rest of the session.

13.1 Participant curses or makes inappropriate comments

The participant starts "cursing" constantly. Perhaps she sprinkles in some rude and discriminatory remarks and jokes. Depending on your political leanings, race, gender, sexual orientation, etc., you may feel personally offended by the salty language or inappropriate comments. In some cases the participant may look to you for affirmation that she's being funny, wanting you to laugh along or share your opinion on the topic.

Method(s): Any
Frequency: Occasional
Pattern(s) to apply: Redirect the participant; Disengage from the participant; End the session early

What to do

➤ If the participant is cursing, consider the severity and frequency of the language. If she's occasionally using a "bad" word, or frequently using less severe language (basically anything not censored on TV), try to ignore it and avoid a visible reaction. If the participant is constantly cursing in an offensive manner or using really objectionable words (the censored kind), simply ask the participant to try to keep her language clean. Be friendly but firm. You can also remind the participant that she's being recorded and/or observed.

➤ If the participant says something discriminatory (i.e., hostile toward race, religion, sexuality, gender, age, disability, etc.), consider the frequency of the comments:

■ If it happens once, ignore it and move on without acknowledging the comment even if her insult felt personal or was directed toward a group you identify with. For example, if the participant makes an aside about how incompetent women are (and you're a woman), just ignore the statement and continue with the session. Avoid placating the participant by laughing along and agreeing. If the participant is looking for an acknowledgment that you heard her, or repeats the comment to make sure, use a polite neutral smile and immediately redirect the conversation to avoid an awkward silence or continued conversation.

■ If the participant uses discriminatory language frequently and you take it very personally, or you feel some moral obligation to say something, think very carefully before responding. If the participant was next to you in the grocery store, you may be tempted to give her a talking to. But you're moderating on behalf of an organization, so it's important to stay cool and professional. Try not to bring your personal life and beliefs into the conversation. Instead, simply ask the participant to stay focused on the topic at hand and avoid any controversial statements.

➤ In conjunction with these tips, think about your body language and moderating style. If you're relaxed and friendly in disposition, now is the time to adapt to a more formal, less responsive moderating style (as discussed in section 1.5) so that the participant knows you're serious.

➤ If asking the participant to stop doesn't help, or her language is still out of control, either take a break to assess the situation with colleagues, or just end the session early. Try to do so in a way that doesn't blame the participant (e.g., use a pretext and blame a technical failure or pretend that you're done with the tasks).

What to say

If the participant is cursing and you feel comfortable using slight humor:

➤ "I just want to let you know that this is a curse-free zone!"

➤ "If you don't mind, let's just keep our words PG-13."

➤ "I like your spirit, but I'll ask you not to curse in this setting if you can help it."

If the participant is cursing, and you want to keep the tone relatively formal:

➤ "*<Participant>*, I appreciate your feedback so far, but since we're being recorded and there may be others listening in, I need to ask you to use clean language for the rest of the session. Thank you! So, let's go back to…."

If the participant is making discriminatory remarks, and you need to redirect:

➤ "Okay, so let's move onto…."

If the participant is making discriminatory remarks and you need to be more explicit:

➤ "I know I told you that you're free to give any feedback, but I'll ask that you do so in a way that is respectful to others. Thank you in advance. Now let's get back to…."

➤ "As I said earlier, we do have some observers and the session is being recorded, so I'll ask you to avoid *<cursing, using profanity, making personal statements about 'kinds of people'>* during the rest of the session."

If you need to end the session, use a pretext such as:

➤ "I'm sorry, but we're going to have to end the session early *<because of pretext, for example, due to some technical difficulties>*. Thank you so much for coming in, and here is your compensation."

What not to do or say

➤ Don't laugh in response to offensive or controversial jokes, even if you want to or feel like the participant is looking for you to respond in some way.

➤ Don't scold the participant, as it may shut her down for the rest of the session and limit the feedback you're able to elicit.

➤ Avoid providing your opinion or engaging in a discussion with the participant.

How to avoid

➤ Make sure that when recruiting, you look for any sign that a participant is especially forthcoming with inappropriate or irrelevant information, and screen her out. For example, if you're recruiting for a financial services website and the participant goes on a long political rant about the current White House administration, that participant is likely to do something similar or worse during the session!

See also

➤ 11.7 Participant becomes insulting or has an agenda

➤ 13.5 Participant does something awkward or uncomfortable

➤ Survival Story: "My best option was to smile" in Chapter 12

13.2 You know the participant, or the participant knows you

> The participant may be someone you know socially, someone you dated, or someone you know from outside of work. She may even be your friend, or someone who you've heard about through personal or professional circles but haven't actually met in person before.

Method(s): Any
Frequency: Occasional
Pattern(s) to apply: Take responsibility; Disengage from the participant

What to do

➤ Acknowledge your acquaintance with the participant and be yourself, but keep any casual conversation to a bare minimum.

➤ Whether it's an ex-partner, old friend, relative, or distant acquaintance, do your best to keep any outside knowledge of the participant out of the session unless that knowledge is related to her not meeting the study criteria.

➤ If you think you know something about the participant that disqualifies her from participating (e.g., your recruit criteria was for HR managers but you know the participant is in a different group), bring up your knowledge as a question to see if it's accurate. If it's accurate and she is not qualified, let her go or, as discussed in section 3.8, see if there's a way to adapt the session.

➤ If you're worried that you'll not be able to treat the participant neutrally (or vice versa), ask another member of your team to moderate the session for you instead, if possible. If that isn't possible, stick closely to your study plan and do your best to put aside your concerns and treat the participant just like any other.

➤ Before the session starts, let your observers know that the participant is someone you know. You don't have to go into detail about how you know the participant, but it's better to let the observers know ahead of time so they aren't surprised or worried if the participant seems like she knows you.

➤ If the participant is overly friendly with you or brings up personal details about you that you'd rather not discuss, remind her that you want to get her feedback as part of the session and that you can catch up with her once the session is over. You can also remind her that she is being observed and recorded.

What to say

➤ "It's so good to see you again. We have a lot to get through during the next *<number of minutes>*, but I'd love to hear more about how you are once we're finished here."

13.2 You know the participant, or the participant knows you (cont.)

➤ "I'm sorry, but I really want to get your feedback on *<topic>*. Let's finish catching up once we're done, if you're able to stick around for a few extra minutes."

What not to do or say

➤ Don't pretend that you don't know the participant—this may frustrate and confuse her, and keep her from providing valuable feedback.

➤ Don't use your session time to catch up with the participant. Stay professional and focused on your research goals.

How to avoid

➤ Monitor the list of participant names provided by your recruiter, and if you see anyone you recognize, plan ahead of time for someone else to moderate the session if possible.

See also

➤ 12.1 Participant is extremely entertaining and friendly

13.3 Participant knows an unexpected amount about you

You greet the participant and she says, "So, how do you like your new car?" or "I saw that you like Jazz music." Perhaps she starts name-dropping people in the organization you're representing. Or she is a remote participant who looks you up on Facebook as you're running the session and shares what she finds. Regardless, the participant clearly has a lot of personal information at her fingertips.

Method(s): Any
Frequency: Rare
Pattern(s) to apply: Redirect the participant; Disengage from the participant; End the session early

What to do

➤ Try to understand the impetus behind the participant's actions. You may need to politely ask how she knows that information. For example, perhaps she was given your name from the recruiting agency you used to schedule her and looked you up to make sure you legitimately work at the organization. If the participant mentions a relatively harmless excuse for her, shall we say, "extensive information gathering," try to ignore any weird comments and move forward with the session.

➤ If the participant starts probing you on your personal life, redirect the conversation back to the session to avoid any awkward discussions. Also use your tone and body language to disengage from the participant by shifting away slightly and using a more formal tone, while still remaining kind and professional.

➤ If the participant seems to be researching you or your colleagues while on a remote session with her, kindly ask her to stop what she's doing and focus attention on the session.

➤ If the participant is going out of her way to name-drop and possibly dig for more information on the organization or your colleagues, feign ignorance. Even if you *do* know the person she's talking about, pretend that you don't or be evasive, at least until the session is over. Use redirection to keep the participant on track.

➤ If what the participant says and how she says it moves beyond awkward into disturbing, you have every right to protect yourself and end the session early. Similarly, if the session starts out fine but over time the participant's actions, words, and/or knowledge of you is coupled with any feelings of extreme discomfort, take a brief break to regroup. At that point either have a colleague take over moderating or end the session early. If ending early, take responsibility with a pretext (e.g., blame the technical setup) so as not to tip off that you're ending the session because of the participant's actions.

13.3 Participant knows an unexpected amount about you (cont.)

What to say

If the participant knows things about you:

➤ "Oh, where did you hear that?"

➤ "Oh, yes, I love my new car *<or other short response here>*. So let's get started...."

If a remote participant is researching you during the session:

➤ "*<Participant>*, I'm impressed with your ability to multitask! If you don't mind, please close your other windows and programs so that we can stay focused on this session."

If the participant knows something about the organization you're representing:

➤ "*<I'm just a consultant/The organization is big>* so I don't actually know that person *<that well/ at all>*. So let's get back to...."

If ending the session with pretext:

➤ "I'm sorry, but we're going to have to cancel the session due to some technical difficulties. Thank you so much for coming in, and here's your compensation. Let me walk you to our exit." Or, "My colleague, *<name>*, will walk you to the door."

What not to do or say

➤ Don't reprimand the participant for looking you up, even if you're uncomfortable or irritated. Treat her in a respectful, professional way.

➤ Avoid getting into a personal conversation about your life. Save that for friends!

➤ Likewise, avoid giving out personal or professional information about colleagues.

How to avoid

➤ Check your social networking settings for LinkedIn, Facebook, and other websites to ensure that you're comfortable with the level of information displayed publicly.

➤ For a remote testing session, ask the participant at the beginning of the session to close out of all nonrelevant windows and applications so she can focus on the session.

See also

➤ 11.7 Participant becomes insulting or has an agenda

13.4 Participant flirts with you

The participant seems to be more interested in smiling at you than actually focusing on the session. She may use subtle hints like smiling and ogling, or perhaps stronger hints like asking you out on a date or propositioning you. It feels awkward or uncomfortable for you, not to mention a little embarrassing if you're being observed and recorded!

Method(s): Any
Frequency: Rare
Pattern(s) to apply: Redirect the participant; Disengage from the participant; Take a break

What to do

➤ If the flirting is subtle (e.g., smiling or ogling), just ignore it rather than acknowledging or drawing attention to the participant's behavior.

➤ If a participant becomes more and more flirtatious throughout the session, try to make your intentions of professionalism clear by redirecting attention to what is being researched, and gently pulling away physically. Adjust your body to be turned slightly away from and behind the participant, and use a neutral, formal tone. Don't give in to her flirting just to be nice or accommodating.

➤ If the situation escalates further (e.g., to direct questions or propositions), use more explicit language to redirect the participant back to your session goals. If you're comfortable using humor, you can use a firm yet humorous tone for the redirection, especially if the participant also has a joking tone. The benefit of this approach is that by responding in a similar tone, you may keep the participant from feeling embarrassed while regaining control of the session. If she continues unabated, let her know that her questions are inappropriate or not relevant to the study and you'd like to bring her attention back to the task question.

➤ If being direct doesn't help the situation, consider using another reason to end the session early, such as getting through your material faster than expected or technical difficulties. Or, if you have someone else who is able to moderate the remainder of the session, you could tell the participant that for the next section of the session, she'll be talking to that person. Leave the room and have your colleague step in and take over.

➤ If the participant revisits any of her flirtatious behavior after the session is over, kindly let her know that you're obligated to keep your relationship with participants professional and thank her again for coming in.

13.4 Participant flirts with you (cont.)

What to say

If complimented in a way that you feel compelled to respond to:

➤ "Thanks. So why don't we look at this area.…"

➤ "Okay. Let's go back to…*<task/question>*."

If you need to redirect a flirtatious participant:

➤ "If it's okay, I just want to stick to the agenda for the session because we have a lot to get through. Let me bring your attention back to.…"

If you're having a colleague take over moderating duties for the session:

➤ "Okay *<participant>*, for the next part what I'm going to do is have my colleague come in and join you. She'll be right in."

If the participant asks you out before or after the session:

➤ "It's been very nice to meet you. But I have an obligation to keep our interaction on a professional level."

What not to do or say

➤ Don't yield to flirting or give the perception that you welcome that behavior! It's important to draw the line and keep the session professional, especially if you're on a site visit at someone's home or if the participant is at your facility after hours when few people are around. Overly friendly or flirty behavior can lead to bad things—like physical danger or legal liability.

➤ Don't embarrass the participant!

How to avoid

➤ There's no easy way to avoid a flirty participant, but if you notice a participant becoming more friendly or starting to flirt, adapt your style immediately to a more disengaged (less friendly) demeanor before it escalates to a more awkward situation.

 Watch Video 4 to see an example of a moderator dealing with a flirtatious participant during a usability study. The participant starts off being friendly but becomes more forward as the session progresses.

Visit our website (http://www.modsurvivalguide.org/videos) or use your QR reader to scan this code.

UNCOMFORTABLE INTERACTIONS: RESPONDING TO AWKWARD SITUATIONS

See also

➤ 12.1 Participant is extremely entertaining and friendly

➤ 14.7 Participant touches you

➤ Survival Story: "You sure are pretty" in Chapter 12

13.5 Participant does something awkward or uncomfortable

At some point during the session, the participant says or does something that makes you uncomfortable. She may ask you to touch her pregnant stomach or if she can take her shoes off. Or maybe she lies down on a couch in the study space. These are just a few real-life examples of countless "Did that just happen?" moments we've encountered or heard about. These actions and requests are somewhat benign—not quite dangerous or crazy—but awkward and uncomfortable nonetheless.

Method(s): Any in-person method
Frequency: Rare
Pattern(s) to apply: Take responsibility

What to do

➤ If the request or action is strange but won't get in the way of the session (e.g., taking shoes off), let the participant do it to avoid any further awkward interactions about it.

➤ If it's a strangely personal request or something that would be more disruptive, politely decline. Try to place the blame on yourself, your study setup, facility, policies, or anything feasible so that the participant doesn't feel bad or stupid for asking. It may be a slight stretch of truth, but will help maintain a connection with the participant. For example, if the participant asks you to touch her pregnant stomach, tell her that there's a no-touching policy at your organization. If the participant starts showing you pictures of a celebrity with a wardrobe malfunction, remind her that the session and screen are being recorded and that there's a lot to cover in the remainder of the session.

➤ You can also use humor if you're comfortable doing so as part of your explanation. Just remember to keep it tasteful, and make sure that your humor cannot be misinterpreted as making fun of the participant. For example, if the participant lies down on the couch, you can gently say, "If this were a sleep study, I'd bring you a blanket and pillow, but for now, I actually need you to sit over here in front of the computer so we can get started!"

What to say

➤ "I'm sorry; our policy is to not let guests *<do that>*. Are you okay to move forward with the session?"

➤ "For the sake of today's study setup, I actually need you to *<describe what you need them to do>*."

➤ "I'm sorry, but we don't usually let anyone *<do that>*. Let's get back to…."

13.5 Participant does something awkward or uncomfortable (cont.)

What not to do or say

➤ Don't scold the participant or do anything to make her feel inadequate, or that would make her more nervous about participating.

➤ Don't laugh or make fun of the participant, even if her request or actions seem ridiculous to you. She may just be trying to be friendly, or is making herself comfortable.

How to avoid

➤ It's hard to see these situations coming! Approach each session with a sense of humor so you can roll with the unexpected.

See also

➤ 13.1 Participant curses or makes inappropriate comments

➤ 13.4 Participant flirts with you

➤ 13.6 Participant makes a strangely specific request

➤ Survival Story: "She tipped me … big!"

13.6 Participant makes a strangely specific request

> The participant asks you to do something that's very specific and slightly unusual. For example, as you start the session and offer a drink to the participant, she says, "Can you please get me a half-regular, half-decaf coffee with one sweetener and fat-free half-and-half?" Or you're asked to clean a participant's eye glasses, find someone to shine her shoes, call her brother, accompany her on a smoke break, or find her a pair of nail clippers.

Method(s): Any in-person method
Frequency: Rare
Pattern(s) to apply: Take responsibility

What to do

Since requests can come in all shapes and sizes, there's no one right answer for this type of situation. We just recommend using the following guidelines:

➤ Accommodate the request, if it's not time consuming, unmanageable, or demeaning. If you don't have exactly what the participant requests, ask if there are suitable substitutions. Even though coffee, water, and tea have been free for guests in many of the facilities we've used, we've had moments of grabbing our own money to get that special Diet Dr. Pepper from the vending machine to make the participant happy. Keep her comfortable as much as possible, especially when minimal effort is required.

➤ If you'd have to spend extra time accommodating her request, or you'd feel uncomfortable in any way, politely let the participant know that you don't have that available (if an item is requested) or you're unable to help (if a service is requested), and offer a substitution if possible.

➤ Keep your professionalism and organization's policies in mind. For example, although it's a little weird to be asked, it's probably fine to clean someone's glasses (we've seen this happen) or provide her with the materials to do so herself, but it's not your job and not a professional presentation of yourself and your organization to shine participants' shoes or call their dentist for them.

What to say

➤ "I'm not quite sure I'll be able to accommodate that request, but let me check into it for you."
➤ "I'm sorry, due to our policies I can't do that for you."
➤ "We're under some time constraints with limited people running this study, so we don't really have time to do <request> today."

13.6 Participant makes a strangely specific request (cont.)

What not to do or say

➤ Avoid giving the participant the impression that you're at her beck and call. Be kind and a good host and listen politely, but remain in control and present yourself professionally.

How to avoid

➤ When the participant is recruited, make sure she knows that she'll be a participant for a user research session with specific goals (rather than a visit or tour as a guest), and what amenities (if any) will be provided.

➤ If you have a waiting area at your facility, provide reading materials and have some common beverages on hand (e.g., water, coffee, tea).

See also

➤ 13.5 Participant does something awkward or uncomfortable

➤ 13.7 Participant makes request during a site visit

➤ Survival Story: "The request caught me off-guard" in Chapter 10

13.7 Participant makes request during a site visit

> You're conducting a study at a participant's house and she asks you politely if you'd like a beverage, or if she can make you some food. Maybe the request is more personal (e.g., asking you to take off your shoes), or it's just plain unexpected (e.g., asking you to take out the garbage).

Method(s): Any in-person method
Frequency: Occasional
Pattern(s) to apply: Take responsibility; Disengage from the participant

What to do

When you visit a participant's home, keep in mind that you're a guest and need to be polite and accommodating. Establishing an amicable yet professional relationship will help set the tone for a fruitful feedback session. However, it's a slippery slope from being polite to getting too involved or friendly with the participant. Doing so can bias the results of your study or get you into a sticky or dangerous situation.

➤ If the participant asks if you want a beverage, feel free to accept as long as it's nonalcoholic, doesn't create a burden on your host, and doesn't take too much time away from the session. Be gracious and thank her for the offer, and remember that the participant is meeting social norms for having a visitor.

➤ Whether you accept a beverage from the participant or bring your own bottle of water, be careful where you place it. Some people are picky about having beverages on their computer desks, or on tables without coasters. Ask the participant where she'd prefer you to place your beverage.

➤ If the participant asks whether you want some kind of food, try to avoid having her go out of the way unless she's very excited or insistent about serving you and it seems offensive to turn her down. Thank her for the offer. However, be aware that if a participant is, say, cooking you up a steak dinner, it sets a precedent for a more friendly relationship, and it may become harder to stay neutral and in control during the session.

➤ If the participant has particular customs or household rules like taking off shoes, be considerate and follow her rules. As a rule of thumb, it's always a good idea to go to a home visit with socks and shoes rather than sandals without socks. Make sure your socks are ready for public viewing with no holes or inappropriate illustrations.

➤ If the participant has a really specific request, be accommodating but try to avoid doing menial tasks for her. For example, out of respect you may take a few minutes of silence for her religious ritual such as praying, but you don't have to agree to take out her trash, answer the phone, or fix her dishwasher in return for her feedback!

13.7 Participant makes request during a site visit (cont.)

➤ Also try to resist any activities that don't relate to the topic you're researching. For example, if the participant tries to show you old home videos, kindly tell her that you'd like to get started with the session. If necessary, take responsibility and say that you packed a lot into your study plan or use some other pretext like having to leave early to help her stay focused.

➤ If the participant seems to be too friendly or eager to connect with you, use the pattern of disengaging from her slightly. Adjust your demeanor and style to be a bit less approachable and more Down to Business, and remind her of your purpose for the session.

What to say

To politely refuse a request:

➤ "Oh no, thank you, I've just eaten but thanks so much for the offer."

➤ "Thank you for offering, but I have a bottle of water right here. If it's okay, I'd like to go ahead and get started."

If asked to take part in some awkward activity:

➤ "That's alright, I actually have a bit of prep work to do here so if it's okay, I'll just be here working quietly."

➤ "Actually, I'd rather just get started if that's okay. I have a lot to get through and need to leave a few minutes early."

What not to do or say

➤ Don't do anything that may be perceived as disrespecting the participant's space, like touching her things, opening her fridge, or sitting on her bed (even in a studio apartment), unless you have explicit permission to do so.

➤ Don't agree to do anything that may put you in danger, such as go into a bedroom or basement alone with the participant unless that location is relevant to the research you're doing. Basically, don't do anything you see innocent victims do in horror movies—use your common sense.

How to avoid

➤ You never know what you'll be asked or offered on a home visit. But one way to get a sense for the participant's personality is to give her a confirmation call personally and chat for a few minutes with her. If the participant seems slightly unusual on the phone, there's a possibility that her living style and habits may follow suit. From there, make a decision on who to bring or even whether to go through with the session. Always bring another colleague with you on field visits.

See also

➤ 13.6 Participant makes a strangely specific request

SURVIVAL STORY: "SHE TIPPED ME … BIG!"
MICHAEL ROBBINS

It started as a routine usability study. Observing behind a huge one-way mirror was my consultancy's director, my boss, a couple notetaker/equipment operators, and the client. The participant and I were seated side-by-side in front of a PC in a cramped, bare-walled testing room. She was a cheerful woman in her fifties and I was a thiry-something-year-old guy.

It was well into the hour-long session before it dawned on me that she might be flirting. She was getting progressively more complimentary and effusive. She cleared up any doubts when she began lightly touching my arm and her eyes shot me that special twinkle. From behind the huge mirror I felt amused grins getting wider. The study wasn't suffering so I kept it moving as before and, besides, she was amusing me too! Everything was fine … until she cranked up the heat after the study ended.

She started with waves of praise about how well I had done, how professional I was, etc. I thanked her for her kind words as I handed payment to her—an envelope of cash. Before I knew what happened, she stuffed $20 into my hand and showered me with a tsunami of praise. She tipped me … big!

My first thought was "Oh no! What do I do now?" Then came a mental flash of our unseen audience transfixing on this rapidly unfolding, live drama. I quickly interrupted her and handed the cash back, asking that she keep it. She refused. I put the cash down on the table in front of her and rationalized that she earned it and it belonged to her. She wasn't having it. I insisted. She counterinsisted. Back and forth it went. Changing tactics, I stuffed the $20 deep into her open purse, got close to her, and explained in an earnest and disarming whisper that, just as an architect is a professional, I wouldn't feel right as a professional accepting her money and I wanted her to keep it … really. And, for some extra oomph, I also assured her I was doing alright with money … really. It worked! She left perhaps even more cheerfully than she arrived. Phew!

I appreciated the knowing smile my director was wearing as she stepped out of the observation room and the good-natured ribbing from my colleagues.

Survival Story (cont.)

Upon reflection, answering her good-natured flirtation with continued friendliness had the best chance of keeping the study running smoothly. Any "correction," however gentle, risked my participant's willing chattiness.

As far as the tip, other than clairvoyance about which approach would work the first time, I'm not sure I would have changed much here either, except perhaps stuffing the money in her purse. That might have gone horribly awry but, as the paraphrased adage goes, it's not what you do that is important, but how you do it.

CHAPTER 14

Safety First:
Minimizing Emotional and Physical Distress

When you or the participant experiences emotional or physical distress, you need to quickly address that distress. Remember your ethical obligations to the participant as well as the need to protect your own well-being and that of your organization. Don't be afraid to end the session if you don't feel comfortable or safe continuing.

14.1 Fire alarm goes off or the facility needs to be evacuated

At some point during your session, a fire alarm goes off or there's some other emergency that requires everyone to evacuate. This may happen during an in-person session or while you're moderating a session remotely.

Method(s): Any
Frequency: Rare
Pattern(s) to apply: Take responsibility; End the session early

What to do

➤ If the session is being held at your facility (or a facility that you've rented), it is your responsibility to bring the participant to safety. Ensure that he gathers all his belongings (if time permits) and then bring him to a safe place outside of the building.

➤ If your observers are unfamiliar with the facility, bring the participant with you and make sure that the observers get out safely as well. Prepare the participant as you're en route by letting him know that you need to make sure your stakeholder team is safe. This gives the participant a heads up that the people he'll see next may have been watching him during the session.

➤ If you're recording the session and the situation doesn't seem to be dire, try to pause the recording before you leave. This shouldn't take long, and will keep you from needing to edit the recording later. Of course, if you're in immediate danger, don't stop to worry about the recording!

➤ If possible, bring the participant's compensation outside with you. This way, if you're unable to go back inside in a timely manner, you can still provide the participant with his promised incentive.

➤ Once outside, stay with the participant until it's safe to go back inside. You can make casual conversation to pass the time, but remember to stay professional.

➤ If the participant seems freaked out by the situation, if the situation is lasting a long time, or if the weather outside is inclement, let the participant leave. Thank him for his feedback and provide him with his full compensation if you were able to bring it with you. If you weren't, let him know that you'll coordinate with your recruiter for a way to get the compensation to him. Give him your contact information as well so he can reach out to you if he doesn't receive the compensation.

➤ If your session is being held at the participant's facility, follow his lead as he evacuates the building. Be sure to grab your belongings in case you're unable to get back into the facility later.

14.1 Fire alarm goes off or the facility needs to be evacuated (cont.)

➤ If the session is being held remotely, let the participant (and the observers) know that you're experiencing an emergency and will need to drop off the call. Ask the participant to disconnect from the screen-sharing application and any associated conference calls, and let him know that you'll get in touch with him again when it's safe for you to return to the building. If time permits, add a note in your screen-sharing application to let any observers who join while you're outside know what is happening.

What to say

For an in-person situation:

➤ "*<Participant>*, that's a fire alarm, so we need to evacuate the building. Please gather your belongings, and we'll go outside."

For a remote session:

➤ "*<Participant>*, our fire alarm is going off so I'll need to leave the building. Please go ahead and exit the screen-sharing application and hang up the phone. I'll contact you again when I'm able to return to the building."

What not to do or say

➤ Don't abandon the participant. Remember that he may be in an unfamiliar location and may not know what to do. Also, once outside, don't leave him by himself. Keep him company, chatting informally but professionally to keep him engaged and distracted from what's going on.

How to avoid

➤ There is no way to avoid this situation. However, you can be prepared by familiarizing yourself with your facility's emergency procedures. If you have control over and consistent access to the space, make sure a copy of the emergency procedures are printed and stored in an easily accessible location. Review these procedures with your team at least once a year, and consider conducting a mock fire drill as well to work out the best way to accommodate participants in case of an emergency.

➤ If you're renting a facility for the study, ask them ahead of time if there are any special procedures that you should follow in case of an emergency.

See also

➤ 14.2 A natural disaster (e.g., earthquake, tornado) occurs

14.2 A natural disaster (e.g., earthquake, tornado) occurs

Your session is interrupted by a natural disaster such as an earthquake, tornado, or severe storm. This may happen during an in-person session or while you're moderating a session remotely.

Method(s): Any
Frequency: Rare
Pattern(s) to apply: Take responsibility; End the session early

What to do

➤ If you receive a warning before severe weather hits, let the participant know. Provide as many details as you know—depending on how far away the weather is, the participant may want to leave immediately to get home. Help him make an informed decision, but let him know that he can stay and wait out the weather in your facility if there's any chance at all he won't make it home safely.

➤ If you live in an area that's prone to the type of natural disaster you're experiencing, you should have a pretty good sense of what to do. Follow the correct procedures for your building and the disaster being experienced, keeping in mind that you and your organization still have responsibility for the safety and well-being of the participant.

➤ End the session, but ask the participant to remain until you verify that it is safe for him to leave.

➤ If you're unfamiliar with what to do for the type of disaster you're experiencing, first, try not to panic. Then,

■ If you're experiencing severe weather or a tornado warning, you and the participant should head toward interior rooms or hallways on the lowest floor of your building (take stairs, not elevators). If you have observers who are unfamiliar with the building, be sure to bring them with you as well. Crouch to make yourself as small a target as possible, and be sure to cover your head with your hands. Avoid windows or glass.

■ If you're experiencing an earthquake, you and the participant need to drop to the ground and take cover (either under a sturdy table or, if one isn't available, move to an inside corner of the room, crouch, and cover your head with your hands). Don't leave the room until the shaking stops. Once the shaking stops, ask the participant to gather his belongings and bring him (and any observers) out of the building, avoiding elevators.

➤ During onsite research at a participant's home or facility, follow his lead. Stay at the location as long as necessary for your own safety, but leave as soon as you safely can, as both you and the participant will probably be very distracted by what is happening.

SAFETY FIRST: MINIMIZING EMOTIONAL AND PHYSICAL DISTRESS

14.2 A natural disaster (e.g., earthquake, tornado) occurs (cont.)

➤ If you forget to give the participant his compensation before he leaves, follow up with the recruiter afterwards to arrange a way to get the compensation to him.

➤ If the session is being held remotely, let the participant (and the observers) know that you're experiencing an emergency and need to end the session immediately. Ask the participant to disconnect from the screen-sharing application and any associated conference calls, and let him know that you'll get in touch to reschedule the session at a later time. If time and conditions permit, add a note in your screen-sharing application to let any observers who join later know what is happening.

What to say

For an in-person session:

➤ "*<Participant>*, we're going to end the session right now. But please stay here while we figure out what's going on—I don't want you to leave unless we're positive it's safe to do so."

For a remote session:

➤ "*<Participant>*, we're experiencing an emergency so I need to end the session. Please go ahead and exit the screen-sharing application, and hang up the phone. I'll contact you later to reschedule the session."

What not to do or say

➤ Don't abandon the participant. His comfort and safety is in your hands.

How to avoid

➤ We highly recommend reading FEMA's guidelines on what to do in case of emergencies, available at *www.ready.gov*. Read them now—you won't have time in the event of an actual emergency!

➤ There's no way to avoid a natural disaster. However, you can be prepared by familiarizing yourself with your facility's emergency procedures. If possible, create an emergency kit in your space that includes a flashlight. If you're renting a facility for the study, ask them ahead of time if there are any special procedures that you should follow in case of an emergency, especially if you're in an area that is prone to disasters that you're unfamiliar with.

See also

➤ 14.1 Fire alarm goes off or the facility needs to be evacuated

➤ Survival Story: "The ground started to move" in Chapter 3

14.3 Participant starts to look ill or otherwise unwell

While the participant seemed fine at the beginning of the session, he starts to seem ill or unwell later on. He may become very pale, start sneezing/coughing uncontrollably, develop motor control difficulties, or faint/collapse.

Method(s): Any
Frequency: Rare
Pattern(s) to apply: Take a break; End the session early

What to do

➤ For minor-seeming symptoms such as coughing or sneezing, offer to let the participant take a break (in case he's just experiencing an allergy attack or something temporary) or end the session early. If he's coughing, also offer to get him some water.

➤ If the participant has collapsed or is showing signs of motor control difficulties that didn't exist before, immediately call for help.

   ■ For a faint or collapse, find someone who can bring water while you stay with the participant. When the participant comes around, offer to call someone to pick him up or offer some other way to make sure he gets home safely (e.g., by arranging a cab).

   ■ For a seizure or other motor control issue, call 911. In some corporate buildings, you may need to call building security first and ask them to call 911. Your first priority is to get the participant the care that he needs. Don't try to restrain the participant, but remove any sharp objects that he may run into. Stay in the room with the participant until help arrives.

➤ If the participant leaves the session abruptly (e.g., in an ambulance), follow up with the recruiter afterwards to see if he's okay and, if appropriate for your study and his physical condition, if he'd like to be rescheduled. You can also arrange a way to get him his compensation.

What to say

If the participant looks pale or is sneezing/coughing:

➤ "<*Participant*>, are you okay? Let me know if you want to take a break, if you need to end the session early, or if I can help in any way."

If the participant begins having serious motor control difficulties or faints, immediately get him help:

➤ "<*Participant*>, I'm going to call 911 (or contact building security) and stay right here with you until help arrives."

SAFETY FIRST: MINIMIZING EMOTIONAL AND PHYSICAL DISTRESS

What not to do or say

➤ Don't ignore the participant's condition. Remember your ethical responsibilities to protect the participant from harm.

How to avoid

➤ Unfortunately, these situations are pretty unavoidable. Within your testing environment, be sure to use antibacterial cleaner and have hand sanitizer available to limit the chance of an ill participant spreading his germs to you (and other participants).

➤ Also, if your facility has a security presence, ask them if there's a recommended protocol for reporting emergencies—some facilities with extensive security services ask you to contact them first so they can coordinate directly with 911.

See also

➤ 14.4 You begin to feel unwell while moderating a session
➤ 14.6 Participant seems to be drunk or stoned

14.4 You begin to feel unwell while moderating a session

While you felt fine at the beginning of the session, you begin to feel ill or unwell later on. Your symptoms are severe enough that you start to have difficulty paying attention to the participant.

Method(s): Any
Frequency: Rare
Pattern(s) to apply: Take responsibility; Take a break; End the session early

What to do

➤ If you're experiencing something like a coughing or sneezing fit, excuse yourself from the room and go to the nearest restroom until the fit is over. Splash cold water on your face and wash your hands before heading back in to the research room.

➤ Take a quick break. Get a cool drink and get some fresh air if possible. If you haven't eaten, have a small snack to keep your blood sugar up. Those small changes may be enough to help you feel better.

➤ If you feel seriously ill, or contagious, and unable to continue, you can do one of two things:

■ If you have another moderator available, have him or her continue the session for you.

■ End the session as quickly as possible, both for your comfort and that of the participant. You can use a pretext if you're not comfortable sharing details about how you're feeling. Be sure to give him his full compensation even if you're ending the session early.

What to say

➤ "Let's take a short break and resume again in five minutes. Can I get you a drink while you're waiting?"

➤ "I feel a sneezing/coughing fit coming on—please excuse me for a few minutes!"

➤ "I apologize, *<participant>*, but we need to end the session a bit earlier than planned due to some technical difficulties with our setup. Thank you so much for your feedback today—what you gave us was extremely helpful. Here's your compensation."

What not to do or say

➤ Don't force yourself to continue the session if you don't feel able to. It's better to end a session early than to collapse in front of the participant!

14.4 You begin to feel unwell while moderating a session (cont.)

How to avoid

➤ Unfortunately, these situations are pretty unavoidable. Within your testing environment, be sure to use antibacterial cleaner and have hand sanitizer available to limit the chance of an ill participant spreading his germs to you (and other participants).

➤ If you have ongoing health problems that require you to sometimes leave a room quickly, give your team a heads up (details are not necessary!). If someone else on your team can fill in for you as a moderator and will be watching your session, consider asking that person to either take over for you immediately or after a few minutes if you have to leave the room in a hurry.

See also

➤ 14.3 Participant starts to look ill or otherwise unwell
➤ 14.5 You notice a bad smell or have an allergic reaction

14.5 You notice a bad smell or have an allergic reaction

A very unpleasant smell distracts you during the session. The smell may be coming from the participant or, if you're at the participant's location, from the environment itself. If you're in the participant's home, the smell may also be accompanied by unsanitary living conditions such as rodents, cockroaches, and unwashed dishes. Similarly, something that either the participant is wearing or that's present in the environment may be causing you to have an allergic reaction.

Method(s): Any in-person method
Frequency: Rare
Pattern(s) to apply: Take a break; End the session early

What to do

➤ Try moving to a different position in the room (e.g., from the participant's right side to his left side). A few inches may make a big difference in how you're being affected by the allergen or smell.

➤ If you're in the participant's home and changing positions in the room hasn't helped, ask if there's another room that you can use for the session. This question can be phrased cleverly so the participant won't feel insulted, ideally by tying in the movement to the reason for the session. For example, you could ask the participant to show you any other locations where he might use the product that you're discussing.

➤ If you don't feel able to end the session (e.g., because you really need this participant's feedback), take a short break and get some fresh air.

➤ If you're in a location where bad smells are par for the course (e.g., an animal testing facility, certain manufacturing locations), consider being honest with the participant and letting him know that you're having a hard time with the smell. He may be able to bring you to a location that's better ventilated and less odorous.

➤ If the smell is making you feel sick and you're unable to continue, go ahead and end the session early. If you still want to get feedback from the participant, you can ask if he'd be willing to talk to you some more by phone.

What to say

➤ "I'm sorry, I think I may be allergic to <*something in this room*>. Is there another location that we could talk in?"

➤ "Let's take a short break and resume again in five minutes. Can I get you a drink while you're waiting?"

➤ "I know you warned me about this ahead of time, but I'm having trouble handling the smell in here. Is there another location we can move to for a little bit?"

What not to do or say

➤ Try not to point out a smell unless it's something that's expected from the kind of location you're in (e.g., a factory or manufacturing facility). Doing so would be rude and potentially insulting.

How to avoid

➤ We wish there was a way to avoid this situation, but especially when it comes to contextual inquiry, there's only so much you can do. For site visits, you can ask ahead of time what kind of environment to expect, but these kinds of olfactory issues may not come up. There's no way (that we know of) to avoid participants with poor personal hygiene.

➤ If you have known allergies (e.g., to cats or dogs), be prepared and have medication with you at all times.

See also

➤ 12.5 Participant has disconcerting or distracting physical characteristic

➤ 14.4 You begin to feel unwell while moderating a session

➤ Survival Story: "I knew what it was like"

14.6 Participant seems to be drunk or stoned

> When the participant arrives, you notice that something seems a little bit off about him. His eyes may be glassy or red, he may smell heavily of alcohol and have slurred speech or difficulty walking.

Method(s): Any in-person method
Frequency: Rare
Pattern(s) to apply: End the session early

What to do

➤ End the session early, and provide the participant with his compensation.

➤ Ask the participant how he got to the session. If he drove himself and you wouldn't be comfortable with him getting behind the wheel, encourage him to take alternate transportation instead (e.g., a cab, calling a friend) and offer to arrange it for him. Remember your responsibility to the participant's safety.

➤ If you have onsite building security, contact them for assistance. They may be able to wait with the participant and provide additional help.

➤ If the participant refuses your suggestions and insists on driving, and you don't have an onsite security team, get his car's make and model, and contact the police right away.

➤ If the participant is making you uncomfortable in any way, trust your gut and end the session as quickly as possible. Contact security and the authorities if you're worried about your safety or that of others in your location (see section 14.9 for more on handling this).

What to say

➤ "Thank you for coming in today. You seem a little distracted, so why don't we reschedule this for a day and time that works better for you."

➤ "Is there someone I can call for you to take you home, or can I call you a cab?"

➤ "I'm sorry, but we're going to have to cancel the session due to some technical difficulties. Thank you so much for coming in and here's your compensation. Let me walk you to our exit. How did you get here today?"

What not to say or do

➤ Don't run a session with a participant who you think is physically unable to give accurate and useful feedback. Let participants who are under the influence go home.

14.6 Participant seems to be drunk or stoned (cont.)

➤ Ensure that you have another person (e.g., an observer or someone from your team) watching your interactions with the participant, especially when you end the session.

How to avoid

➤ There's little you can do to avoid this situation. Make sure that you're not running sessions alone and have the number for onsite security handy just in case.

See also

➤ 14.3 Participant starts to look ill or otherwise unwell
➤ Survival Story: "You sure are pretty" in Chapter 12

14.7 Participant touches you

At some point during the session, the participant deliberately touches you. The touch may be something like a brief touch on your arm or hand. Or, when you're both leaned in to look at something, his shoulders touch yours and he doesn't move away. Or maybe he not-so-briefly touches your leg or your back.

Method(s): Any in-person method
Frequency: Rare
Pattern(s) to apply: Redirect the participant; Disengage from the participant; Take a break

What to do

➤ If the participant's touch was more of a grab or threatening movement, or he deliberately ignores your request to not be touched, end the session as soon as you can. If you were feeling uncomfortable with him already and the touch made you more uncomfortable, do the same. Trust your gut! If you don't feel safe staying in the room with the participant, leave the room and find a team member to end the session for you.

➤ If the touch seemed harmless (e.g., the participant is very expressive and his arm movements result in an infrequent touching of your arm) or accidental (e.g., mistaking your foot for the leg of the table), just carry on with the session. You can also reposition yourself or the participant so that you're further away. For example, you can scoot your chair behind him in a usability study or contextual inquiry, or go into another room to moderate over a microphone if your setup allows it. If making a physical shift would seem like an abrupt change, you can first take a break. Then, when you resume, assume a different position.

➤ If the touch is intentional but subtle (like a flirtatious participant touching your hand or leg), slowly and steadily pull away to show that it's not okay. Then try the repositioning approach. Turn your body slightly away from the participant, minimize eye contact, and use a more formal tone. You could also ask the participant to adjust his position (e.g., by moving to a different chair in the room).

➤ If you're uncomfortable continuing with the participant, switch moderators if someone else is available or end the session early.

What to say

To reposition yourself or the participant:

➤ "I'm having a hard time getting a view of what you're doing while beside you, so I'll just scoot behind you and watch what you're doing."

➤ "I just realized that your chair is one of the most uncomfortable ones we have—I'm sorry! Why don't you switch over to that chair instead for the rest of this interview."

14.7 Participant touches you (cont.)

To take a break:

➤ "Let's take a short break and resume again in five minutes. Can I get you a drink while you're waiting?"

➤ "I need to check on something before the next part of the session, so let's take a brief break."

What not to do or say

➤ Try not to disengage immediately after the touch happens. If it's an awkward touch, slowly and steadily pull away. But you don't need to jump right to sitting elsewhere in the room or taking a break. This can make things more awkward. Just continue with the task, question, or thought you're on, and then find the next natural breaking point to either move positions, take a break, or switch moderators.

How to avoid

➤ Although it's always important to disclose to the participant that there are observers, we don't usually draw much attention to it. However, this is a rare case where it's helpful to *emphasize* that there are observers and video cameras—it will usually keep participants within bounds.

➤ At the beginning of the session, position yourself a comfortable distance away from the participant where it will be hard for him to touch you without going out of his way. In studies involving computers, it's helpful to have the computer setup so that you have a second keyboard and mouse wirelessly connected. It allows both you and the participant to have your own controls, so you can change anything on the screen without having to reach over the participant or ask him to move or get up.

➤ Never run research alone, especially at night and in others' homes. Always have at least one person observing, and if you're going onsite, bring a buddy!

See also

➤ 13.4 Participant flirts with you

14.8 Participant's environment contains dangerous items

While entering the participant's home or work space—either in person or through a virtual view established by a webcam—you notice the presence of materials that are dangerous (e.g., guns or weapons) or potentially offensive (e.g., porn or racist propaganda).

Method(s): Contextual inquiry; Interview
Frequency: Rare
Pattern(s) to apply: Take responsibility

What to do

➤ If you feel uncomfortable or that you're in even the slightest bit of danger, trust your gut and end the session as quickly as possible. We strongly recommend that you trust your instincts when it comes to potential warning signs—again, your safety is more important than gaining an additional data point.

➤ If you do end the session, for your safety, try to end the session in a subtle way that doesn't make it obvious that it's due to the participant's environment. For example, wait a couple of minutes and use a pretext like you forgot some study materials, or check your phone and pretend there's an emergency that you need to leave for.

➤ If you feel safe continuing the session (again we suggest that you to err on the side of caution here, but we leave that at your discretion—for example, if the participant is a collector of medieval weapons that are in a locked case and you're not picking up any odd vibes from him), ask him if he can move any dangerous materials to another area of the house or if you can talk in a different location. If he's unable to make an accommodation that you feel comfortable with, end the session. Be respectful when drawing attention to any of these items, regardless of your personal feelings toward the questionable items.

➤ If the materials are offensive, but not dangerous, try not to mention them. While this may be difficult, keep in mind that you're out in the field to see the reality of your user's environment, and that reality isn't always what you expect.

➤ If you're video recording the session or taking pictures, remind the participant of this before you start. The participant may realize that he has materials visible that he wouldn't want a wider audience to see and move those materials on his own.

What not to do or say

➤ Avoid engaging the participant in a discussion about the dangerous/offensive materials unless the participant brings it up on his own and the material is somehow connected to your research

14.8 Participant's environment contains dangerous items (cont.)

goals. For example, if you're talking with the participant about how he spends his free time and he brings up his antique gun collection, you can ask him follow-up questions just as you would for any other answer.

What to say

➤ "Thank you so much for letting me come talk with you today. Before we get started, can I ask you to move that *<dangerous item>* into another room while we're talking in here? I really appreciate it."

➤ "Before I take this picture, I want to remind you that this will get shared with other members of the project team. Is it okay for me to continue?"

How to avoid

➤ There's not much you can do to avoid this—ideally, a participant who knows he is having visitors will make the environment safe. However, this isn't always the case. Keep in mind that the beauty of field research is that it lets you see the reality of a user's environment, and that environment may not be what you expected.

See also

➤ 12.2 Something personal, inappropriate, or confidential is visible

➤ 14.9 Participant is doing something illegal or threatening

➤ Survival Story: "We didn't know much about them"

14.9 Participant is doing something illegal or threatening

At some point during the session, you realize that the participant poses some kind of threat to your well-being and that of others at your location. You may notice that the participant is stealing items from your facility. Or, the participant may seem unstable or potentially violent and you no longer feel comfortable proceeding with the session.

Method(s): Any in-person method
Frequency: Rare
Pattern(s) to apply: Disengage from the participant; Take a break; End the session early

What to do

➤ If you feel that a participant may be unstable or a danger to you or others (e.g., paranoid, violent, extreme mood swings), trust your gut and end the session as quickly as possible. We strongly recommend that you use your instinct when it comes to potential warning signs—again, your safety is more important than gaining an additional data point.

➤ If you do end the session immediately, for your safety, try to do so in a subtle way that doesn't make it obvious that it's due to his behavior. For example, wait a couple of minutes and use a pretext such as technical troubles with the product or not having the right study materials.

➤ If the participant is doing something illegal, take a break as soon as you can, again citing a pretext like technical difficulties, and ask a coworker or observer to alert the appropriate authorities (police, security, etc.) to the situation. Depending on what the participant is doing (or has done), you may ask the authorities to just be aware as the participant leaves the facility, or you may ask them to confront the participant (e.g., to regain stolen goods). Follow the guidance provided by the authorities when you describe the situation.

➤ Once you have some kind of backup available, end the session with the participant. Provide him with his compensation to keep the session proceeding as normally as possible from his perspective.

➤ Do your best to look and sound neutral when interacting with the participant, even if you're scared or nervous.

➤ Remember that you need to look out for your comfort and safety, so if you're not comfortable for any reason, end the session.

What to say

To the participant, to end the session:

➤ "I'm sorry, but we have to end the session early due to some problems with our equipment. Thank you so much for coming in—here's your compensation. Let me walk you out."

To police or security:

➤ "This is *<name>* in *<location>*. I'm running a research study with a participant and I'm worried about my safety because of what the participant is doing. *<Describe the participant's actions or behavior.>* I am going to end the study, but I want you to be aware of what's happening. Do you have any recommendations on what I should do?"

What not to do or say

➤ If at all possible, avoid handling the situation on your own (e.g., by confronting the participant about what he has done). These rare scenarios are also one of the main reasons we recommend never performing research alone.

How to avoid

➤ Have all emergency numbers posted and ensure any observers and team members know where those numbers are located.

➤ If you have onsite security at the facility where you're performing research, let them know ahead of time that you're running a research study. This way, if you need to contact them in case of emergency, they will already have some knowledge about who you are and what you're doing.

➤ Check with your building's security team about any policies they have about weapons, as they may have specific procedures to follow if you notice an armed participant.

See also

➤ 14.8 Participant's environment contains dangerous items

SURVIVAL STORY: "WE DIDN'T KNOW MUCH ABOUT THEM"
BOB VIRZI

We were doing a usability evaluation of some home networking gear. We had completed a series of lab studies, but our customers were still reporting problems with the installation in the field. In response, we initiated a field study where we observed customers attempting to install the equipment in their homes.

When we contacted people to participate in the study we explained that the interview would be conducted in their home, using their equipment, and they would be expected to try to install the networking gear while we observed. We collected some information from them like their age and type of equipment, but other than that, we didn't know much about them. We always sent two people for safety and liability reasons, usually two usability experts. But in this case it was one usability expert (a man in his forties) and a business partner (a woman in her late fifties).

They arrived at the home of the participant, a man in his thirties, and were brought to his study where his computer was. Apart from a generally messy room, the other thing that was striking to the researchers was that the walls and the home screen of the computer were plastered with porn. While the two researchers were dumbfounded at this casual display of sexually explicit material, our interviewee was not at all put off and seemed to think everything was normal. After a quick private conference, the researchers decided the participant seemed genuinely interested in participating in the study and, apart from his sensibilities about what is appropriate content for wall art, he appeared to be a reasonable test participant. As a result, they went ahead with the session.

A few takeaways from this are, (1) that is why we send people out to homes in pairs, (2) you need to be prepared for anything when you enter an unknown person's home, and (3) trust your gut—if it doesn't feel right, get out of there quickly.

SURVIVAL STORY: "I KNEW WHAT IT WAS LIKE"
JACQUELINE STETSON PASTORE

I was working on an ethnography project with a pharmacology client, designing software to manage the development of tumor models. To do my job correctly, I had to go into the labs where scientists performed their tumor research on mice to see where the work was being done.

I should also point out that I had a brain tumor as a teenager and had surgery to remove it. As the date for the lab visit came closer and closer, I felt a strong bond with the mice I hadn't met yet because I knew what it was like to have a tumor cut out of you. I was nervous about seeing the racks of animal cages. I imagined myself multiplied by the thousands, sitting in little boxes and growing tumors to be removed. Also, I'm a flaming animal lover and on- and off-again vegetarian who can't bear to see blood or needles, so I honestly didn't know if I would be able to emotionally handle the lab.

The day finally came for our first lab visit. We tagged along behind a few of the scientists to learn what their typical day was like. When it came to prepping for the lab, they showed us how to put on the jumpers, hair nets, safety goggles, booties, and gloves. We would have to double-glove and double-booty once we entered the work room.

Because I know that I am a ninny about animals, I had to be extra careful about not projecting my personal beliefs during the sessions. When I saw the first surgery, my nerves got the better of me and I got a bit woozy. I thought about the strategies they trained us for—where the trash can and vents were and how to safely exit the room by stepping onto certain areas and removing double booties and gloves. I reminded myself what I tell my observers: you're an alien in a strange world and you have no preconceived ideas. You're there to learn and do your job. So I marched myself over to the air conditioning vent and got cold air blown on me. This cleared my head and I was ready to focus again.

After watching a few more surgeries to make sure I understood the ergonomic and workflow concerns, I positioned myself to focus on the scientists' faces so the surgical area was out of my view. We had planned to use iPhones and iPads to take notes since notebooks, pens, and laptops were not allowed. However, once we were in the lab, we discovered that touchscreen devices don't work when you're double-gloved. Since we were not allowed to use recording devices, we solved this by doing debrief sessions immediately afterwards to write down everything we saw. All in all, it was an amazing experience. I was lucky to be able to go into a lab and help design software that may cure diseases one day.

Part 3
Improving Your Skills

CHAPTER 15

An Ounce of Prevention:
Avoiding and Mitigating Situations

Many of the situations described in Part 2 can be mitigated earlier in the session or prevented entirely ahead of time. This chapter compiles the tips we provide in each situation's "How to avoid" section to help reduce the chances of you encountering, or make it easier to deal with, many of the situations discussed earlier, especially the occasional and rare situations. This isn't intended to be a comprehensive list of everything that you need to do to prepare for a successful study, but instead highlights the key topics—from expectation setting to technical tinkering to practicing and preparing your space.

15.1 Recruiting process

We hate that horrible feeling you get when you realize that the participant had completely different expectations for your session, or you have a room full of high-level observers who are antsy because the participant is running late. These tips help you set expectations with participants and plan ahead for situations where you absolutely cannot have a late or no-show participant.

Specify your recruit criteria

It doesn't matter how carefully crafted your study plan is or how sharp your moderating skills are if the participant doesn't meet the necessary criteria. As you prepare for your recruit, think carefully about the must-haves that your participants need to provide the desired feedback. Craft your list of criteria carefully to avoid any deal-breakers.

Potential must-haves may include participants who:

➤ *Have the desired experience or role.* You can't rely just on job titles to figure out if a participant is really who you're looking for. Instead, think of the specific tasks or attributes that you need her to have. For example, if you need to get feedback on a new timesheet approval system, it will not be enough to recruit managers—you need to verify that participants have direct reports whose timesheets they approve.

➤ *Are representative users.* Recruiting *unrepresentative* users often happens when you ask someone within your organization to recruit internal employees. For example, if you need to interview sales managers, the person scheduling participants may only find you the top performing managers. Communicate that you want truly representative users—an average sample.

➤ *Are set up to show you what you need.* For example, if you're visiting participants at home to watch their process for doing laundry, you need to make sure that participants will have dirty laundry at the time of the scheduled session.

By being specific about these criteria ahead of time, you'll hopefully avoid any unpleasant surprises once your session starts!

Appendix B summarizes the steps in this chapter, and Appendix C lists books that go into more detail about planning user research studies.

For additional tips on how to build a recruiting screener and find qualified participants, see Rubin and Chisnell (2008).

Set participant expectations through the recruit

To avoid a mismatch between your expectations and those of your participants, it's important to be crystal clear during the recruit about what participants will be doing during the session. Important elements to highlight include:

➤ *The type of research* (e.g., a usability study, an interview), along with a brief description of what this means. Participants are sometimes intimidated to find out that they will be working through tasks in a usability study when they assumed they would just be chatting in an interview.

➤ *The length and location of the session.* If the session is taking place at the participant's location, confirm her contact information and address, and ask if there are any special things you need to know about parking, entering the building, or anything you might not be allowed to bring into the building (e.g., cameras or other equipment).

➤ *The session will be one-on-one*, so there will only be one other person (you) interacting with the participant. If participants expect to be in a focus group, they may wrongly assume they would be able to hide behind others or cancel without advance warning.

➤ *If the session will be recorded*, and what will be recorded (e.g., both the computer screen showing the product and a capture of the participant's face).

➤ *The amount and type of compensation being provided*, as well as how and when they'll receive it. For example, some organizations compensate in cash immediately following or before a session, while other organizations use recruiting agencies and have the agency send a check in the mail after the session is complete.

Be sure to send a confirmation letter to participants either via mail or email so they have the study details in writing. The letter should also include your contact information on the day of the scheduled session (or whoever should be contacted in case the participant is running late or can't make it). If possible, call the participant a day before the session to verify the details about the study and answer any last-minute questions she may have.

Take extra measures if you have internal employees as participants

When using internal employees of an organization for research, you'll probably encounter a hornet's nest of politics that have little, if anything, to do with your project. Internal employees may be chosen because they're the target users of an internal product, or as surrogate users (who can play the role of your target users). They may be recruited as part of a convenience sample—they're chosen because the person managing the recruit can easily find them rather than because they represent a diverse sample of users. Often they're recruited by managers who tell them almost nothing about the project. As a result, they have no expectations or the wrong expectations (e.g., that it's a training session). These participants may feel, or actually be, pressured into participating, so they may come into the session with a chip on their shoulder. Also, many organizations prohibit internal employees from receiving compensation for their participation, so participants may be doing your research for no additional incentive.

To help ensure a smooth session when you have internal employees as your participants:

➤ If someone else recruited the participant for you, spend a bit of extra time at the beginning of her session explaining the purpose of the study and how the feedback will be used. Reinforce that you'll keep her information confidential and will not use her name or any other specific identifying information, and that she is not required to participate. The participant may not have been told much, if anything, about the research.

➤ Avoid having the participant's direct manager, people from the same team as the participant, or employees from human resources observing a session. This can make the participant feel even more nervous or that she is being evaluated.

➤ Disclose whether you have observers and that it's possible any of them may recognize her, but emphasize the point that they're all happy for any feedback she has to give and that she is not being evaluated at all. Reinforce that none of the observers are from her team. Also make sure to brief your observers on how to behave in a manner that respects the participant and maintains her confidentiality (see section 15.4 for more observer guidelines).

➤ Sincerely thank the participant for her time, and stress that her feedback is extremely valuable.

Also, keep in mind that the same guidelines that apply to regular participants still count for internal employees! You still have an ethical responsibility to look out for their physical and emotional safety.

Consider scheduling backup or floater participants

Sometimes it's critical not to have an empty timeslot during a study. Stakeholders may be traveling to observe sessions, or the project may be very time constrained so there is no way to schedule replacement sessions. In these situations, consider recruiting either:

➤ *Backup participants.* A backup participant is double-booked for a timeslot, so you actually have two people scheduled for the same timeslot. Use the backup if the regular participant doesn't show up or is late. If the regular participant shows up, compensate the backup and let her leave.

➤ *Floater participants.* A floater participant is available as a backup for a period of time that stretches across multiple timeslots, and usually is compensated more for doing so. If you have floaters, but end up not needing them, you might still have a colleague conduct an interview to get some useful data, or give them a survey, an unmoderated study, or some other independent activity from which you can collect feedback.

If you schedule a backup participant, we recommend not telling her that she is a backup. She may be more likely to skip the session if she doesn't think she is needed.

When discussing backup and floater participants with your stakeholders and other user researchers, be sure to clarify exactly what you mean. Sometimes these two terms are used interchangeably.

It also helps to discuss with your stakeholders if surrogate users who are internal employees from your organization might be appropriate floaters or backups in case of a no-show participant. If you don't have floaters or backups, set expectations that no-shows are a fact of life and plan accordingly (e.g., by recruiting ten participants to ensure that at least eight show up).

15.2 Your study plan

Sometimes you have to do some creative juggling within a session. Maybe you have to shift the focus of the research because your product is experiencing technical difficulties. Or, maybe the participant spent more time than expected answering your first few questions or tasks and you realize that you won't get through everything else in your plan. You also need to think about how you'll brief the participant, present your questions or tasks, and when and how you'll provide compensation.

Prioritize the study plan and create a backup plan

As you're writing your study plan, structure the protocol in such a way that it's easy to identify the high-priority tasks and questions. Work with your stakeholders to determine what, if any, material can be comfortably cut if necessary. This way, if you know you need to end the session early for some reason, you can adapt on-the-fly while making sure you hit all the necessary areas.

The shift the focus pattern talks more about when and why you might adapt a session. See section 3.8 for more on this.

Once you have your study plan in place, also think about additional questions or tasks that you can prepare as a backup. This backup content can be used if you need to shift the focus of a session or take an extended break, and will let you continue to get feedback related to your research. Depending on the length of your study plan, you may already have several lower-priority tasks and questions that can be easily repurposed. For example, if you're planning a usability study or contextual inquiry, review your study plan and consider what additional questions you can ask if you need to shift the focus to an interview. These techniques are all ways to make use of a session that may otherwise have been wasted.

Another type of backup you can create is a paper or online questionnaire. The questionnaire can contain questions related to your project (e.g., demographics and product usage) or anything else that would be helpful, but not vital, to know about your participants. If appropriate, you can plan to give the questionnaire to all participants at the end of the session, but have it ready to use earlier in case something goes awry and you have to take an extended break.

If you're asking participants to interact with a product, think about any extra tasks that you can keep in your "back pocket." These may be lower-priority tasks related to the project or more general tasks that always apply to any user who participates. These tasks may come in handy if the product breaks in the middle of a session, or you realize that the participant doesn't meet your criteria and would not provide the right kind of feedback on your intended tasks.

Prepare your presession briefing

When the participant arrives for her session, greet her warmly and make some casual conversation to help her feel comfortable. Once you arrive in your study space, transition to your presession briefing. The briefing should:

➤ Explain your goals for the session.

➤ Set clear expectations for how the session time will be used.

➤ Let the participant know that she can take a break or end the session at any time.

➤ Reiterate the points highlighted in your consent form including any recording that is being done and how the findings from this research will be used.

Appropriate casual topics include the weather, the traffic, any difficulty experienced finding the location, and if she has participated in any user research studies before.

Set up the briefing in whatever format will be easiest for you to read without missing any key elements. Some researchers prefer to have a bulleted list, while others write everything out — find what is most comfortable for you. Even if you have your points memorized, make sure you refer back to the list often so that you aren't forgetting important points; forgetting one important point may open the door for a tricky or sticky situation to occur later. To make things less awkward, you can preface the briefing by saying, "I'll be referring to my notes here to make sure I don't miss anything."

If you have a detailed script, practice it ahead of time so that you can easily deliver it in a comfortable tone while making eye contact with the participant. If you read it word for word, looking down at your clipboard and with a monotone voice, participants may zone out, get irritated, or get more nervous. Newer moderators who feel more comfortable reading directly from a script can preface to the participant that you'll do so, but may want to write in reminders for you to "LOOK UP!" after every few lines.

If you have a lot of points to cover in your briefing, find a way to keep it broken up and engaging. For example, ask some background questions in between sets of briefing points, stop periodically to ask if everything makes sense so far and whether the participant has questions, and use your intonation and delivery to keep the participant listening carefully. Sometimes it also helps to warn the participant by saying something like, "I have a lot of points to go over, so forgive me in advance for throwing a lot of information at you! I just want to make sure you have a clear understanding of what we're doing here today."

Consider keeping the tasks "close to your vest"

Letting usability study participants know ahead of time how many tasks you'll be asking them to attempt may create complications. If the participant sees the number of tasks, she may start self-timing and rush through some tasks or take more time on others instead of approaching them naturally. Another challenge is that in some situations, like those described in sections 10.4 and 10.7, you may not get through everything you'd planned. She may then feel bad about not being able to give you all the feedback you wanted.

Divulging tasks one by one is a useful way to mitigate these issues. After the participant completes a task, you hand her the next task or move on to another part of your study plan. However, this method presents its own challenges: not being able to send tasks to remote participants to print ahead of time, having to read tasks to participants, or needing to be in the room with the participant to hand her the next task. Think about the needs of your study and choose accordingly. If the participant has to have the tasks ahead of time, it's not the end of the world! As she starts each task, encourage her to go at her natural pace and not speed up or slow down for your sake (and write this into your study plan so you don't forget to say it). Warn her that for the sake of time you may push her along sometimes, but that you don't expect to get through everything (even if you do expect to), so she doesn't feel bad if the session ends before all tasks have been attempted.

Decide when you'll provide compensation

You'll notice that in many situations, we recommend providing the full compensation amount to your participant even if she doesn't stay for the full session or if she doesn't meet your recruit criteria. We've found that it's easier to provide the compensation no matter what than trying to define the specific instances when it's not appropriate. It's too difficult to figure out where to place the blame for a participant who does not meet your recruit criteria or why a participant arrived late, and we'd rather pay a little extra in compensation to keep participants satisfied than get into an argument with an uncompensated participant.

Compensating the participant is also consistent with the pattern of taking responsibility wherever possible, which is described in section 3.1.

Obviously your mileage may vary on this recommendation. However, if you do implement a policy that would prevent the participant from receiving her compensation, be very clear with her about those circumstances during the recruiting process and allow a bit of tolerance. For example, if you let participants know that they won't be compensated if they arrive more than 15 minutes late, and the participant arrives 17 minutes late, she should still receive her compensation. Be reasonable and understanding.

Also, think about when in the session—the beginning or end—you'll provide compensation to participants. Most researchers provide compensation at the end of the session. However, providing compensation at the beginning of the session reassures the participant that she really is free to leave at any time and that she is not going to be penalized for leaving early.

15.3 The product, space, and technology

If you're planning to have the participant interact with a product—whether a released/ live version or a prototype—during the session, follow these tips to limit the possibility of technical or product-related situations.

Preparing a live website or application

If you're getting feedback on a live website or application, talk with your development team to ensure that no updates will be applied during your research. Explain that you need participants to all give feedback on the same version of the product. If it's a website and any A/B testing is being done, see if there is a way for you to either have that functionality turned off during your research or for you to consistently see the same version of pages (e.g., always the A design). If these guarantees cannot be made, see if you can run your research from a developer sandbox, quality assurance link, or some other staging area with the extensive functionality of the live product.

If you're getting feedback on the released public-facing version of an application or software product, check to see if any updates are scheduled to be released between now and your study. For most research you want feedback on the most recent version, so you may be able to get access to a test or beta version of the upcoming release so you can plan ahead.

If you're unable to talk with the development team (e.g., because you're running a competitive study and have no way to contact a team), check the product every day for a couple of weeks before the study to see what, if anything, changes. This due diligence will help you get a feel for what you might expect on your study days. However, keep in mind that you might come in to find that a brand-new redesign has been rolled out. Be sure that your stakeholders are aware of this as a potential complication.

Preparing a prototype

The features needed in a prototype (typically used for a usability study) vary widely depending on the domain, product type, and goals of the study. However, the following tips will help make your prototype (i.e., an interactive environment beyond static images) be successful during a study:

➤ Make the prototype as functional as possible. The situation described in section 11.4 is a good example of why: participants can be frustrated by a low-functioning prototype. Developers or prototypers new to user research often mistakenly think of the study as a demo that will be performed in a very structured and linear fashion. This mindset may lead them to create a prototype that has only the correct answer-paths working, and sometimes in only a set order. Participants will catch on to which areas are working and which aren't, which can lead to frustration and bias. It may influence the way they think about the design and the actions they take.

➤ If the prototype can't be completely functional, make it adequately functional. In the real world, participants will try lots of crazy paths to an answer and sometimes you can't anticipate all of them. So "adequately functional" means that the prototype includes more than just a linear flow of clicks or steps, and more than just the correct paths are working. The prototype should provide alternate and anticipated wrong paths or steps that the participant can then explore and attempt.

➤ We recognize that most teams have time and resourcing constraints. If you can't get more than the correct paths or steps working, provide the *illusion* that the prototype is more functional. One example of this is, in a website prototype, make all of the links on the page *look* clickable even if they're just null links that don't go anywhere. Doing this prevents the mouse "drive-by," where participants can catch onto what is working based on where they get the hover-hand icon.

As with running your study on a live product, talk with your designers/developers to ensure that no design changes are made to the prototype during the study. Let them know that any changes they want to make need to be discussed with and approved by you first, as those changes may have an impact on your study protocol, the data you're able to collect and compare to previous participants' results, and the prototype's stability.

If you're doing your research in an agile environment, you may be planning to update the prototype after just one or two participants. Even so, we recommend that the changes are discussed with you first so you're not surprised the next time you open the prototype.

Test and document the technical setup

To avoid, or at least minimize, technical difficulties during your study, do a full walkthrough of your technical setup for the session. This walkthrough should including turning on and off any cameras, screen-sharing applications, and recording devices. Test the order in which each item needs to be turned on or off and document the order that works best. Depending on the complexity of your setup, consider including a checklist of your setup steps in your study plan so you can easily reset if anything changes during a session.

If you're running a remote session:

➤ Familiarize yourself with options to mute others on the call or eject them from the screen-sharing session to avoid observers interrupting the session.

➤ Do a dry run with participants to ensure that your screen-sharing software works on their computers, which will save time during their sessions.

➤ In your technical setup checklist, include screenshots of what the participant will experience as she joins the remote session. These screenshots will help you provide instructions to the participant to perform basic troubleshooting.

For more ideas on what to look at in your technical setup, see the sidebar "Troubleshooting Skills Are a Lifesaver."

TROUBLESHOOTING SKILLS ARE A LIFESAVER

A key skill for a user researcher is technical troubleshooting. Given how integrated technology is with our work, it's in your best interest to learn as much as possible about:

➤ Recording technologies, including software like Morae or Camtasia, and old-school recording technologies such as DVD burners and video cameras.

➤ Screen-sharing technologies, such as WebEx and GoToMeeting.

➤ Built-in and external web cameras, their drivers, and how they're used through recording and screen-sharing programs.

➤ Phone conferencing systems, including voiceover IP systems that integrate into programs like WebEx.

➤ General computer basics, such as networking, extended and clone desktop, and changing screen resolution. Try to be at least familiar with both Macs and PCs.

➤ Cables and connection types, including VGA, DVI, and HDMI.

➤ Usability lab settings, the specifics of which depend on the lab but usually include changing camera views, routing screens, and sound.

➤ Any other devices you plan to use to capture participant feedback, such as eye-tracking equipment.

No matter the problem, the most valuable troubleshooting tip we have is to isolate the variables! For example, if your audio is not working, avoid changing five settings at once. If the audio still is not working after making multiple changes, you don't know anything more about the problem than when you started—and if it did work, you lost a chance to identify the most efficient solution. Change one thing at a time and see if it solves the problem. Only consider trying combinations of things if, based on prior experience, you think you need to and individual changes didn't make a difference.

Knowing these basics will help you keep your sessions running smoothly without waiting for someone else to help you. Tinker with the equipment and settings before a study. Ask someone who knows the equipment to deliberately break something (e.g., disconnect a cable or change a camera setting) and try to troubleshoot it for practice. If you have a team of researchers, you can set up troubleshooting exercises for each other to help increase your competence and confidence. The next time something goes wrong during a session, you'll have the skills to handle it!

Familiarize yourself with the space and its safety options

Before your study begins, familiarize yourself as much as possible with the space that your research is being performed in. Are there security guards? Where is the nearest fire exit? Don't be afraid to ask questions, especially if you're in an unfamiliar space. By knowing these answers ahead of time, you'll be able to more quickly respond to anything that requires a bit of "native" knowledge.

If there is building security, notify them about any participants who may be coming for your research. Again, if something happens, their advance knowledge of what you're doing may save precious time.

Also, make sure at least one other person from your team, whether a team member or stakeholder, is available to watch each session. We highly recommend avoiding running user research on your own because, if an uncomfortable or potentially litigious situation arises, you need another set of eyes, and hands.

Once you have another person who can join you for the session, consider creating a "safe phrase." This is a phrase that you share with the person observing the session, and that you use only if you need that person to interrupt the session. For example, if you've been getting a very bad feeling about the participant, and the participant has positioned himself between you and the door, you may want to use the phrase to notify your observer that you need her to knock on the door and provide an excuse for you to leave the room. Since it may be difficult to tell exactly how serious a situation is from another room, the safe phrase is your way to request assistance.

Investigate cultural customs and taboos

If you're doing research in other countries or cultural regions, do your due diligence and learn about the customs ahead of time. For example, some cultures require you to take off your shoes before entering. Others may take offense if you don't accept tea, or if your knees and shoulders aren't covered. Some cultures expect you to exchange business cards in a certain way. The more you can be prepared, the less uncomfortable or awkward the situation will be.

A good resource with more tips for conducting user research with different cultures is *The Handbook of Global User Research* (Schumacher, 2010).

But also be careful not to assume anything solely based on what you read or hear—that could be offensive too. Try to take cues from your participants—for example, if the participant has her shoes off and there is a shoe rack at the door, that is probably a good sign that it's important to respect that rule in the household. Put your empathy and observational skills to good use!

15.4 Your observers

By sharing your moderating approach and establishing ground rules ahead of time, you can decrease the odds of your observers disrupting your session.

Communicate your moderating approach

As you work with your team to create the study plan, set expectations with your potential observers about how you're going to moderate during the session. The detail level you need to go into will vary depending on how familiar they are with user research in general, the specific method you're using (e.g., contextual inquiry), and your particular moderating approach. Here are some things to consider going over:

➤ You may not follow the study plan in its exact order, or use its exact wording (if you're confident and experienced enough to take this approach). You might reprioritize goals on-the-fly based on what the participant says or does, or probe with follow-up questions wherever necessary.

➤ You may let the participant go off on brief tangents and act interested in irrelevant things to let the participant feel heard.

➤ You may not answer the participant's question, or might pretend not to know an answer even if you do (and that is not an invitation for someone to come in and give you the correct answer!).

➤ When probing for something specific—a goal, or understanding more behind something the participant did or didn't do—you may start with broad questions and narrow down to more and more specific questions. For example: "What did you think of that?" "What did you think of how this area worked?" "What do you think this button does?"

➤ You might drop a topic, redirect to another as a diversion, and come back to the first topic later (see Chapter 3 sidebar "The Diversionary Assist").

➤ If you're doing a usability study:

■ You may let the participant struggle for the sake of uncovering findings, but ultimately the participant's comfort is the first concern. There will be times you need to sacrifice "data" or be especially strict about observer behavior for the participant's well-being.

■ Explain what an assist is, and when and how you give participants assists.

By setting these expectations, you can hopefully prevent an observer from making assumptions (e.g., assuming that you were being leading when you were giving an assist). It will also keep them from interrupting a session because they don't understand what you're doing and think you need additional information or assistance.

Provide ground rules

Another way to avoid or minimize observer interruptions is to provide a set of ground rules for observer behavior during a session. You should share these ground rules with your observers before the session so they have a chance to read them ahead of time. Also, print the list of rules and give it to your observers if they're in the room with you during the session, or post the rules on the wall of their observation space.

Here are some ground rules for observers in another room (e.g., usability lab observation room):

➤ Keep any conversation or discussion to a minimum. No loud laughing! Even supposedly soundproofed walls can be surprisingly permeable.

➤ Keep the participant's identity and personal information (e.g., company) confidential, especially if an observer knows her personally. The observers should also refrain from revealing the identity to others.

➤ Avoid making fun of the participant.

➤ Keep cell phones silenced (not on vibrate).

➤ Leave the room quietly if a call must be taken.

➤ Avoid slamming doors.

➤ Avoid talking about the research study outside of the observation room for as long as the sessions are running. This includes not talking to the participant about the study if observers run into her in the hallway or restroom before or after the session.

➤ Stay for an entire session, and attend as many sessions as possible.

➤ Follow agreed-on guidelines for asking questions to the participant. These guidelines should be based on a conversation you had with the observers before the session and should cover if, when, and how they can ask questions. However, be careful to set expectations that you may not always get to asking their questions, or ask their questions in the way they posed them.

For example, you may want to set up an instant message (IM) session where observers can IM their questions to you. Section 9.5 includes additional options for gathering observer questions.

➤ Follow agreed-on guidelines for how to communicate with you. Again, these guidelines should be based on a conversation you've had before the session about if, when, and how to get in touch with you during the session. For example, you may set the expectation that if they see something that isn't working in the prototype, they can quietly knock on the door of your study space so you can excuse yourself and talk to them, but otherwise they should hold their questions until you come talk to them toward the end of the session.

➤ If you've asked them to take notes or help in some other way with data collection, include a short summary that observers can refer to throughout the session.

When an observer is in the room with you and the participant, most of the previous points apply. Some exceptions and additions include:

➤ There should be *no* conversation or discussion, and absolutely no laughing or even throwing meaningful looks at other in-room observers.

➤ Avoid multitasking (and the appearance of multitasking). Pay attention!

➤ Avoid disruptions (stepping out, etc.) unless absolutely necessary.

➤ Be careful of body language and any physical or audible reactions.

➤ Know if, when, and how to interact with the participant, based on a conversation before the session. For example:

▪ The observer should not help the participant complete tasks or answer questions.

▪ Is the observer experienced talking to users? If so you may let her ask questions to the participant directly either during the session or at the end. Or, if you're less comfortable with that, have her write down her questions on notes and (subtly) pass them to you.

When observers are observing remotely, include additional ground rules:

➤ Keep the phone or voice over IP (VoIP) functionality on mute at all times unless told otherwise. This includes situations when it seems like the participant has dropped off the call or has hung up. As with in-person observing, the observer should know if she can interact with the participant at all, and when (e.g., at the end of the call when the moderator opens up the line for questions).

➤ Know how and when to interact with you, as described in the preceding points. Communicating via an IM application can be very useful when you have remote observers. As discussed earlier, be clear with the observers about whether or how you might react to their IM requests and questions.

 Watch Video 5 to see an example of a moderator dealing with an interrupting observer during a contextual inquiry. The moderator pulls the observer out of the room to reiterate the session ground rules.

Visit our website (http://www.modsurvivalguide.org/videos) or use your QR reader to scan this code.

15.5 Your technique

Before you moderate your first session for a study, review:

➤ The list of prefabricated phrases from Appendix A. If you're new to moderating, jot a couple of the phrases in your study plan to reference throughout the study.

➤ The guidelines for your language and tone from section 2.5.

➤ The list of moderator behaviors to avoid from section 2.3.

Once you have a study plan almost finalized, you can also run a practice session with a colleague acting as your participant so you can get a better feel for how the session will go and any areas that you feel like you might struggle with. This practice will help you refine your study plan and help you feel more comfortable with the protocol by the time your first session comes around. Of course, also be sure to run a pilot session with an actual participant using your study plan and the product (if applicable) before your first full day of sessions. You'll feel more confident and will appreciate the additional familiarity with the protocol in case anything unexpected happens and you need to adjust.

Chapter 16 provides additional suggestions for improving your moderating skills.

YOUR MODERATING "INSTINCTS"

The user research field draws personality types who are curious about, and enjoy observing, the world and human behavior. These natural instincts help you pick up on the participant's emotional state.

With practice, you start to notice the subtle body language cues coming from the participant, and adjust your own body language, tone, or study plan accordingly. This unspoken feedback can help you understand how the participant feels about a product, and provides an opportunity for you to follow up with questions if she is not articulating the issues clearly on her own. Carolyn Snyder (2003) defines one of the roles of the moderator as a "sportscaster" who helps make observers aware of what is going on in the session. Using your intuition to identify opportunities to probe is central to this role. Practice will also help refine your ability to understand whether a behavior is related to the design or the research situation, so that you can respond appropriately.

Although there is no easy way to "teach" instincts, our advice is to try to broaden your research lens outside yourself when you moderate. In other words, don't just focus on your research goals but turn it into a challenge to also research the participant's demeanor. Try to develop an awareness of what is happening during the session. As G.I. Joe says, "knowing is half the battle."

Also, try turning other experiences with the outside world into opportunities to improve these instincts. Watch people interact with each other at your local coffee shop, and try to gauge their emotional states based on their body language. Watching others will help you refine your awareness of how the participant may be feeling and will help you adapt appropriately. Plus, it's fun to people watch!

CHAPTER 16

Sharpening Steel:
How to Improve Your Skills
and Help Others Improve Theirs

Since you're reading this book, you're already aware that moderating is a skill that can always be improved. You may have noticed that user researchers rarely talk to each other about our moderating skills. Instead, we commiserate with each other about challenging participants or unique situations. This commiseration is valuable, but it can be difficult to translate those stories into actionable ways to improve yourself. Think of your moderating skill as a blade that needs to be sharpened on a regular basis if you want it to work efficiently. If you've ever gone a few months between moderating sessions, you've probably felt a bit rusty and like you were off of your game. This chapter focuses on how to get feedback on your moderating, and how to give feedback to others. These techniques will help you improve and refine your moderating skills whether you're a novice or an expert.

16.1 Working on your moderating skills

No matter how experienced you are, at various times in your career you'll inevitably say or do things while moderating that you'll wish you hadn't. You'll say something outrageously leading or give away something about how a task can be accomplished, and watch in horror as those words float out of your mouth. Even the most experienced moderators among us can get sloppy and fall into bad habits. We all make mistakes. But mistakes don't make you a bad moderator as long as you recognize when you could have done something better and take steps to avoid those mistakes in the future.

The following are some ways in which you can elicit feedback and improve your own moderating skills.

This recognition and self-reflection helps you grow and succeed as a moderator.

Watch yourself

First, watch a recording of a session that you've moderated. Yes, this may be painful, especially if you're fairly new to moderating. You may hate the sound of your voice and cringe at the verbal tics you never noticed before. But, take a deep breath and remember that you're doing this to be better and more successful at your job! Watching yourself is the easiest way to build a realistic awareness of what your moderating is really like. For specific ideas on what to look for while watching the recording, see the sidebar "What to Look for in a Moderating Critique."

If you can plan ahead of time to record a session specifically for this purpose, and your facility has the appropriate setup, adjust the cameras so you can capture both you and the participant. This view will let you watch your body language and give a wider lens to your interactions with the participant.

Ask a colleague to watch

One of the best ways to get feedback on how you're doing is to ask a trusted colleague with user research experience to watch while you moderate. If possible, and your confidentiality policies allow it, have him watch you with a real participant, but if that's not possible, ask another colleague to be your practice participant. Offer a friendly incentive, such as taking him out for a coffee, especially if you're asking him to help outside of his normal work hours.

If you can't work out a time when your colleague can watch you actually run a session, see if you can have him watch a recording instead. You can either sit with him as he watches to receive his feedback in context of the recording, or talk with him afterwards.

If you're not sure how to ask your colleague to watch you and provide feedback, consider something like:

> ➤ "I'd really like to get some feedback on my moderating. Do you have some time to watch one of my sessions? I'd really appreciate your perspective and recommendations about my tone, my questions, body language, and anything else you think might help me improve."

If you feel comfortable taking it a step further, consider asking him to also:

➤ Take notes while watching. This will help him document and remember concrete examples of things you did well and could do better.

➤ Be as candid as possible, because you value constructive criticism.

➤ Spend some time debriefing with you, rather than just handing off his notes. Ideally, you'd like to have a conversation.

➤ Pay attention to specific areas that you would like advice for, especially if you're showing a recording. Ask him to think about what he would do in certain situations in which you struggled. Also, consider giving him a copy of the sidebar "What to Look for in a Moderating Critique."

You could also ask multiple colleagues (who ideally have experience moderating research sessions) to watch a session. We recommend that you know and trust your audience if you do this, as it is humbling to have a group of people scrutinizing your work! It may be more comfortable to have colleagues who you've worked with repeatedly and whose judgment you trust, rather than a random group of people who don't know you or have limited experience with user research. We recommend asking an individual colleague to take notes while watching and debrief with you afterwards.

Depending on your colleagues, they might feel more comfortable if you broaden the scope to have them comment on anything related to the study setup and protocol in addition to your moderating interactions.

Be sure not to violate participant confidentiality for recordings by sharing outside of your project team (or whatever the agreement established). If you're at all uncertain whether this is allowed, run and record a practice session that you can share instead.

Even better than asking for feedback as a one-time thing, consider finding one or more colleagues to be recurring "moderating mentors." Ask your mentors to observe your user research studies, either via real time or recordings, and pay attention to the items previously listed. Having a mentor at every study will help you understand how you're improving over time. The benefit of having multiple mentors is receiving feedback from moderators with multiple perspectives and styles so you can begin to calibrate your own approach.

However, we know that not everyone has the luxury of working with a team of user researchers. If you are a "team of one" and don't have any colleagues who can provide feedback, reach out to local (or national) user experience groups to see if they can pair you with a more experienced mentor. Even if your mentor is in a different physical location, the Internet has made it easier than ever to share recordings and watch sessions remotely.

For a list of user experience groups and resources, see Appendix C.

Practice with someone

If you're just starting your research career, you may be nervous about moderating with a real participant in front of your stakeholders. The best way to reduce your nervousness is by practicing as much as you can! Grab a colleague or family member as the participant. If you're not sure what to ask, try something like:

➤ "Do you have time later this afternoon? I need a participant for a practice session. I'd go through the script I'll use with actual participants, but I wouldn't be recording you or using any of your feedback."

You can use a study plan that you've used for a recent study as long as you don't violate any confidentiality agreements you have in place with your stakeholders. Another option is to adapt a study plan for a product that is publicly available (for a usability study or contextual inquiry), or a different topic (for an interview).

Go through the session end to end, starting with welcoming the participant and going all the way through thanking him for his time. Do your best to pretend that this is an actual session with a participant who you don't know.

Record the session to watch later, although if you do so, be sure to provide the participant with a consent form explaining how his recording may be used (e.g., you'll not share it publicly, it will only be viewed by yourself and possibly a few respected colleagues with the purpose of improving your skills).

Practicing isn't just for new or inexperienced moderators. Even experienced moderators can benefit from additional practice, especially if you give the participant free reign to act unexpectedly at various points throughout the session. When we've held practice sessions, some of the types of things we've asked the participant to do at random times include:

➤ Forget to think aloud.

➤ Ask "Am I doing this right?"

➤ Blame himself for not being able to do something.

➤ Ask personal questions or flirt.

➤ Become extremely angry at the product/company.

You can even let the participant flip through this book's situation chapters to get ideas on what he might want to do during the session. We also recommend watching the companion videos provided on our website for additional ideas: http://www.modsurvivalguide.org/videos. Watch one of the videos, and then act the same scene out with someone playing the participant. Take the suggested approach and apply it to your own style of moderating. How does it feel? What might you need to adjust to better suit your personality and comfort levels?

Think of all of these practice sessions like workouts before your big game. This kind of role-playing lets you experience situations in a relatively safe zone and can better prepare you for what might happen during a real session.

Observe others moderating and ask questions

If you're lucky enough to work with other user researchers, sit in on as many of their sessions as possible. Even experienced moderators can pick up tips, tricks, and reminders about behaviors they want to try to emulate (or avoid) by watching others. Take notes while you watch so you can review later.

If you're unsure about why a moderator did something during a session, ask him about it afterwards. Remember to keep your tone curious and courteous, not accusatory.

See section 16.3 for more on providing feedback to other moderators.

Seek out resources

While there aren't a ton of resources focused on moderating, the topic is discussed in almost any book about user research. Find books on the research methods that you're most interested in, and read their tips on moderating for those methods. There are also many articles that pop up on this topic in professional magazines and journals.

Many user experience conferences that focus on methodology and research techniques will include presentations or tutorials about moderating. Dumas and Loring (2008) also recommend attending a short course on conducting usability tests, although these are usually focused on new or inexperienced practitioners and may be less useful for someone who wants to refine their skills.

Listen to stories from other moderators

The great thing about listening to stories from other moderators is that you can learn something without needing to go through the experience yourself. It's not as powerful as experiencing it yourself, even in a practice setting, but learning vicariously gives you a framework for thinking about how you might deal with similar situations. While we hope this book is helpful in this respect, we encourage you to reach out to others in your research community so you can learn from each other.

16.2 Integrating tips and feedback

Of course, becoming a better moderator isn't as simple as taking feedback and tips and *just doing it*. These techniques won't immediately make you a superstar moderator—like most skills, moderating takes lots of practice, over a long period of time.

Once you've sought out all available resources, practiced, and received feedback on your moderating, take an incremental approach rather than trying to change everything all at once. You have a lot to think about during research sessions, and you don't want 80% of your brain power going to overanalyzing your performance. Revisiting the metaphor of improvisational comedy, the best improvisation scenes come when the players are not "in their heads." In other words, if you're thinking too hard, you're blocking the passageways for the instincts formed by all of the training, practice, and feedback you've received up until that point. The same is true for moderating—don't get stuck on acting and reacting perfectly, or you'll just freeze up.

Instead, plan out the incremental changes that you can make. When you run your next session (even if it's just for practice), focus on one or two small things that you want to improve about your moderating. Make a note for yourself about it in your study plan so you have an additional reminder. Aside from those small things, free yourself up to think on your feet and use your instincts to respond genuinely to the participant and acquire solid research findings. Focus on the same thing across a few sessions or even an entire study. Then, for the next session, focus on another area you want to improve.

As an example of how to plan out these changes, let's say that you've received feedback from a colleague saying you tend to cut off the participant, answer questions too soon, and unconsciously tap your pen on your clipboard. In your next session, focus on addressing the problem of cutting off the participant. Try deliberately to let him finish his thoughts before saying anything. You may have to do this for a few sessions until you feel like you're not

Refer to Appendix C to see a list of user research resources that focus on specific methods.

Each change is a baby step, but those small steps are incredibly effective.

THE MODERATOR'S SURVIVAL GUIDE

thinking about it so much. Then introduce the next change—addressing the fact that you answer every question a participant asks right away. So in preparation for the next session, write a note that says "WAIT FIVE SECONDS!" at the top of every page of your study plan. Every time the participant asks you a question, count to five in your head before doing or saying anything. Continue working on this for a few sessions until it too feels natural. Then, focus on the pen-tapping for the next go-round.

16.3 Giving feedback to other moderators

Giving solicited feedback

If someone asks you to give feedback on his moderating, take it as a compliment—that person thinks enough of your skills to want your perspective. Congratulations! Be sure to take his request seriously; don't respond with "Oh, your moderating is fine," even if you think it is. As we've mentioned before, even good moderators can improve and need to keep their skills fresh.

For tips on how to give feedback, see the sidebar "What to Look for in a Moderating Critique."

WHAT TO LOOK FOR IN A MODERATING CRITIQUE

Here are some pointers on what to look for when watching your own moderating or giving feedback to other moderators (in which case, replace "you" with "the moderator"). Pay attention to:

➤ *How you start the session.* The first encounter and introductions set the stage for the rest of the session. If you're nervous, that might be reflected in the participant's behavior.

➤ *Where you're positioned relative to the participant.* Are you too close or too far? How might your positioning be affecting the research? For example, is sitting directly beside the participant encouraging him to fraternize too much?

➤ *What you're saying to the participant.* Are you asking leading questions? Are you using terms that are visible in the interface you're testing? Are you being kind, yet in control? Are you talking too quickly, or too slowly?

➤ *The tone of what you're saying to the participant.* Do you sound condescending? Conversely, do you sound unsure or reluctant?

➤ *Anything about your behavior that you find annoying or distracting.* Are you playing with your watch, your hair, or your clipboard?

➤ *Anything unnecessary that you're doing or saying.* Is there something you could stop doing that either gets in the way or doesn't add value to the session?

> ➤ *The participant's reactions in particular situations, both his body language and what he is saying.* If necessary, go back a bit in the recording and replay it. Did you do (or not do) anything that made the participant react? What did you miss about the participant's behavior and attitude while you were sitting with him? Which of his reactions are you surprised by?
>
> ➤ *If, and how, you adapt your behavior throughout the session.* How might you adapt your moderating style based on the participant's reactions? Should you?
>
> ➤ *Examples of what you did well.* What should you continue to do in the future?
>
> If you encountered a situation that's listed in this book, go back and look at that section. How did you do compared with what is listed there? If you deviated from our suggestions, did it make sense to do so based on your circumstances? Every scenario is unique, and real-life scenarios can include a confusing combination of situations. You may encounter times when the goals and strategies for handling one situation conflict with the goals and strategies for the other, combined situation. If that is the case, use your best judgment and the suggestions in Chapters 2 and 3 to help decide what should take priority. If you're unsure about whether you did the right thing, start a discussion with colleagues about the best course of action and the trade-offs you had to make.

Giving unsolicited feedback

You may find yourself needing to give feedback to someone who hasn't asked for it. Maybe you're working with a consultant who is moderating some research for you, and you've noticed some behaviors that are influencing the participant. Or, maybe you have junior team members helping with a study who need a reminder to avoid asking leading questions.

You may feel nervous if the person you need to give feedback to is more senior than you, or is someone who is well-known in the field. One approach you can take to avoid sounding confrontational is to ask the person about why he handled the situation the way he did, taking a curious and conversational tone:

➤ "I noticed that when the participant asked how he was doing, you told him that other participants had the same problems he had. I'm curious about why you answered that way—is that a standard response?"

➤ "During the session, the participant seemed really upset about how poorly he thought he was doing. I've seen other sessions where the moderator offers to let the participant take a break when the participant gets that upset. What do you think about that—is that ever appropriate?"

If you feel that you have a strong working relationship with the person you'd like to give feedback to and aren't worried about his reaction, you can try a more direct approach. But don't just start giving him feedback; start by asking if he'd like to hear it:

➤ "I had a chance to watch one of your sessions, and thought you did a good job. There were a couple of things that I noticed while you were moderating. I know you have a lot going on, but would you be interested in hearing my feedback?"

➤ "Hey *<moderator>*, great session! I know that if it were me, I'd want to hear any feedback that other moderators have for me (and please do let me know any time you have feedback for me!). So I do have a couple of ideas to bounce off you about what I noticed while watching you moderate, if you're up for hearing them."

Of course, a less direct way of giving the feedback is to present it in a funny way. For example, "Heh, that was funny when you asked, 'Are you having a problem?' and the participant got upset and was like, 'Um-NO!'" We've received feedback veiled in humor before and we've gotten the message and were glad to hear it! But of course using humor can be touchy, so if the person you're giving feedback to doesn't respond, or responds negatively, avoid using that approach with him in the future.

Also, keep in mind something you've hopefully learned when presenting user research findings: discussing what worked well can help the more negative feedback be received more smoothly.

Another way to exchange feedback is to set up a process where you and your colleagues can submit your feedback. For example, if you work on a large user research team, you could create an anonymous survey to fill out after each study. Or the survey could capture "suggestion box" ideas, collecting generalized feedback that is not specifically targeted to any one researcher or study. The entire team can then get together and discuss the comments. It's a great way to continually discuss moderating techniques and improve everyone's skills.

If you're hiring a consultant to work with or for you on a project, his agency might solicit feedback on his performance after the project has ended. If this mechanism is in place, make sure to include feedback on his moderating. If something like that is not in place, consider working with the agency to instate a feedback loop for this purpose.

16.4 Spread your wings

We hope this book has provided you with the confidence to handle anything that gets thrown your way while moderating user research. Even if many of the situations listed are uncommon, we recommend that you flip through them anyway. You should be able to make connections between the patterns, steps, and best practices we've presented to you, and our recommended courses of action in the many normal, abnormal, boring, interesting, common, intimidating, zany, funny, and scary situations you've read about. Internalizing those connections and recommendations, and continuously working to improve your skills as discussed in this chapter, will help you handle any new situations that arise—with confidence.

When your colleagues sing your praises about your improved moderating techniques, first pat yourself on the back because you're the one who made that happen. Then, tell them that this book helped and point them to our website: http://www.modsurvivalguide.org. There are lots of additional resources available there, including those that you find in the appendices of this book, to get anyone started and keep you sharp. And by all means, we want to hear your stories too! Visit http://www.modsurvivalguide.org/stories and let's keep the conversation going about how to learn and evolve as moderators.

APPENDICES

APPENDIX A: WHAT TO SAY

Knowing what to say, and when, is one of the biggest challenges in moderating, especially when you're just starting out. Here are some of the phrases that we've found to be effective throughout a session. You'll notice that in many cases, we show a lot of different ways to say the same thing. Try them all and see which variations feel most comfortable for you.

Desired Effect	What to Say
Set expectations	"If you ask me questions, I may not really answer you or I may be vague. If I'm doing that, I'm not being unfriendly; I'm just trying to stay neutral."
Provide a neutral acknowledgment	"Mmhmm." "Okay." "Okay, thank you." "Okay, thanks for that." "That's good to know." "That's helpful for us to know."
Turn a question around	"I want to stay neutral here, so I'm going to turn that back on you— what are your thoughts on this?" "If you were doing this at home, and I wasn't sitting there next to you, what would you do?" "I'm not sure, but tell me more about what you're thinking here...." "What matters is your experience, which we can learn from. Tell me more about what you're experiencing here...." "My opinion isn't important to the team—we're here to talk about yours. What do you think?"
Prompt a silent/ nonresponsive participant	"What are you trying to do right now? "May I ask what you're thinking about right now?" "What are you thinking right now?" "What is going through your mind right now?" "What are your thoughts on this?" "What are your thoughts on how that worked?" "I'd like to remind you to try to think out loud as you go through these tasks. I know it may feel uncomfortable at first, but it helps us understand more about how you're approaching the tasks."

Desired Effect	What to Say
Clarify behavior	"I noticed you doing something that I couldn't quite follow. Could you help me understand better what you were doing and why? It was when you <*did thing*>...."
	"How did this compare with your expectations?"
	"What would you expect?"
	(If the participant encountered a limitation of the prototype): "This section isn't built out for us today—what were you expecting to happen?"
	"That link isn't working for today's session. What would you expect to happen if you clicked it and it was working?"
Provide reassurance and build engagement	"There are no wrongs here; you're here to help us."
	"If we didn't see what areas work well or not so well for you, we wouldn't learn anything."
	"Please know that your candor is appreciated. Nothing you say will hurt anyone's feelings. You're here to help us make the product better for yourself and future users."
	"This is just the kind of feedback we want to hear...."
	"Thanks so much for participating. I know it is taking time out of your busy day, but your feedback is very helpful."
	"All of this has been very helpful to hear and see. Thank you for your continual feedback."
	"You're here to help partner with us to evaluate the design, so all of this is really helpful for us to see and hear."
	"Have you ever tried to do this before? Tell me about your experience."
Redirect or cut feedback short	"We have a lot to get through, so I may at times gently push you along so that we can make sure to cover everything."
	"This is all very helpful to see and hear. Just for the sake of time, I'm going to ask you to go to the next task/go back to...."
	"Thank you for going into that level of detail. For the sake of time though, I'd like you to return to attempting/answering task/question...."
	"I'm sorry, I just want to interrupt you here for a second. For the sake of time I'd like you to return to the task/question, and we can revisit this topic at the end of the session if time permits."
	"Let's move on for now. I wanted to ask you about what you did earlier...."
	"Why don't we stop this task here, because I wanted to ask you about...."
	"Let's stop this here and we can come back to it later. Read the next scenario...."
	"That's as far as we need to go with that. Why don't we...."
	"I'm interested in hearing more about this. I do want to make sure we cover everything we have planned, so if there is time, let's come back to this at the end of the session...."

Desired Effect	What to Say
Assist (purposeful help)	"What if I were to tell you that...."
	"Let me draw your attention to this area. What are your thoughts on it being here?"
	"I'll just let you know that there is a way from here to do that...."
	"I will point out that you can find that functionality here. Talk to me about that versus your expectations."
	"It's good to see your thought process in doing that. I will just let you know that there is actually a different way of doing that task. I'm curious to know what you think of it <point him to correct way>."
Take a break, using a mild pretext	"I apologize, but it looks like there's something wrong with our system. Please excuse me for a few minutes while I go to the other room and see if anyone from our team knows what is going on."
	"Excuse me for just a moment, but I just noticed that there's something wrong with our equipment. Let's take a short break so I can get it working again."
	(For a user test with a multiroom setup): "It seems like we may be having technical issues. Let's take a short five-minute break while I run nextdoor to look into it. Feel free to leave the room to get a drink or go to the restroom while I'm gone."
	(For an onsite session): "I'm so sorry, but would you mind if I took a quick five-minute break to get a drink?" or "This seems like a good stopping point. Why don't we take a quick five-minute break?"
	"Thank you for your feedback so far. Let's take a quick five-minute break so I can see if any of our observers have any questions for you so far."
	"I need to check on something before the next part of the session, so let's take a brief break."
Shift focus	"It looks like our prototype is not working as we planned it to, so if you don't mind I'm going to just ask you some questions."
End a session early	(If you're skipping sections of your script, and the participant can see that there are more tasks/questions than what you're asking): "The rest of these tasks/questions aren't applicable to you/your role, so we're going to skip them."
	"You went through everything faster than expected, so we're going to get you out of here early."
	"That's actually all I had for you today, so you'll get some time back in your day! Thank you so much for your feedback, and here is your compensation."
	"I'm sorry, but we're going to have to cancel the session due to some technical difficulties. Thank you so much for coming in, and here is your compensation."
	"I'm sorry, but we have to end the session early due to some problems with our equipment. Thank you so much for coming in—here is your compensation. Let me walk you out."

APPENDIX: PREPARING FOR A SUCCESSFUL SESSION

Follow this checklist as you prepare for your research study. These tips will help make sure that you do everything possible to reduce or minimize the chances of something unexpected or sticky happening. While we always hope for the best when it comes to our participants and study setup, it never hurts to plan for the worst.

For more information about these topics, refer to Chapter 15.

One Week in Advance

- Discuss the recruit criteria with your stakeholders:
  - How many participants do you need (remember to account for possible no-shows)?
  - Do you need floater or backup participants?
  - If you don't recruit floater or backup participants, are there surrogate users at your study location who may be able to fill in for a session on short notice?
- Identify your key participant criteria, whether in a formal recruiting script that can be used by external recruiters or a checklist that you can use when scheduling participants on your own.
  - Explain who and what the study is for, how long it will take, where it will be held, and what (if any) compensation will be offered.
  - Make sure they understand that it will be one-on-one.
  - Specify if the session will be recorded (and if so, what exactly will be recorded) and observed.
  - Be specific about the experience/skills required.
  - Ask about the criteria in a way that makes it hard to tell what your desired answer is. For example, ask "What is the make and model of your car?" not "Do you have a Toyota Prius?"
  - Check to make sure you can understand the participant.
  - If you (or someone else at an organization) will be scheduling internal employees:
    - Reiterate that they are not required to participate.
    - Recruit a representative sample of users rather than just the best or most vocal.
    - Assure them that they'll not be watched by their manager or members of their own team.
  - Ask for the best phone number that you can use to contact them, and give them a way to directly get in touch with you if necessary.
  - If you'll be going to the participant's location, ask if there are any restrictions on what you can bring with you (e.g., cameras, USB flash drivers) or if you'll need to arrive early to go through any additional security.

APPENDIX B: PREPARING FOR A SUCCESSFUL SESSION

Follow this checklist as you prepare for your research study. These tips will help make sure that you do everything possible to reduce or minimize the chances of something unexpected or sticky happening. While we always hope for the best when it comes to our participants and study setup, it never hurts to plan for the worst.

For more information about these topics, refer to Chapter 15.

The recruiting process

➤ Discuss the recruit criteria with your stakeholders:

■ How many participants do you need (remember to account for possible no-shows)?

■ Do you need floater or backup participants?

■ If you don't recruit floater or backup participants, are there surrogate users at your study location who may be able to fill in for a session on short notice?

➤ Identify your key participant criteria, whether in a formal recruiting script that can be used by external recruiters or a checklist that you can use when scheduling participants on your own:

■ Explain who and what the study is for, how long it will take, where it will be held, and what (if any) compensation will be offered.

■ Make sure they understand that it will be one-on-one.

■ Specify if the session will be recorded (and if so, what exactly will be recorded) and observed.

■ Be specific about the experience/skills required.

■ Ask about the criteria in a way that makes it hard to tell what your desired answer is. For example, ask "What is the make and model of your car?" not "Do you have a Toyota Prius?"

■ Check to make sure you can understand the participant.

■ If you (or someone else at an organization) will be scheduling internal employees:

• Reinforce that they are not required to participate.

• Recruit a representative sample of users rather than just the best or most vocal.

• Assure them that they'll not be watched by their manager or members of their own team.

■ Ask for the best phone number that you can use to contact them, and give them a way to directly get in touch with you if necessary.

■ If you'll be going to the participant's location, ask if there are any restrictions on what you can bring with you (e.g., cameras, USB flash drives) or if you'll need to arrive early to go through any additional security.

➤ Monitor the recruit—ask to receive updates as frequently as possible and double-check the answers provided by the scheduled participants.

➤ Send a confirmation letter or email to scheduled participants before the session:

  ■ Highlight the date, time, and location of the scheduled session. Include parking and transportation directions.

  ■ Ask them to arrive 15 minutes before the scheduled start time.

  ■ Remind participants that the session will be recorded and observed (if applicable).

  ■ If remote, include any requirements about the technical setup.

  ■ If the session will be at the participant's location:

    • Detail how many people will be with you (e.g., you plus one note-taker).

    • Remind them if you need them to have anything set up or available for the session.

  ■ Reinforce that the session is one-on-one.

  ■ Provide your contact information including your phone number on the day of the session.

➤ Reconfirm with participants the day before the session:

  ■ If you have the time, take this opportunity to test the screen-sharing applications with remote participants.

➤ Take extra measures if you have internal employees as participants:

  ■ Make sure none of their team members will observe their sessions.

  ■ Add extra reminders to the observer ground rules about respecting the participants' confidentiality.

Your study plan

➤ Work carefully on the wording of your tasks and questions to avoid leading or influencing the participant's responses.

➤ Prioritize the study plan so you know the highest- and lowest-priority tasks/questions.

➤ Create a backup plan. Consider creating a paper questionnaire that you can give participants if you experience technical difficulties.

➤ Think about any additional questions or tasks you may want to use if you have to shift the focus of the research in the middle of a session.

➤ Prepare your presession briefing:

  ■ Set clear expectations about the session:

    • The purpose of the session.

    • How you want them to provide feedback/think aloud (if applicable).

    • You're not a subject matter expert.

- You may cut short certain areas of conversation to make sure you cover everything you need to.
- You may not answer their questions right away.
- The prototype may not be fully functional (if applicable).
- They can take a break or end the session at any time.

■ Reiterate the consent form, including how the data and recordings will be used.

■ Ask the participant to turn off the ringer on her cell phone.

■ Use a format that is easy for you to read.

➤ Consider how you'll provide tasks to the participant. Will you read the tasks aloud? Will you send the tasks ahead of time (if the participant is remote)?

➤ Decide when you'll provide compensation:

■ Unless you specify otherwise as part of the recruit, plan to provide compensation to participants even if they're late or do not seem to meet your recruit criteria.

■ Decide if you'll give the compensation at the beginning or end of the session.

The product, space, and technology

➤ If you're using a live website or application:

■ Ensure that no updates will happen during your research.

■ If A/B testing is performed on the website, see if there is a way for you to consistently access the same version (e.g., always the A version).

➤ If you're using a prototype:

■ Work with your developers to make the prototype as functional as possible.

■ Build the illusion of functionality (e.g., by making all links look clickable) for areas that cannot be prototyped in time for your study.

➤ Test and document your technical setup, including:

■ Any recording technology you'll be using (e.g., Morae, camcorders) and the resulting files.

■ The product, on the device that the participant will use. For example, if you're using a prototype of a website, open the prototype on the computer and in the web browser that the participant will use.

■ Any links and passwords required to access the product.

■ Any phone or audio conferencing systems you'll be using.

■ Other devices that you plan to use to capture participant feedback (e.g., eye-tracking equipment).

■ Your screen-sharing application (both your process as the moderator and what the participant will experience when she joins the session).

➤ Make sure you have someone (a colleague or stakeholder) who can watch every session, especially if you're doing onsite sessions.

➤ Familiarize yourself with the study space:

■ Find the nearest fire exit.

■ Research evacuation procedures.

■ If there is building security, give them a heads up about your study and your scheduled participants.

■ If you're going to a different country or cultural region, learn as much as you can about customs and taboos ahead of time.

Your observers

➤ Communicate your moderating approach so observers understand that you may:

■ Jump around in your study plan depending on what happens during a session.

■ Avoid answering a participant's question directly.

■ Provide assists to participants.

■ Redirect participants from a topic but revisit it later.

➤ Establish and distribute ground rules for observer behavior during the session, including:

■ Keep conversation to a minimum—no laughing!

■ Keep the participant's identify and personal information confidential.

■ Avoid making fun of the participant.

■ Keep cell phones silenced.

■ Leave the room quietly if a call must be taken.

■ Avoid slamming doors.

■ Don't talk about the research study outside of the observation space at any point while sessions are running.

■ How to ask questions to the participant (e.g., you'll check with them 10 minutes before the end of the session to gather any questions).

■ How to communicate with you during a session, if necessary.

■ If you want them to take notes or help with data collection, include a short summary that they can refer to during the session.

■ If observers will be in the room with you and the participant, also include:

  ● No conversation or discussion with other in-room observers during the session.

  ● Avoid multitasking.

  ● Avoid disruptions.

  ● Be careful of body language and any physical or audible reactions.

  ● Do not help the participant complete tasks or answer questions.

- ■ If your observers are remote, also include:
  - Stay on mute unless you explicitly ask them to unmute.
  - Avoid using a screen-sharing application's chat feature to communicate with you, as the participant might see it as well.

Your technique

- ➤ Review the prefabricated phrases in Appendix A and include any that you think will be useful in your study plan.
- ➤ Review the list of moderator behaviors to avoid from Chapter 1.
- ➤ Review the steps to take during a session from Chapter 2.
- ➤ If time permits, use some of the techniques discussed in Chapter 16 to further refine your moderating technique.
- ➤ Run a practice session with a colleague acting as your participant.
- ➤ Run a pilot session with an actual participant at least one day before your first scheduled session.

APPENDIX C: RESOURCES

As we discussed in the Introduction, this book deliberately avoids getting into the fundamentals of individual user research methods. This appendix compiles some of the best resources that you can use to learn more about these methods, as well as professional organizations that you may find helpful in your role as a user researcher.

Please check our website (*http://www.modsurvivalguide.org/resources*) for additional and updated resources.

Books to help you plan, run, and analyze your user research session

Usability study	Dumas, J. S., and Loring, B. A. (2008). *Moderating Usability Tests: Principles and Practices for Interacting.* Boston: Morgan Kaufmann.
	Krug, S. (2010). *Rocket Surgery Made Easy: The Do-It-Yourself Guide to Finding and Fixing Usability Problems.* Berkeley, CA: New Riders.
	Rubin, J., and Chisnell, D. (2008). *Handbook of Usability Testing: How to Plan, Design, and Conduct Effective Tests,* 2nd ed. Indianapolis: Wiley Publishers.
Interview	Portigal, S. (2013). *Interviewing Users: How to Uncover Compelling Insights.* Brooklyn: Rosenfeld Media.
Contextual inquiry	Beyer, H., and Holzblatt, K. (1998). *Contextual Design.* San Francisco: Morgan Kaufmann.
	Hackos, J., and Redish, J. (1998). *User and Task Analysis for Interface Design.* New York: John Wiley and Sons.
	Holtzblatt, K., Burns Wendell, J., and Wood, S. (2004). *Rapid Contextual Design: A How-to Guide to Key Techniques for User-Centered Design.* San Francisco: Morgan Kaufmann.
Multiple methods	Bolt, N., and Tulathimutte, T. (2010). *Remote Research: Real Users, Real Research.* Brooklyn: Rosenfeld Media.
	Courage, C., and Baxter, K. (2005). *Understanding Your Users: A Practical Guide to User Requirements.* San Francisco: Morgan Kaufmann.
	Hanington, B., and Martin, B. (2012). *Universal Methods of Design: 100 Ways to Research Complex Problems, Develop Innovative Ideas, and Design Effective Solutions.* Beverly, MA: Rockport Publishers.
	Kuniavsky, M. (2012). *Observing the User Experience: A Practitioner's Guide to User Research,* 2nd ed. San Francisco: Morgan Kaufmann.
	Patton, M. (2002). *Qualitative Research and Evaluation Methods,* 3rd ed. Thousand Oaks, CA: Sage Publications.
	Schumacher, R. M. (2010). *The Handbook of Global User Research.* Boston: Elsevier.
	Sharon, T. (2012). *It's Our Research: Getting Stakeholder Buy-In for User Experience Research Projects.* San Francisco: Morgan Kaufmann.
	Tullis, T., and Albert, B. (2008). *Measuring the User Experience: Collecting, Analyzing, and Presenting Usability Metrics.* Boston: Morgan Kaufmann.
Prototypes for user research	Snyder, C. (2003). *Paper Prototyping: The Fast and Easy Way to Design and Refine User Interfaces.* San Francisco: Morgan Kaufmann.
	Warfel, T. (2009). *Prototyping: A Practitioner's Guide.* Brooklyn: Rosenfeld Media.

Professional organizations and conferences

Professional organizations	These organizations have annual conferences as well as a number of online resources. They also have local chapters so you may be able to find a group somewhere nearby.
	User Experience Professionals Association (UXPA): *http://www.usabilityprofessionals.org/uxpa/*
	ACM's Special Interest Group on Computer–Human Interaction (SIGCHI): *http://www.sigchi.org/*
	Human Factors and Ergonomics Society (HFES): *http://www.hfes.org*
	Interaction Design Association (ixDA): *http://ixda.org/*
Conferences	In addition to the conferences provided by the organizations above, the following sites can help you find other events that focus on improving the user experience.
	Interaction Design Foundation's list of conferences and events: *http://www.interaction-design.org/calendar/*
	Lanyrd's list of user experience conferences and events: *http://lanyrd.com/topics/user-experience/*

Web resources

At the time this book was written, these web resources were available.

Online magazines	Johnny Holland: *http://johnnyholland.org/*
	The UX Booth: *http://www.uxbooth.com/*
	UX Magazine: *http://uxmag.com/*
	UX Matters: *http://www.uxmatters.com/*
Usability measurement	Jeff Sauro's Measuring Usability blog and articles: *http://www.measuringusability.com/blog.php*
	Tom Tullis and Bill Albert's Measuring User Experience website: *http://www.measuringuserexperience.com/*
Interesting anecdotes	Steve Portigal's "War Stories" from the field: *http://www.portigal.com/series/warstories/*
Emergency preparedness	FEMA's guidelines on what to do in case of emergencies: *www.ready.gov*

REFERENCES

Boren, M., & Ramey, J. (2000). Thinking Aloud: Reconciling theory and practice. IEEE Transactions on Professional Communication, *43*(3), 261–278.

Dumas, J. S., & Loring, B. A. (2008). Moderating Usability Tests: Principles and Practices for Interacting. Boston: Morgan Kaufmann.

Loring, B., and Patel, M. (2001). Handling awkward usability testing situations. Proceedings of the Human Factors Society, 45th Annual Meeting. The Human Factors Society, Santa Monica, CA.

Macefield, R. (2007). Usability studies and the Hawthorne Effect. Journal of Usability Studies. Retrieved from http://www.upassoc.org/upa_publications/jus/2007may/hawthorne-effect.pdf.

Retrieved April 17, 2013

Rubin, J. and Chisnell, D. (2008). Handbook of Usability Testing: In: How to Plan, Design, and Conduct Effective Tests (2nd ed.). Indianapolis, Wiley Pub.

Schumacher, R. M. (2010). The Handbook of Global User Research. Boston: Elsevier.

Sharon, T. (2012). It's Our Research: Getting Stakeholder Buy-in for User Experience Research Projects. Boston: Morgan Kaufmann.

Snyder, C. (2003). Paper Prototyping: The Fast and Easy Way to Design and Refine User Interfaces. San Francisco: Morgan Kaufmann.

Sun Tzu. (n.d.). The Art of War. Retrieved April 17, 2013, from http://suntzusaid.com/.

INDEX

Note: Page numbers followed by "f" denote figures; "t" tables; "b" boxes.

Related Titles from Morgan Kaufmann

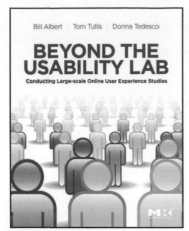

Beyond the Usability Lab
Bill Albert, Tom Tullis, Donna Tedesco
ISBN: 9780123748928

Moderating Usability Testing
Joe Dumas & Beth Loring
ISBN: 9780123739339

Usability Testing Essentials
Carol Barnum
ISBN: 9780123750921

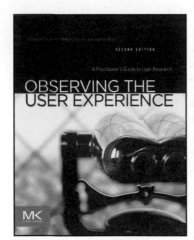

Observing the User Experience 2E
Elizabeth Goodman, Mike Kuniavsky, and
Andrea Moed
ISBN: 9780123848697

Measuring the User Experience 2E
Tom Tullis & Bill Albert
ISBN: 9780124157811

Quantifying the User Experience
Jeff Sauro and Jim Lewis
ISBN: 9780123849687

mkp.com

Printed and bound by CPI Group (UK) Ltd, Croydon, CR0 4YY

03/10/2024

01040325-0014